THE KLAN UNMASKED

Stetson Kennedy after being released by Capitol police following his unsuccessful attempt in 1946 to interest the House Un-American Activities Committee in his evidence against the Ku Klux Klan. Photo courtesy AP/Wide World.

THE KLAN UNMASKED

Stetson Kennedy

FLORIDA ATLANTIC UNIVERSITY PRESS
BOCA RATON

Other Books by Stetson Kennedy

Palmetto Country, Duell, Sloan & Pearce, 1942
Florida A&M University Press, 1989

Southern Exposure, Doubleday, 1946

Jim Crow Guide, Jean-Paul Sartre, Paris, 1955
Lawrence & Wishart, London, 1959
Florida Atlantic University Press, 1990

The Florida Atlantic University Press is a member of University Presses of Florida, the scholarly publishing agency of the State University System of Florida. Books are selected for publication by faculty editorial committees at each of Florida's nine public universities: Florida A&M University (Tallahassee), Florida Atlantic University (Boca Raton), Florida International University (Miami), Florida State University (Tallahassee), University of Central Florida (Orlando), University of Florida (Gainesville), University of North Florida (Jacksonville), University of South Florida (Tampa), University of West Florida (Pensacola).

Orders for books published by all member presses should be addressed to University Presses of Florida, 15 NW 15th St., Gainesville, FL 32603.

Library of Congress Cataloging-in-Publication Data

Third printing, 1991

Kennedy, Stetson.
    [I rode with the Ku Klux Klan]
    The Klan unmasked / Stetson Kennedy.
        p.   cm.
    "Originally published as I rode with the Ku Klux Klan by Arco Publishers Ltd."—T.p. verso.
    ISBN 0-8130-0986-3 (alk. paper)
    1. Ku Klux Klan (1915-   ) I. Title.
HS2330.K63K46   1990
322.4'2'092—dc20   89-29033
[B]   CIP

To
all those who ever have or ever will stand up to and
struggle against the
Ku Klux Klan
and the bigotry for which it stands;
and also to
all those who shared with me the risk, anxiety,
deprivation, and work which went into this
investigation and book.

Americans of many races, creeds, and faiths are joined in the continuing struggle against Ku Kluxery recorded in these pages. In the preparation of this book, however, special contributions have been made by my fellow anti-Klan agent " Bob " who has risked his life many times, Edith Ogden and my son Loren who lived through the investigations, Patricia Hemberow who believed in the material enough to put it in order, and Marika Hellstrom who made possible the writing.

Stetson Kennedy.

CONTENTS

The author in his uniform of the Columbian brownshirt terrorists, sometimes called the "juvenile delinquents of the KKK."

CHAPTER ONE

THE FIERY SUMMONS

I AWOKE with a start, my hand already instinctively reaching for the ·32 automatic I kept under my pillow. No sooner did I have the comforting cool steel in hand than I became aware that the ringing of a bell had awakened me. It was dark, and my first thought was that the alarm clock must have gone off ahead of schedule. Cursing under my breath, I flicked on the bed light. It was 2 a.m. Then I realized that the bell had stopped ringing, and I knew it was the telephone.

Trouble, I thought. But I knew that failure to answer it might mean worse trouble, so I stumbled out into the hall and picked up the receiver.

" Who is this? " asked the caller. I recognized the voice—rather like a cement-mixer running at half speed—as that of Cliff Carter, " Chief Ass-Tearer " of the hooded Ku Klux Klan's Klavalier Klub murder squad.

"John Perkins," I replied, giving him the alias under which I had lived ever since I joined the Klan as a secret undercover agent to gather evidence against it.

" What's your number, Perkins? " asked the voice bluntly.

" Seventy-three," I replied, this being the number on my Klavalier Klub membership " Kard."

" White—" he said, giving me the first half of the Klan's current secret password.

" —man," I replied, returning the countersign.

" Native—" he continued.

" —born," I concluded.

Satisfied that I was indeed his " Brother Klansman " and Klavalier, Carter dropped the recognition ritual we Klavaliers always used for telephonic conversations.

" This is Clearwater," he said solemnly, giving the code

9

name by which he as Chieftain was known to us. " And this is a Fiery Summons! Remember your oath to be ready when called! The call is imperative! Bring your robe and *come prepared*—to Black Rock! "

Wide awake now, I was thinking hard. When Carter said " come prepared," I knew he meant for me to bring whatever deadly weapon I had available. " Black Rock " was our secret code name for the Atlanta suburb known as Buckhead—one of the key mobilization points which the Klavaliers had designated throughout the city. Someone— Negro, Jew, Catholic, or labour unionist—had been tagged for a KKK flogging or worse that night. Or perhaps I was literally being invited to my own funeral—which was always a possibility when I attended a Klan function.

I wondered whether I could rouse Dan Duke—the state's Assistant Attorney-General under whom I worked as an anti-Klan agent—in time to nip the Klavaliers' projected flogging or lynching party in the bud.

" Clearwater," I said weakly, " you know I've been very sick with the flu lately. I don't think I would be much good to you tonight."

" Klansman! " Carter roared. " You know the oath as well as I do! And I happen to know you are not bedridden! No other excuse is tolerated! *You must go!* " There was a click as he hung up.

I knew there was no way out—that I myself would be subject to " banishment " as a " citizen " of the Klan's " Invisible Empire " if I failed to respond to the summons. " Herein fail ye not! By mandate of His Lordship, the Imperial Wizard " is the way the little printed cards read in red ink, when a Fiery Summons is sent by mail. All action undertaken by the Klavalier Klub, which serves as the " Military Department " of the KKK, has the approval of the Wizard or Grand Dragon. All Klansmen are sworn not only to obey the edicts of the hierarchy but to enforce obedience upon any Brothers who fail to live up to this oath. I had seen one Klansman, who chose punishment to banishment, forced to run nude through a gauntlet of Klan belts. I had no desire to let myself in for the same thing.

I put in a rush call for Dan Duke, using the direct private

telephone he had installed in his home to keep our Klan probe out of the hostile ears of telephone company switchboard operators. Duke had been out of the city on official business, and I had an anxious moment until I heard his sleepy voice on the phone. Briefly, I relayed to him the details of the Fiery Summons I had received.

" Got any idea who they're after this time? " Duke asked.

" Not the least," I had to admit.

" Well, I'll do my best to get my men out to Buckhead in time," Duke said. " If you get a chance to call me back without making anybody suspicious, phone me when you get more details."

" Right," I said. " I'd better get moving—it isn't healthy to be late for one of these affairs."

A few minutes later I was speeding in my car through the city's deserted streets—my automatic in my pocket and my black Klavalier's robe tucked under the seat.

As I approached Buckhead I could see, scattered over an area of several blocks as we had been trained to do to avoid suspicion, the cars of other Klavaliers who had arrived ahead of me.

Cars were still converging on the intersection, so I knew I would not be the last arrival. I wondered about Duke's men—whether they were somewhere on hand. Our whole " Operation Anti-Klan " was so ticklish that Duke had kept my identity from his other hand-picked undercover agents of the Georgia Department of Law, and I in turn had no idea who they were. So deep was the KKK infiltration inside the state's law enforcement agencies that my cheque was even drawn from a special account, as a precaution against real Klansmen on the state payroll discovering my identity.

Parking my car in the shadows of a side street, I went around to the parking lot behind an abandoned theatre which was our meeting place. I estimated that there were nearly forty Klavaliers assembled there, each one carrying his robe in small briefcase-like bags (which the Dragon sold at a neat profit for $10 each) or in paper bags or simply wrapped in newspapers. They were just standing there, smoking and talking in low tones, waiting for Carter to give them their riding orders for the night. Carter was checking those present by a list of numbers he carried. Finally he was satisfied that all those who had been summoned—thirty-seven, hand picked for reasons known only to himself—were present. Raising a hand as a signal for us to gather around him, Carter said:

" So far so good. You are all to be commended for getting here in good time. Keep your robes off for the time being, disperse, and proceed to Wingo's Café. Take your robes in with you. And keep a sharp lookout to see whether you are being followed! "

Wingo's Café was a joint in the East End of Atlanta, specializing in steaks, and open all night. We Klavaliers met there for steak dinners and corn liquor one night each month, but I couldn't imagine why we should be ordered there at two-thirty in the morning. I wondered if Carter were mean enough to do a job on the Negro chef, who on our last visit had refused to cook when he detected that we were Klansmen.

I decided to try to give Duke a ring on the way to Wingo's. Starting off slowly, I waited until I had turned the corner before cutting on my lights. Adjusting my rear-view mirror, I looked back to see if I were being followed. Just as I was about to relax, I saw that I was being tailed by a car without lights. Was it Duke's men—or Brother Klavaliers keeping an eye on me? The car kept too far behind for me to recognize it.

I tried speeding and I tried slowing down. Neither worked. Finally, putting all the distance I could between us, I careened around a corner, cut my lights and motor, and coasted far up into the dark driveway of the first house I came to. Immediately, a dog inside the house began to bark. I had visions of what might happen if lights began to go on inside. It seemed a long time before the following car turned the corner, and I held my breath in anticipation that it might spot me and slam on the brakes. It roared on down the street, hesitated at the corner, and then disappeared in a cloud of red Georgia clay dust.

The dog inside the house was barking louder than ever, and I wondered whether I had escaped my pursuers only to be accosted by an irate householder. I stamped on the starter and accelerator simultaneously. As the motor roared, the lights in the house flashed on, but in a matter of seconds I had backed out and was off down the street—on my way to an all-night drug store where I could telephone.

The tailing episode bothered me chiefly because, had my pursuers turned out to be Klavaliers, it would have meant I was under suspicion as the much-sought-after " spy " in the Klan. It would also have prevented me from tipping off Duke to the new mobilization point at Wingo's Café, in case his men failed to get there on their own.

I circled the drug store twice before deciding it was safe to make the call. Inside, I made certain that no one was in the adjoining phone booths. Duke said he had just had a call from his men, who had lost the trail after trying to tail a Klavalier car from Buckhead. They had been shaken, he said, without getting close enough to the car to describe it.

" It's a good thing you called," Duke said. " They're going to phone me back in five minutes, and I'll send them on to Wingo's! "

All this had taken time, and I raced to Wingo's without seeing any further signs of being followed. Most of the Klavaliers were already assembled in the private dining-room where we always convened. Carter was at the door.

" Enrobe, but do not put on your mask," he ordered.

The Brothers were all seated around a long table which had been formed by placing a number of tables together. Most of them had ordered hamburgers, and Carter had provided half a dozen bottles of cheap " drinking whisky " as a reward for their " faithfulness." Even with their masks off, they were an awesome sight. I was the last to arrive, and Carter, taking his place at the head of the table, lost no time in asking:

" Were any of you followed? "

" I was," I said promptly. " A carload of Duke's men got in behind me without any lights, and I had one hellova time shaking them. That's why I was late getting here. There's no doubt about it—the damned spy is still on the job."

Carter looked at me and blinked.

" Are you positive you shook them? " he asked finally.

" Absolutely," I replied.

" Anybody else followed? " Carter asked, looking around the room.

" Yeah, they tried to tail me too," said a Klavalier named Nathan Jones, " but I finally got rid of them. Somebody ought to pay me back for all the gas I had to burn."

This got a laugh from the brethren, but Carter cut it short.

" This is no laughing matter! " he roared. " The Judas we've been trying to catch so long is sitting right here at this table tonight! At last I know who he is! That's why you men were summoned here—to close the trap and mete out fitting punishment! "

It was a cold January night, but I began to sweat under my robe.

" Name the s.o.b.! " several Klavaliers shouted—and I joined in the chorus with what little enthusiasm I could muster.

" Take it easy," said Carter with a grim smile. He was playing cat-and-mouse, studying each man's face carefully. For a brief moment I thought of making a break for the door. It was closed, and while no guard had been posted outside of it to my knowledge, it occurred to me that Carter might have locked it. I wondered, too, about the odds of backing out of such a room even if I could succeed in getting the drop on them all with my automatic. The odds, I decided, were not too good—and when I noticed that Carter was keeping one hand under the table I decided to sit tight and sweat it out.

" I told you all to come prepared! " Carter said. " Let's see what you've got to work with! "

From under his own robe he pulled a ·45 Police Special revolver, and laid it on the table in front of him. Amidst a tumult of curses to "let us at him," the Klavaliers followed suit. Soon the table was covered with an assortment of pistols, switch-blade " nigger-killer " knives, blackjacks, brassknucks, and a flogging whip made by sewing a piece of sawmill belt to a sawed-off baseball bat handle. Adding my automatic to the collection, I decided that the chances for a getaway were now non-existent.

" We're prepared, all right! " shouted one Brother.
" Just name him! "

Carter only smiled, and the clamour arose like the frenzied
" treed " baying of a pack of hounds gathered for the kill—
gnashing their teeth in anticipation of rending their prey
asunder. Carter kept smiling and watching.

" What are we gonna do with the rat? " one man shouted.

" You know the penalty," Carter spoke up. " Death,
death, at the hands of a Brother! " He was quoting the oath
we all took upon joining the Klan, wherein we swore to
accept the death penalty if we ever betrayed the Klan's
secrets.

" Let's take him out in the woods, fasten him to a log
with a staple over his testicles, set fire to the log, give him a
knife and tell him to ' Cut or burn! ' " shouted one enthusiast.

Other proposals came thick and fast, each more blood-
curdling than the other. I tried without much conviction to
make some suggestions of my own.

Every now and then Carter would toss them some more
bait.

" We've waited a long time to corner the rat," he said,
" and every one of you who is paid up in his dues can have
a free hand in working him over. I'm going to start things
off by standing him in front of a Klan altar and wearing off
both my arms up to the elbows! "

" Don't you think we ought to banish him from citizenship
in the Invisible Empire first? " one stickler for protocol asked.
Banishment proceedings are a long-drawn-out ceremony,
including a mock trial and concluded by a symbolic
" burial " of the banished Brother.

" When we get through with him he won't need banish-
ing! " Carter said solemnly, still watching.

But he had stopped smiling.

Suddenly, I almost smiled with the realization that
Carter was bluffing—that he had no idea whom to put his
finger on. Fortunately, I didn't smile, for Carter was clever
enough to have interpreted a smile at that moment. But I
kicked myself mentally for not having considered the possibility that Carter had merely set a trap and hoped that
someone would make a break and dash into it. I took a

long pull at the " drinking whisky " and rejoined the debate with far more enthusiasm than before.

At last, when he could stall the men no longer, Carter stood up.

" Brother Klansmen and Dirty Rat," he began sardonically, " I'm sorry to have to disappoint you, but we're going to have to put off the killing a little while longer. I don't know who the rat is, but I hoped that by giving him a little rope here tonight he would hang himself by trying to make a break for it. I wish he had. Knowing the penalty, I can't understand how any man would dare rat on the Klan! Anyway, we've narrowed the prospects down to thirty-seven men—the men right here in this room. We're hot on his trail, and it's getting hotter all the time. We know he's here tonight, or we would never have been followed. Our Klokann investigating committee is made up of the best detectives on the Atlanta police force, and we'll catch the rat yet!

" I want to congratulate you all for your quick mobilization tonight. There is plenty of good work that needs to be done, and we will attend to it just as soon as we get rid of the rat. As long as he is in our midst, our hands are tied. Catch him, and I promise you we'll light up the skies with fiery crosses! There'll be something doing every night!

" Disrobe now, and go back to your homes. And if any of you are stopped by Duke's men, remember the marks of a Klavalier—not only to be ready when called, but to have guts and a tight lip! Sew up your mouths, and they can't hold you! Disperse! "

There was a scrambling for what was left of the whisky, and a great deal of profanity, but nothing new was proposed by way of punishing the " rat."

I was never so happy to disperse in my life.

CHAPTER TWO

WHY I JOINED THE KLAN

I DIDN'T get much sleep the rest of that night. Instead, I lay there in bed thinking about some of the things that had led to my joining the Klan and getting into such a hot spot. . . .

I remembered how as a kid my first knowledge of the Klan came when I discovered my Uncle Brady Perkins' flowing white robe and mask tucked away in a closet. I slipped the hood over my head and peered through the eye-slits—little anticipating then that so much of my adult life was to be spent behind a Klan mask.

" Is that white gown in the closet your ghost costume for Hallowe'en? " I asked Uncle Brady when he came home that night.

" No, sonny," he replied, more than a little miffed that I had discovered his secret. " Some of us grown-up menfolks have a club we call the Ku Klux, and we wear those robes when we have to go out and scare or spank bad people to make them behave! "

Sometime later, my family took me one night to see my first Ku Klux parade. We were standing on the kerb of Jacksonville, Florida's, Main Street, when the Klansmen came into view. At the head of the procession were two Klansmen mounted on horseback. The horses were also clad in flowing white, with masks over their faces very much like those I had seen in my history books on the steeds of tilting medieval knights. One of the mounted Knights of the KKK bore a flaming fiery cross, while the other blew long mournful blasts on a bugle. At each intersection they would jerk on their reins, and the horses would rear up and paw at the air, neighing shrilly. It was an awe-inspiring spectacle, and I was duly impressed.

17

As the Klansmen marched past, six abreast, I kept my eyes glued on the feet protruding from beneath the robes.

" There he is—that's Uncle Brady! " I cried out finally, when I spied his old-fashioned hook-top shoes.

" Shhh . . . ! " my mother said, looking around to see if anyone had heard.

" Where are they all going? " I asked, as the last of the robed figures disappeared from sight.

" Oh, probably over to coloured town to throw a scare into them," my mother said.

At the time, the whole thing seemed harmless enough to me, and I thought how lucky grown-up men were to be able to play Hallowe'en on such a grand scale whenever they felt like it. It was not until a few years later that something happened to change my mind—something that undoubtedly started me down the trail that eventually led me to join the Klan in the hope of breaking it up. . . .

I had boarded a trolley with my family's Negro maid, Flo, a lovely young woman in her middle twenties. Flo had been working for my family since she was very young, and had nursed, bathed and fed me from the day I was born. I had spent more time with her than any other adult—and loved her accordingly.

I saw Flo hand the trolley conductor half a dollar—and he gave her change for a quarter.

" I gave you fifty cents, mister," Flo said, politely enough.

" It was a quarter! " the conductor said with finality.

" No, sir, it was half a dollar," she insisted.

" I'll teach you not to call white folks liars, you impudent black bitch! " he yelled.

Pulling the heavy iron handle with which he steered the trolley from its socket, he struck at Flo's head. She ducked and what otherwise might have been a fatal blow was a glancing one which opened a wound on her forehead that bled profusely. With renewed curses, the conductor drove us from the trolley. With me holding her hand, Flo staggered back to my home. My mother drove her to the county hospital, where they sewed up her wound.

One morning about a week later, Flo failed to come to work. About noon, my mother decided to drive to Flo's

home to find out what was wrong. I went with her. We
found Flo in bed, moaning.

" What's the matter, Flo? " my mother asked.

" The Ku Klux came on me last night—" she groaned.

" The Ku Klux? What on earth for? "

" It was that trolley conductor who put them on me.
While they was beating me I kept asking them what I had
done, and finally one of them said I had been sassing white
folks."

" What did they switch you with? "

" They didn't switch me, ma'm—they beat me with a
heavy leather belt. I mean something awful, too—they kept
passing the belt around, taking turns. I'll show you what
they did to me."

She turned back the sheet. Her thighs were a mass of
bruises, and in half a dozen places the skin was torn and
clotted with blood.

" Merciful heavens! " my mother exclaimed. " They
had no right to do a thing like that! "

" That's not all they done to me. . . ."

" Not all? "

" Couldn't you run and get away from them? " I asked
Flo.

" I wanted to," she said, trying to smile, " but they tied
my hands around that big pine tree out in the front yard,
and pulled my gown up and went to beating me! "

" You said there was something else they did to you? "
my mother asked again.

" Yes, ma'm. After they had gone away and left me tied,
one of them came back and had to do with me right there. . . .
There wasn't a thing I could do to fight him off. He was
drunk and just as mean as he could be—pulled my womb
down so I don't know if I'll be able to walk."

I didn't understand everything that was being said—but
I had seen enough to turn me against the Klan for ever. We
left Flo moaning quietly. It was almost two weeks before
she came back to work.

As the years went by, more and more of the Klan's
handiwork came to my attention, and the hatred I had

formed for it at Flo's bedside was confirmed and re-confirmed.

My first chance to strike a major blow against the Klan came in writing my first book *Palmetto Country*, published on the eve of World War II. In it I nailed the Big Lie—to be found in most American history books—that the original Ku Klux Klan was founded in 1865 to " save the South " from " rascally Negroes, Scalawags, and Carpetbaggers." That fairy-tale, especially as it found expression in the book and film *Birth of a Nation*, may make comfortable reading, but it is very far from the truth.

My careful researches into the post-Civil War Reconstruction Period—including many talks with people who actually lived through it—revealed that the Negro Freedmen, the poor white Southerners, and the inspired Northerners who came down to assist in the Reconstruction, were actually laying the foundations of a real democracy when the big planters launched the KKK to break it up. The publication of these findings in *Palmetto Country* was altogether unpalatable to some Southern newspaper editors, who denounced me as a " galvanized Yankee," " the renegade scion of a respected Southern family " and " a traitor to his region and his race."

All this was too much for my relatives, many of whom were high in the councils of the United Daughters of the Confederacy. I was literally drummed out of the family circle. Not only was I ostracized socially, but economic sanctions were imposed against me, so that it was difficult for me to find or hold a job.

In delving into both old and new outrages perpetrated by the Klan, I was soon struck by one all-important fact— almost all of the things written on the subject were editorials, not exposés. The writers were *against* the Klan, all right, but they had precious few inside facts *about* it. Their punches consequently lacked the dynamite I knew it would take to score a knockout against the Klan.

The need, obviously, was not just for more words, but legal evidence on the Klan's inside machinations—evidence which could be taken into court and used to put the Klan's leaders behind bars where they belonged. To get such evidence—just as obviously—somebody would have to go under a Klan robe and turn the hooded order's dirty linen inside out for all the world to see.

I decided to volunteer for the job. While I was fully conscious of the dangers involved, at that time people all over the world were fighting in the front lines in defence of democracy. They knew they were going to be shot at and possibly killed, so the prospect that this might also happen to me if I crossed swords with the Klan did not seem a sufficient reason to hold back. That there seemed to be no other volunteers for " Operation Anti-Klan " made it all the more imperative that I undertake to carry it out.

Having made my decision, there remained the problem of putting it into effect. I was living in Miami, Florida, at the time, where the Klan's John B. Gordon Klavern No. 5 (named after a Confederate general) was active enough. But I was aiming higher—I wanted to penetrate the Klan's top-level, top-secret councils in the Imperial Palace—the clearing-house for Ku Kluxery all over the country. To do this I would have to move to the Imperial City of the KKK's Invisible Empire—Atlanta, Georgia.

I had to change, of course, much more than my place of residence—I needed a whole new identity. There is nothing illegal about changing one's name, I knew, provided it is not done to defraud anyone. In casting about for a suitable " alias," I decided to become " John S. Perkins." In the South one must have not only a name, but kinfolks; and the name of Perkins had the advantage of linking me with my Klansman uncle—who by this time had passed on " from the Invisible Empire to the Empire Invisible," as the Klan says of its deceased brethren.

It was a delicate mission that I had assigned myself and I wanted to take every precaution against being tripped up. If the Kluxers discovered that I was Stetson Kennedy, whose anti-Klan writings had already been a thorn in their sides for years, they would not handle me gently even if they caught on to me at the outset. With this in mind, I proceeded to put into mothballs my shirts with their " Kenn " laundry marks, and my felt hat with " S.K." stencilled inside its band. Next, I arranged with a friend to receive all future mail for Stetson Kennedy, and to forward it to me in an outer envelope addressed to John Perkins.

And so it was that I left my white flannels behind in Miami and went to Atlanta in search of a white robe. . . .

Upon arriving, I took a room in the East Point neighbourhood, where Ike Gaston, a white barber, had been flogged to death by the Klan several years earlier. Then, in order to have what would appear to be some reasonable means of support—actually I was living on a modest income from my book—I took a commission job selling encyclopædias from house to house, for $1 down and $1 per week. I never sold any, but the sample copy looked impressive, and gave me a good excuse to knock on any door at almost any time.

With the groundwork thus carefully prepared, I felt that I was at last ready to make contact with the Klan. But how? I had already decided not to waste time with rank-and-file hate-mongers, but to " start at the top " if at all possible.

" What," I asked myself, " is the shortest route into the Klan's inner councils? "

The answer I got was: " Eugene Talmadge."

At that time Ole Gene—having already served three terms as Governor of Georgia—was out of office but hot on the comeback trail. Though he was smart enough never to take out actual membership in the Klan, he liked nothing better than to speak at the KKK's fish-fries and barbecues. As the South's uncrowned " Champion of White Supremacy," Ole Gene was regarded by the Klan as its very best friend and spiritual leader. A recommendation from Ole Gene, I thought to myself, would open the doors to the Klan's inner dens in a hurry.

But how was I to make the approach? After thinking about it for some time, I picked up the telephone and called him.

" Governor," I said, " my name is John Perkins. I'd like to stop by and talk to you whenever it's convenient—I think I might be able to help out some in your campaigning."

" Be glad to see you, Mr. Perkins—come by at any time after dinner," he said.

A Southerner myself, I knew he meant early in the afternoon. I went to his law office in the Wm. Oliver Building, and sat down in the reception room. Through the transom, I could hear Ole Gene sounding off.

" The way to handle an ox," he was saying to whoever was with him, " is to pop him on the nuts with a whip! I'll guarantee he'll move then! "

When I was finally ushered in, I found Ole Gene looking not only very old, but ill. He had the same pallor about him that I had seen on cancer victims in a mortuary operated by one of my friends. His eyes, however, still had a foxy gleam.

" What can I do for you, Mr. Perkins? " he asked, chewing on the stub of a cigar and expectorating with an accurate " boing! " into a brass spittoon in the corner.

" I was hoping I might be able to do something for you," I countered. " I get around a great deal from house to house selling encyclopædias, and would be glad to put in some good words for you and hand out campaign literature as I go."

" Well, now, that's mighty nice of you—I'd appreciate that a whole lot. Whereabouts in Georgia did you say you come from? "

" My folks all live over around Statesboro."

" Bullock County always votes for Gene. I always did say I can carry any county that ain't got streetcars. Tell me, Mr. Perkins, how does it look to you—the election, I mean? "

" Oh, I'm sure you've got it in the bag! But what's all this I hear about your coming out in favour of repealing the poll tax? "

" Yeah, I'm a convert on that," he replied with a sly grin. " Done decided the best way to keep the niggers from votin' is to let all the white folks vote, and then pass the word around that Mr. Nigger is not wanted at the polls! Sure, let all the white folks vote—makes a kind of mob, and you can sway their emotions! "

" Of course Governor Ellis Arnall claims the credit for getting rid of the poll tax."

" Oh, well," he said with another grin, " you know credit is like water—it sort of flows around."

" How do you suppose things are going to be when the war's over? "

" Oh, we're gonna have riots and bloodshed and

insurrection! " Ole Gene said with a wink and a wave of his hand. " Blood will flow in the streets! Be lots of people killed —lots of poor innocent Nigras! "

At this point a young man about my own age entered the room. I knew at a glance that it was Young Hummon, Ole Gene's son. He had the same cowlick of hair hanging over his forehead, and was also chewing on a black cigar. His aim at the spittoon was not as good as Ole Gene's, however.

" Mr. Perkins, meet my boy Hummon. Hummon, Mr. Perkins here has offered to hand out some literature for us."

" Every little bit helps," Hummon said, shaking my hand. " How about taking a stack along with you right now? "

" Suits me," I replied.

He reached into a cabinet and pulled out a sheaf of leaflets. I looked at one—it was a vicious attack upon the Rosenwald Foundation, which was accused of promoting political and social equality in Georgia. Actually, the Foundation simply built schools for Negroes where no such schools existed.

" This is hot stuff! " I said. " I can get rid of these in a big way! How many more have you got on hand? "

Hummon and Ole Gene grinned at each other, delighted with the zeal of their new legman.

" Must be three or four thousand left," Hummon said.

" I'll take 'em all," I said, opening my briefcase, and stuffing them in.

" Thanks a lot, Mr. Perkins," Ole Gene said as I took my leave. " We may be able to use a man like you in our Press department. Drop in to see us any time! "

" I'll sure do that," I promised.

Walking a few blocks down a side street with my heavily laden briefcase, I dumped its contents into an open sewer. ...

Having built my fences with Talmadge, I felt I was ready to make contact with the Klan. I did not, of course, want to walk up to the front door of the Imperial Palace and ask to be let in; I wanted to be invited to join the Klan. With this in view, I scouted about until I found a combination bar and pool-room whose habitués had the frustrated, cruel look of the Klan about them. After a good many games of pool and an uncounted number of beers, I was sitting at the bar one afternoon when I suddenly heard what I had been waiting to hear.

" What this country needs is a good Kluxing—that's the only way to keep the niggers, kikes, Catholic dagos and Reds in their place! "

The man who muttered this in my ear was perched drunkenly on the bar stool next to me. A slim, hard-drinking cab-driver, I knew him only as " Slim."

" My uncle used to be a big shot in the Ku Klux down in Florida," I said off-handedly, " but they're dead now, aren't they? "

" Don't kid yourself! " he said, reaching for his wallet. From it he pulled a small printed card and slapped it down on the bar in front of me:

Here Yesterday, Today, Forever!
The Ku Klux Klan Is Riding!
God Give Us Men!
Nathan Bedford Forrest
Klavern No. 1
P.O. Box 1188
Atlanta, Georgia.

" Well, well," I said. " Have you got one of those cards to spare? I might be interested in joining some day, and could write in to that post office box number."

" No need to do any writing," Slim said importantly. " Just say the word, and I'll take care of everything."

" What are you—an organizer or something? " I asked, trying to hide my eagerness.

" A Kleagle, we call it in the Klan."

" Probably costs more to join than I can afford," I said dubiously.

" It ain't so bad. The Klectoken—that's the initiation fee—is ten bucks, but right now we've got a membership drive on, so you can get in for eight dollars."

" How much of that do you spend on beer? " I asked grinning.

" The Kleagle gets a two-dollar commission on every man he brings in," Slim admitted, only half sheepishly.

" What about dues? "

" Three dollars per quarter, or ten dollars a year if you pay up in advance."

" I'd have to buy a robe too, I suppose? "

" The Grand Dragon sells 'em for fifteen dollars."

" Fifteen dollars for a bedsheet and pillow-case? " I snorted indignantly. " I can make up my own robe for less than that! "

" You must have never looked at one close up," Slim explained patiently. " They've got a cape, and a belt, and a hood and tassel, and a lot of pretty embroidering besides. The Betsy Ross chapter of the Klan's ladies' auxiliary does all the needlework free, so you really get a bargain. A robe will last you a long time if you just take care of it and don't tear it up on the brush when you're out on a job some night."

" Don't know where I can find a good second-hand one, do you? "

" Look," Slim said, losing his patience, " haven't you heard the expression, ' once a Klansman, always a Klansman ' ? Nobody just walks out on the Klan. If you're ever banished from citizenship in the Invisible Empire, you won't be taking your robe with you. I'm beginning to think you're not serious."

" I really am," I said, thinking I had gone too far with my game of hard to get. " It's just that I don't have a Klectoken on me right now. I'll let you know just as soon as I can see my way clear."

" O.K.," Slim said, obviously disappointed at not raking in his two dollars commission then and there. " But you're liable to miss some fun. I belong to the headquarters Klan— Nathan Bedford Forrest Klavern No. 1, named after the Confederate cavalry general. We've got the best bunch of boys there is, and I think I can get you in. It'll take some time even after I put your name up. The names of applicants have to be read before the full membership two weeks in a row, to see if anybody has anything against letting you in. Besides that, the Klokann—that's our five-man investigating committee, made up of Atlanta's best police detectives—has to check up on you."

" Don't worry—I'm as clean as they come," I said, and let it go at that. What I wanted was for Slim, in handing in my Klectoken, to say, " Here's one from a guy named Perkins; I had one hellova time talking him into joining! " After waiting about a week, I decided the situation was ripe enough.

" O.K., Slim," I told him, " if that bargain price is still on I'll take you up on your proposition."

" Good man! " he exclaimed, his eyes lighting up. " Let's go back to the lavatory. I don't like to do business out here in the bar—no telling who's going to look over your shoulder."

We went back to the men's room. There was no one else there, but a royal stink permeated the air. An appropriate atmosphere for joining the Klan, I thought to myself.

" I've got an application blank right here in my pocket," Slim said, pocketing my eight dollars. He pulled out a dog-eared blank and handed it to me. It was titled " Application for Citizenship in the Invisible Empire, Knights of the Ku Klux Klan." I began to read:

" To His Majesty the Imperial Wizard—I, the under-signed, a native-born, true and loyal citizen of the United States, being a white male Gentile person of temperate habits, sound of mind and a believer in the tenets of the Christian religion, the maintenance of White Supremacy and the principles of a pure Americanism, do most respect-fully apply for membership in the Knights of the Ku Klux Klan through *Klan No. 1*, Realm of *Georgia*.

" I guarantee on my honour to conform strictly to all rules and requirements regulating my naturalization and the continuance of my membership, and at all times a strict and loyal obedience to your constitutional authority. . . . If I prove untrue as a Klansman I will willingly accept as my portion whatever penalty your authority may impose."

The time for hesitation had passed. I signed with a flourish—but not without some trepidation as to what I was letting myself in for.

" We've got to have two other names on here of people who will vouch for you," Slim said. " I'll sign for one. Anybody else you know in the Klan? "

"Well, I don't know if he's actually a member or not,"
I replied, playing my ace slowly, "but I do know Gene
Talmadge pretty well."

It worked like magic.

"You're a friend of Gene's?" Slim exclaimed, instantly
respectful. "That's all the recommendation anybody could
ask for. We'll put his name down."

"How about my uncle who was Grand Titan of the
Florida Klan?" I asked. "He's dead now, but do you
suppose his name would help any?"

"Shucks, I reckon! The Wizard's got a rotary card file
with over nine million names of former Klan members on it,
going all the way back to the 1920s. What was your uncle's
name?"

I told him, and he wrote: "Nephew of Brady Perkins,
former Grand Titan Florida Realm. Check inactive file."

"You shouldn't have any trouble at all," he said.

"How will I know when I've been passed on?"

"Don't worry—we'll get in touch with you! Just sit
tight. . . ."

So I sat, and wondered how the Klokann was progressing
with its investigation of John Perkins—and what might
happen if they discovered I was really the anti-Klan author
Stetson Kennedy. . . .

While my application to join the Klan was still pending, I
occupied myself with making another connection which I
thought would stand me in good stead in the course of my
investigations. I had long made it my business to subscribe
to all the hate sheets being published in the South. One of
the most virulent of these was the *Southern Outlook*, printed
in Birmingham, Alabama. Calling itself the "Feature
Newspaper of the American Way of Life," the *Outlook*
scrambled its pro-Klan, anti-Negro, anti-Semitic, anti-
union propaganda with generous helpings of comics, car-
toons, sexy photographs, mystery stories, and crossword
puzzles. In a copy which came to me in Atlanta I came
across the following advertisement:

WANTED.—Full-time agents, Gentile, who can earn
up to $500 per month handling the *Southern Outlook*.

This intrigued me in more ways than one. While I had no intention of peddling hate at any price, I was curious to know how anyone could make $500 per month in the subscription department of the race racket. It also occurred to me that a connection with such a sheet would give me further prestige for gaining entrée to the Klan's high councils. Accordingly, I packed my bag and caught a bus to Birmingham, thinking that if the Klokann called on me during my absence it would be just as well to be " away on business."

I walked into the office of the *Southern Outlook* and introduced myself to its publisher, T. E. Blackmon, a giant of a man with a shock of bristling grey hair.

" Encyclopædias aren't selling too well these days," I told him, " and I'd like to get into something with more of a future."

Blackmon was obviously interested in having someone handle his hate sheet in Georgia, but it wasn't until I said casually that I was " doing a little work on the side for Gene " that he really pricked up his ears.

" You know Gene Talmadge? " he said. " I've always been a great admirer of his. How about having lunch with me, Mr. Perkins? I'd like you to meet my business manager, Raymond Parks."

This was a pleasant surprise, which I accepted. As I looked over the menu, I decided then and there to make it a matter of principle to make hate-mongers pay through the nose for my having to listen to their mouthings. So I proceeded to order the most expensive items on the menu. Blackmon winced every time I called for something, but said nothing.

We were soon joined by Parks, a very smooth operator in his middle thirties.

" Parks used to handle the Press for Kingfish Huey Long in Louisiana," Blackmon said. " He knows his business, and is doing a great job with the *Outlook*. After lunch, you two can go to his office and he can brief you on how this thing works."

Parks' office turned out to be a whole suite of swank rooms on the top floor of Birmingham's finest hotel. Working for him was a whole bevy of luscious girls, who looked more like artists' models than secretaries. Each room had a battery of telephones, and these girls did nothing but sit there with card files and call up business men and turn the heat on them for contributions for the *Outlook*.

" I always make the first call myself," Parks said to me. " If they don't come across right away, I hand them over to one of these girls, and they keep after them until they give. As soon as they say yes, I send a girl over to pick up their cheque. I'll show you how it's done in a few minutes. But first let's have a highball."

He ordered up a pitcher of ice and a bottle of soda, and extracted a quart of straight Bourbon from a well-stocked cabinet.

" It's not a half-bad life," he said, winking at one of the girls in the next room and handing me a stiff drink. " Why don't you stick around, and we'll pick a couple of the girls and have a little celebration tonight? They're all good sports—I hired them myself! "

" I'll think about it," I said vaguely.

" Here, take a look at this—" Parks said, as the drink began to take effect. Unlocking the top drawer of his desk, he pulled out a cheque and showed it to me. It was made out to the *Southern Outlook* in the amount of $250, and was signed by Paul Redwing, president of Ollossa Mills, one of the South's largest textile trusts.

" I've really got him trained! " Parks gloated. " He gives me two hundred and fifty dollars every month that rolls by. Doesn't like to give cheques, though—usually just hands it to me in twenty-dollar bills."

" A few more like that, and you'd be fixed," I said suggestively.

He bit. " Redwing's not our only big backer—there are some others as big or bigger, who also let us use their names. You've probably heard of ' Bama's Big Mules '—meaning the top industrialists of the state. Well, we've got 'em hitched! For instance, there's C. F. De Bardeleben, Junior, head of the Red Diamond Mining Company, and Prince De Bardeleben, head of the Alabama Mining Institute. I could name a lot more."

He picked a card from a file on his desk.

"Here's a batch of selected prospects taken from a directory of Alabama industrialists," he said. "Just listen, and I'll show you how it's done." He dialled a number.

"Hello, Mr. Moore? . . . This is Raymond Parks, circulation manager of the *Southern Outlook*. I'm calling at the suggestion of several gentlemen who are well known to you—the De Bardelebens, Mr. Redwing, Mr. Rosser, and some others. We started sending you a complimentary subscription to our paper last week, and if you've had a chance to look it over you know that we've made it our business to save the South for free enterprise! Maybe you've been having trouble with union organizers in your own plant. I don't have to tell you that if those fellows are allowed to have their way, they will socialize and mongrelize the South in no time!

"Now, Mr. Moore, the service we're providing Southern industry is to get the truth to the workers. We're inviting leaders of Southern industry like yourself to join in this crusade by taking as many block subscriptions as possible. The cost is only two dollars per year for each subscription. You can provide us a list of your own workers if you like, or we'll send the papers you order to workers in other plants where unions are trying to muscle in. Can I put you down for two hundred dollars' worth? . . . One hundred and fifty? . . . Yes, thank you very much. . . . No, you needn't worry about your name being used in any way. May I send over for the cheque tomorrow morning? . . . Thank you, Mr. Moore!"

"Ye gods!" I said as he hung up. "A hundred and fifty bucks just like that?"

"Just like that!" Parks replied with a broad grin, pouring into our glasses. "Absolutely nothing to it! These guys hate the unions so, they'll pay any amount for protection. That bird isn't going to get away with just a hundred and fifty dollars. He's a large operator, and I'm going to jack him up and nick him every month!"

"What commission would I get on this proposition?"

"You won't believe it, but for every two bucks you take in, you can stick one in your own pocket! That gives you enough leeway to hire some girls to do the dirty work for you if you feel like it."

" It's a deal," I said. " When do I start? "

" Not so fast," said Parks, obviously pleased with my avariciousness. " Blackmon says you're a friend of Gene Talmadge. You won't mind if I try to reach him on the telephone, will you? After all, this is a responsible position and we ought to have some reference."

" Go right ahead—Gene ought to be in his office about now," I said. This was an unexpected development, and I began to perspire a bit as I considered the possibilities. Suppose the Klokann had found out that Perkins was Kennedy—and had told Talmadge? Having let me in on his top secrets—enough to put him out of business when I got around to publishing the names of his " angels "—Parks would doubtless be in a very ugly mood if he learned from Talmadge who I really was.

For the first time I began to size up Parks physically. He had about sixty pounds edge on me. But a beating would not keep my mouth shut, and he would know it. There was a scar on the back of Parks' neck, which looked like the result of a knife wound—probably a souvenir from his days as a Huey Long henchman. I decided he would be a tough customer.

" Mr. Eugene Talmadge . . ." Parks said into the telephone. " . . . When is he expected back? . . . Any time? . . . Well, keep trying, operator."

" I don't see how I can wait," I said, thinking it might be more healthy to check with Parks by telephone as to Ole Gene's recommendation. " There are some people I've got to see while I'm in town."

Parks stiffened, immediately suspicious.

" Don't rush off like that, Perkins," he said, trying to calm his own apprehensions. I could literally see him visualizing my exposing the names and cheques I had seen. " We'll get the call through in a minute. Here, have a cigarette—pour yourself another Bourbon."

" I ought to see these people this afternoon," I insisted, edging toward the door. This really threw a scare into him. He came between me and the door. It would be difficult to say which of us was perspiring the most.

"Take it easy," he said, taking hold of my elbow and ushering me back toward my chair. He poured a couple of drinks and handed me one, his hand shaking. Then came a cigarette, and I made the mistake of offering him a light— my hand was shaking a bit too. We were obviously making each other very nervous.

Then the phone rang, and Parks leapt for it. This put the desk between us again, and I let my hand rest on the handle of my briefcase, thinking I would make a bolt for the door at the first indication that things were going wrong.

"Yes, yes, go ahead—hello, Mr. Talmadge? . . . This is Raymond Parks, of the *Southern Outlook* over in Birmingham. . . . You do get our paper, don't you? . . . Thank you, sir— and that's a fine paper you get out too! Now the reason I called you, sir, is that we have a Mr. John Perkins here in our office, who we would like to have handle our paper over in Georgia, and he has given us your name as a reference. . . ."

I tightened my grip on my briefcase, and glued my eyes on Parks' face. The sweat was pouring from his forehead. But as I watched I could see him relax, and then begin to smile.

"Well, that's all we wanted to know, sir! Your word is all we need! Thank you very much, and I hope I didn't disturb you. Goodbye!"

"Perkins," he said, charging round the desk to slap me on the back, "you're all right! The job's yours! I'll make out your credentials and issue you some supplies first thing in the morning. Now what do you say about that double date? To hell with your other appointments—you've got a new job now!"

By this time my resistance was at a low ebb.

"O.K.," I said.

"Attaboy! Which one would you like? I saw you giving the eye to that little blonde!"

He opened the door and called into the next room.

"Hey, Myrtle—whadaya say we knock off and have a party? You and Dottie come on in, and tell the other kids they can go home."

Happily, Parks poured out four drinks. Myrtle and Dottie came in and closed the door. Myrtle promptly settled down on the arm of Parks' chair, while Dottie perched on the edge of the desk, crossed her legs, and looked at me coyly over her highball. I leaned back, telling myself that as Georgia circulation manager of the *Southern Outlook* I was entitled to some relaxation in life. . . .

Two days later, I was back in Atlanta with a large box of *Outlook* stationery, pads of subscription blanks, and a bale of sample copies. Seldom was anyone so ready for business —with no intention of transacting any.

It was exactly two weeks and a day after I had signed the Klan application that my phone rang and I heard Slim's voice.

" Perkins, at six-fifteen tomorrow evening you are to be standing on the north-west corner of Peachtree Street and Auburn Avenue! Don't fail! "

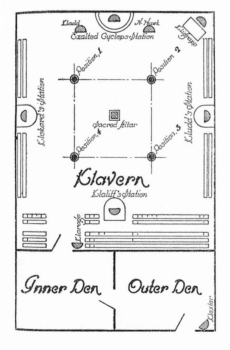

Diagram from the Klan's *Koran* (1915, revised 1925) showing standard arrangement of outer and inner dens, klavern, seating, officers' stations, sacred altar, flag and fiery cross, lockers for storage, and so on. On meeting rituals, see Wyn Craig Wade, *The Fiery Cross: The Ku Klux Klan in America* (New York: Simon and Schuster, 1987), pp. 405–26, and an original copy of the *Klavern* in the Stetson Kennedy Papers, Schomburg Center for Research in Black Culture, New York Public Library.

CHAPTER THREE

BEFORE THE ALTAR OF HATE

I was there, a half-hour ahead of time.

The station where I had been ordered to take my stand was at Five Points, the busiest intersection in Atlanta, and the rush hour was already beginning. Why the Klan had chosen such a spot for a rendezvous was beyond me.

As I stood there scanning the faces of the people who passed by, expecting Slim to appear, I wondered what chance there was that the Klokann, in spite of all my efforts to take on a new identity, had discovered who I really was. Perhaps I was waiting to be taken for a ride instead of an initiation! If I were ever going to turn back, this would probably be my last chance to do it with impunity. But then I remembered the cruel flogging the Klan had given Flo, and recalled too the many outrages which had taught me to hate the hooded hate-mongers. . . .

I was still standing there when, at exactly six-fifteen, a large black sedan screeched up to the kerb beside me. In it were four robed, hooded and masked Klansmen! The back door was flung open, and a voice from behind a mask—the first such I had ever heard—ordered:

" Get in! "

Taking a deep breath, I got in, squeezing between the two Kluxers on the back seat.

The crowds pressing by had stopped in amazement, but the policeman who was directing traffic in the centre of the intersection pretended not to have noticed anything. The Klansman at the wheel, I noticed with something of a start, was wearing a scarlet satin cape instead of the white ones attached to the robes of the other Kluxers. He was an enormous man, his huge bulk almost filling the front seat. Fortunately the other Klansman up front was a small man.

The driver threw the car into second gear, and we plunged into the traffic of Peachtree Street, leaving a crowd gaping on the kerb. This didn't look like the beginning of any initiation I had ever heard about, Klan or otherwise.

" Slim . . . ? " I said tentatively, looking from one Klansman to the other, trying to see through the eye-slits to the faces behind the masks.

" Shut up! "   commanded the red-caped Klansman. " You'll speak only when spoken to! "

This did not make me feel any better. With every moment that went by, I became more convinced that I had been discovered and was being taken for a ride. I wondered, with a half smile, what the reaction would be if I were to say: " You can let me out at the next corner."

Actually, I toyed with the notion that I might be able to make a leap for it at the first red traffic light. But this question was answered for me when the man at the wheel began to tap out bursts of three blasts on the horn, and drove at full speed towards the red light. A policeman leapt out from the kerb blowing his whistle shrilly; but instead of halting us, he stopped the cross traffic and signalled us on.

So that's how these gangsters work, I thought. With the police giving them right of way, it was no wonder they rode rough-shod over the country.

The car turned off in a westerly direction, weaving through traffic and ignoring red lights whenever we caught one. Eventually we passed through the suburbs, picking up speed all the time, and at length emerged on an open highway through the countryside.

The driver stepped on the accelerator, and I looked at the speedometer. It hovered between eighty and ninety.

" Brother Night Hawk, how about slowing down to seventy on the curves? " the little Klansman on the front seat said in a nervous voice that I recognized immediately as Slim's. " There's two things I like in this world, and Kluxing is one of 'em. But I don't like it so well as to get killed in the process. I do love to Klux, but anytime it interferes with that other, I'm gonna give up Kluxing! "

The Night Hawk chuckled, but if he slowed it was imperceptible. On and on we sped, farther and farther from the city. It was dark now, and the lights from farmhouses were few and far between. If they intended to do a job on me, this thinly settled countryside would be a logical place for it. So far as I knew, Klan initiations were conducted inside the Klaverns in Atlanta.

Such discomforting thoughts as these were interrupted by a sudden "whoosh-whoosh!" The car trembled, but the Night Hawk held it in the road.

"Sideswiped some goddam nigger driving a cotton cart!" he cursed. "I tried to skim him close just to give him a scare. If my car's tore up any I'll skin him alive!"

He brought the car to a halt and leapt out to inspect the damage.

"Could have been worse," he said with relief. "The bumper caught most of it. We ought to take the black bastard along to entertain the boys!"

He climbed back into the car, and backed it rapidly to where the overturned cart was lying in the ditch. The cotton was dumped in the red clay mud, and one cartwheel was some distance off in the field.

"Sarah, baby, they done killed you!" an anguished voice cried out in the darkness.

A grey-haired Negro man, tears streaming down his cheeks, was sitting on his haunches in the ditch, holding the mule's head in his lap. One of the wagon tongues had been driven into its side.

"You had no business bein' on the highway at night without lights!" the Night Hawk shouted at him.

"I had light," the old man said simply, nodding to where a small grass fire was springing up beside the ditch where the kerosene tail-lamp had exploded.

The Night Hawk looked down the highway in both directions.

"Here, uncle," he said, reaching into his pocket and pulling out a ten-dollar bill. "You look like a good nigger— take this and buy yourself another mule."

The old man just looked at the money in silence, until finally the Night Hawk let it drop into the ditch.

"Ten bucks won't do me no good, the fix I'm in," the old man said. "Sarah cost me fifty dollars, and there ain't no 'nother one like her in the world. Besides that, my cart's busted all to smithereens, and my year's share of cotton is lying in the mud."

"To hell with you and your mule!" the Night Hawk said bitterly, picking up the money, wiping it off, and putting it back in his pocket. "If you say so much as one word to the police about who hit you, it'll be your last!"

He got back in the sedan, and we drove off into the night, leaving the old man sitting there in the ditch, crying quietly over his dead mule.

"Don't know what's gettin' into niggers nowadays," the Night Hawk grumbled. "They don't appreciate nothin' you try to do for 'em. It's just as well he didn't take the ten bucks—I'd probably have had a hellova time gettin' it back from the Klan's charity fund."

Remembering the Night Hawk's remark about taking the Negro along "to entertain the boys," I began to wonder if I was scheduled to provide such entertainment—on the receiving end of a bullwhip, or worse. At least it was obvious that we were on our way to meet some other Klansmen.

"We're gonna be late if we don't step on it," the Night Hawk said, pushing the sedan back around ninety. We zipped past a car going in the same direction, and the wail of a siren caught our ears. Looking back, I saw the car had flashed on a red spotlight, and was coming after us in hot pursuit.

"Don't suppose that nigger back yonder has already talked, and they radioed ahead to pick us up?" Slim whined.

"Don't worry," the Night Hawk said confidently, slowing down.

The police car quickly overtook us, pulled alongside—and then sped on ahead with siren still wailing and red light flashing.

"I thought so!" the Night Hawk exulted, stepping on the gas and following in the wake of the police car. "That's some of our Brother Klansmen on the Rockledge County police force giving us an escort. We can stop worrying about that little accident down the road. I was hoping we had already crossed over into Rockledge when it happened. We're among friends here, and we have nothing to fear from the law!"

I was worrying plenty when we skidded around a curve, and my eyes caught sight of an enormous fiery cross far ahead, seemingly suspended high in the sky.

" They must be dragging a flaming cross through the skies behind an aeroplane! " I thought.

" Ain't she a beaut? " the Night Hawk asked proudly. " That oughta put the fear of the Klan in all the niggers for ninety miles around. I worked all day draggin' them oil drums up the mountain."

Then I knew our destination. We were headed for Stone Mountain, where a cross-burning in 1915 had marked the " reincarnation " of the modern Klan, and where Imperial Klonvokations had traditionally been held since! Tonight's events, whatever they might be, were certainly going to be something more than an ordinary local Klan initiation.

As we drew nearer, the huge size of the cross which blazed in the sky became all the more evident. Entering the small hamlet of Stone Mountain, we found the streets lit up by the glow. Craning my neck, I looked out and up. Made by stringing oil drums at intervals across the face of the mountain, the cross was at least 300 yards long.

Beneath the cross, carved into the solid chunk of granite that is Stone Mountain (its presence in the rolling Georgia Piedmont plain has never been understood by geologists), I saw the half-finished heroic-size figures on horseback of Robert E. Lee and other Confederate generals. The work of the noted sculptor Gutson Borglum, the ill-fated memorial was sponsored during the 1930s by the United Daughters of the Confederacy and surreptitiously by the Ku Klux Klan; but no one was able to collect enough money to complete it.

As we approached the base of the mountain, we came upon a robed and masked Klansman standing in an intersection directing traffic. In a highly professional manner, his cape flowing like that of a French gendarme, he halted the cross traffic and signalled for us to turn off down a dirt road that wound around the side of the mountain. Looking down at his feet, I saw the trousers of a police uniform protruding from beneath his Klan robe.

" Flump . . . flump . . . flump-flump! " A strange sound

filled the night, rather like the wing beats of some enormous bird from a prehistoric era.

" Just listen to those oil drums rumble! " the Night Hawk said happily.

We drove slowly over the rocky road, past tumbledown shacks of Negro cotton pickers. The occupants—men, women and children—were standing along the road, as though watching a parade. I saw several of the young men wearing U.S. Army shirts, indicating that they were veterans of World War II. All of the spectators' faces were immobile.

" What's wrong with these niggers, anyway? " the Night Hawk growled. " They ought to all be out hidin' in the woods, or at least under their beds! Don't they know enough to be scared? Just look at their sassy faces! I've half a mind to stop off on the way home and teach 'em more respect! "

The road we were travelling wound up the mountainside. It was lined now, on both sides, solidly with parked cars. Trying not to make myself conspicuous, I kept both eyes open for out-of-state licence plates. This was my first opportunity to spy on the Klan, and I tried to remember all the licence numbers I could. Though the majority of the cars were from various parts of Georgia, I could see there were sizeable contingents from such states as Florida, Alabama, Tennessee, the Carolinas and Ohio. While I succeeded in tucking some numbers away in my head, most of them were to evaporate before the night was over. . . .

We came at last to a large field, where hundreds of additional cars were parked, together with seven Atlanta buses marked " Charter." Obviously, there were literally thousands of Klansmen on the mountain.

In the centre of the field we came upon a campfire. Around it were four robed, hooded and masked Klansmen, clad not in regulation white but resplendent satin robes of purple, gold, green and red, with dragons and other such emblems embroidered upon their chests. The top dogs of the Klan, I thought to myself.

As our car came to a stop the Klansman in purple rushed towards us.

" What the hell's been keeping you, Cliff? " he demanded.

" The boys have been drawn up in formation up on the mountain nearly an hour, and are freezing to death! "

" We had a little accident on the way out, Your Majesty," the Night Hawk said apologetically. " But your idea for staging a fake kidnapping at Five Points went over big! You can bet your boots the whole city is buzzing, and the papers will be full of it tomorrow! "

" I'm glad something is turning out right," the purple-robed man I now knew to be the Imperial Wizard said. " But if we don't get started soon those drums will run out of fuel oil, and we'll be stuck up on the mountain in the dark."

" I was all over the mountain today," the Night Hawk said. " I think I know a short cut up to the glade."

" Lead on, Night Hawk, and we'll follow! " the Wizard ordered. " But don't forget to bring the fiery cross."

The Night Hawk went over to his car and unlocked the boot. From it he took a cross, heavily wrapped in burlap. Removing the wrapping, he extracted a red neon cross about four feet high, complete with dry cells which he strapped over his back under the red cape.

" Fall in, you! " he shouted at me.

The Night Hawk started slowly up the steep mountainside, followed by the Wizard and gold, green and red Klansmen. I followed them, and the three white-robed Klansmen made up a rearguard.

" Don't y'all want a cup of hot coffee before you go? "

A frenzied little man had dashed up and shouted the question at us. Looking back, I could see on the outskirts of the field an improvised refreshment stand.

" Got no time! " the Wizard shouted back.

" Dammit to hell! " I heard the little man curse beneath his breath. " First the Wiz tells me to be prepared for four or five thousand, and then barely a couple of thousand show up. I'm gonna lose my shirt on this deal! "

He slouched on back across the field, while we continued up the mountain, picking our way slowly between large boulders and pot-holes which loomed suddenly in the darkness. Overfed and pot-bellied, the satin-robed Klan leaders were soon puffing and grunting from the unaccustomed exertion.

"Blast it, Night Hawk, are you sure you know where you're going?" the Wizard demanded.

"Don't worry, Your Majesty—I can see like a cat in the dark!"

As he spoke, the liquid whistle of a chuck-will's-widow (Southern cousin of the whip-poor-will) sounded in the darkness to our right.

Strange, I thought, for such a bird to be on this treeless slope. Then there came an answering whistle to our left— and another and another, until it was clear that the whistles were human signals, and that we were surrounded by a dozen or more men.

"My Klavaliers are on the job!" the Night Hawk gloated. "There won't be no alien eyes prying on our ceremony while they're guarding the mountain!"

"They're closing in on us!" the Wizard exclaimed, a note of fear creeping into his voice. "Do something, you dam' fool—signal them quick!"

The Wizard pursed his lips, but he was so excited his whistle got no further than "Whip" before it petered out.

A rifle cracked up the mountain, the projectile knocking splinters from a boulder near the Wizard's head, and then ricocheted with a vicious whine off into the night.

The Wizard hastily scooted around to the other side of the boulder, hugging it.

"Take cover!" he cried, hoarsely and belatedly; but the rest of us had already done so on our own initiative. At the sound of the Wizard's voice, a volley of rifle and pistol fire swept around us from all directions. Boulders, obviously, were inappropriate. The Wizard and I caught sight of the same pot-hole simultaneously, and flung ourselves into it. The others speedily disappeared into other holes in the ground.

"Don't shoot! It's us—me—the Imperial Wizard!" the Wizard shouted at the top of his lungs.

The mountain echoed his cry, and then was silent except for the "flump-flump" of the oil drums as the wind whipped the flames of the fiery cross.

"I don't think they believe me," the Wizard croaked in a very small voice, gazing at me balefully through one eye-slit of his mask.

" Flash your cross, Night Hawk—that'll show 'em! " he called out in a burst of inspiration.

The Night Hawk, ensconced in an adjoining hole, reached for the cross and held it on high. He pressed the switch, and the area all around us was lit with a roseate glow.

Into this glow in a matter of seconds there stepped a Klansman clad in a robe and mask of black. Then, from behind boulders in every direction, other black-clad figures emerged, until we were surrounded by about a dozen of the ominous crew.

" My God, Chief," the first of the black-robed men called out. " What are you doing here? "

The Wizard and all the other satin-covered dignitaries began to climb out of their holes.

" Ye gods and little catfish! " the black-robed Klavalier exclaimed. " The Wizard and all his official family! "

" I'll teach you to disobey my orders! " the Wizard roared, his courage apparently recovered. He rushed at the Klavalier and shook his fist in his face, while the other Klavaliers shrank back visibly into the shadows. " I've given you Klavaliers strict orders not to fire at everything that stirs in the bush but to see what you're shooting at first! Get me? "

" Yes, Your Majesty—we were trying to see, but couldn't."

" Cliff, this is your responsibility! " the Wizard said, turning on the Night Hawk. " If you can't get some discipline into your men, I'm going to have you up on charges! "

" I've tole 'em time and time again, Your Majesty, but they're a hard-headed bunch," the Night Hawk said remorsefully.

" I can lead you to the glade," the Klavalier offered eagerly. " Back to your stations, Klavaliers! "

The black-robed figures disappeared silently, and we resumed our trek up the mountain, led by the Klavalier with a flashlight.

At length, emerging from a defile, we came suddenly into a wide, open plain on the side of the mountain directly beneath the huge fiery cross. Drawn up in the centre of this field were over a thousand white-robed Klansmen. In lines three deep, with arms interlocked, they formed an impenetrable barrier to a huge square. It was by far the largest assemblage of Klansmen I had ever seen, and the impression was one of power.

At one end of the field there was another group of men, nearly a thousand strong, clad in ordinary civilian clothes. These, I gathered, were like myself candidates for naturalization as citizens of the Klan's Invisible Empire. They were lolling about, some sitting on rocks or their haunches, smoking. As we came into view there was a murmur from the ranks of both the Klansmen and the candidates. Then the Klansmen parted ranks, and through the gap a Kluxer clad in blue trotted towards us.

" Thank God you're here at last, Your Majesty! " he exclaimed. " The altars are all in readiness. I only hope we don't run out of fuel oil! "

" Well done, Faithful Kludd! " said the Wizard. " Let the ceremonies begin! "

" Follow me! " the Night Hawk ordered me, leading me off to the group of probationers. Looking back over my shoulder, I saw the satin-clad officers disappear into the centre of the square, while the three white-robed Klansmen who had been in the car with me fell into line with their brethren.

I joined the group of candidates, and wandered among them, studying them closely. Judging from their clothes, I guessed that most of them were unskilled or semi-skilled tradesmen and farm folk, with a sprinkling of white-collar and professional men. There were also many men in police uniforms—city, state and county.

As for their ages, I was disappointed to see so many young men of my own generation. The group was almost equally divided between young men, middle-aged men and old-timers. I had hoped that the spread of public school education, and the experiences of World War II, would make my own generation less susceptible to the appeals of Ku Kluxery than were their fathers and grandfathers before them. But this was obviously not the case; many of the young men were wearing portions of U.S. Army uniforms, indicating that they were veterans. A sad commentary, I thought, on Army orientation courses!

Sidling up to an old-timer, I said:

" First time I ever knew the big shots wore such fancy-coloured robes."

" That's so you'll know they're big shots," he chuckled. " Each one of the Kloranic officers has his special colour of robe."

" The Wizard is the one in purple, the guy with the red cape is the Night Hawk, and the one in blue is called a Kludd—that much I already know," I said.

" You're right," the old man nodded. " The Kludd is the chaplain of the Klan. Them others, the one in gold, he's the Klaliff or vice-president, the green one is the Klokard or lecturer, and the red one is the Kladd of the Klan, or conductor."

" How come you to know so much about it? " I asked with a show of respect.

" I'll give you a clue," he said with a wink, leaning over to whisper in my ear. " I've helped put on many a Klan initiation in my day. There wasn't enough new candidates to suit the Wizard for tonight's ceremony, so he ordered a bunch of us old-time members to leave our robes at home and go through the initiation with you. I reckon he aims to make it look like the Klan is growing faster than what it is."

Our little gab-feast was interrupted when the Klan square broke, and the red-clad Kladd came through.

" Every man who has in his possession a firearm of any kind will step forward and surrender it for the duration of the ceremony! " he shouted at the group of candidates.

Several men came forward and handed him revolvers and automatics.

" Us too? " a probationer in police uniform asked.

" Every man-jack! " the Kladd barked, obviously enjoying his ability to disarm police officers.

A steady procession of assorted police came forward, unbuckled their revolver and ammunition belts, and handed them over to the Kladd. I began to count. Soon the Kladd's arms were filled, and the Night Hawk stepped forward to help. When all weapons had been turned in, both men had their arms full. I had counted thirty-seven policemen. The Kladd and Night Hawk staggered off with their burdens, and the Klan square opened and swallowed them up.

In a moment they were both back.

" Attention! " the Kladd bellowed. " Fall in—single file, right hand on the shoulder of the man in front of you! "

Thinking it might be a good idea for me to be in the forefront of the proceedings, I took a stand at the head of the line. As the men stamped out their cigarettes and shuffled into place, a cloud of choking red clay dust arose. The Night Hawk charged up and down the line, cursing like a top sergeant. The long line curled like a serpent down the mountainside. Finally the Kladd drew himself up at the head of the line, and the Night Hawk attached himself to the rear.

" Aliens of the Outer World! " the Kladd addressed us. " You are now candidates for naturalization as citizens of the Invisible Empire, Knights of the Ku Klux Klan! Before we pass on into the delectable realms of Klankraft, if there is one among you who, in his secret heart of hearts, knows that he harbours some ulterior motive, and will not remain loyal to all the obligations and duties of Klankraft, I command him to step aside and go no farther! "

There was a long silence, but needless to say no one spoke up. I merely gulped a time or two.

" Forward march! " he finally ordered, taking me by the left arm and leading the line to a corner of the Klan square. The Kladd was carrying the red neon cross now, and its glow gave a roseate hue to the white robes. So intense was this glow, in fact, that I looked around and discovered that the Night Hawk at the end of the line was now carrying a brilliant red flare—stolen, no doubt, from some railroad train. I had to admit it made a colourful procession.

" Who seeks to enter here? " a voice from within the square demanded.

" Aliens of the Outer World of darkness, who seek citizenship in the Invisible Empire, Knights of the Ku Klux Klan! " replied the Kladd.

" Have they at all times shown themselves to be loyal to their God, country, race and home? "

" They have been so reported! "

" Have they the password? "

" They have it not; but I have and am authorized to speak it for them."

" Pass, Kladd, and candidates for citizenship in the Invisible Empire! "

At these words the Klan square opened up, and the Kladd took me by the arm once more and led us inside. As he led us off in a circle to the right, I looked around me. Midway in front of each side of the square a crude stone altar had been erected, and beside each of these altars blazed a fiery cross about five feet high. In the centre of the square was a larger, more elaborate, altar, flanked by the American flag on a staff, and an unlit fiery cross.

" Halt! " the Kladd commanded, drawing us up in front of the first altar. So long was the line of candidates that he had to break it up into three rows.

" Right face! "

Several of the candidates were so nervous they turned left instead of right.

" What's wrong with you dumb-bells? " the Night Hawk cursed. " Don't you know right from left? "

Behind Altar No. 1 stood the blue-robed Kludd, arms folded solemnly in front of him.

" Faithful Kludd, I present candidates seeking elevation to the primary order of knighthood! " intoned the Kladd.

" Have they proven themselves devoted to the principles of True Americanism, Protestant Christianity and White Supremacy? "

" Since that moment when first they came under the scrutiny of the eye of the Unknown, it is reported that they have been worthy."

" Honour to those who are honourable! Advancement to those worthy of advancement! Conduct them to the Klokard of the Klan! "

Leading us on in our counter-clockwise circle inside the square, the Kladd called us to a halt in front of the altar of the green-robed Klokard directly across from the Kludd.

After substantially the same question and answer, we were led to the third altar, that of the gold-clad Klaliff.

" Have they always been loyal white Christian Americans? " the Klaliff demanded.

" There is among them not one who even in the slightest act, so far as we know, has ever been a traitor," the Kladd responded.

" Good words, for treason is the crime that blackens every other. You may escort your charges to the altar of His Majesty the Imperial Wizard! "

Around we marched like a troop of convicts, the red clay dust rising in a cloud, until we were called to a halt at the far end before the altar of the Wizard.

" Your Majesty, I present candidates seeking entrance into the Knights of the Ku Klux Klan. On their way hither, they have passed under the scrutinizing eyes of the Kludd, Klokard and Klaliff, who believe them to be worthy! "

The Wizard was about to speak, when the fiery cross beside his altar spluttered and went out. There was a bit of disconcerted muttering, until finally a white-robed Klansman stepped forward with a can of fuel oil, dashed it on the burlap with which the iron-pipe cross was wrapped, and ignited it again.

Regaining his dignity, the Wizard intoned:

" Are you each and every one ready and willing to take a fourfold solemn oath of allegiance binding you for ever to the Invisible Empire? "

" I am! " prompted the Night Hawk, and we all echoed him.

Speaking over our heads to the massed Klansmen, the Wizard called out:

" My Ghouls and Terrors, what is the penalty sufficient for betrayal of the secrets of the Klan? "

" Death, death, at the hands of a Brother! " their answering chant replied, causing my knees to waver a bit.

" Knowing this, do you still wish to proceed? " the Wizard demanded of us.

" I do! " we all replied.

Even as I spoke, I noticed for the first time that all the pistols which the Kladd and Night Hawk had collected from the candidates now lay in a pile at the Wizard's feet.

" Faithful Kladd, you will conduct the candidates to the sacred altar! " he commanded.

This time we were led out into the centre of the square, and laboriously assembled to form three sides of a square around the altar. A table-like affair constructed of field stones, the altar was about waist high, and was draped with a Confederate flag, in the centre of which lay an open Bible.

" Principal Terrors, you will assist me in conferring the Order of K-Uno! " the Wizard called out. Stepping from behind his own altar, he waited until the Klaliff, Klokard and Kludd had joined him. Together they then marched up behind the altar in the centre of the square. The Klaliff, who was carrying a sword, came around in front of the altar, carefully took the lower right-hand corner of the draped flag and folded it back over the Bible to the upper left corner of the flag. Then he laid the sword across the altar above the flag, its tip extending to touch the fiery cross, which still had not been ignited. This done, he unfolded the flag once more. Then the Night Hawk stepped forward, ignited the cross, saluted the Wizard and reported:

" Sir, the necessary changes have been made in the Sacred Altar! "

Raising his arm, the Kludd spoke the following prayer:

" God of our fathers, we thank Thee for these tall, sun-crowned men who are about to become Knights of the Ku Klux Klan! May they so live as Klansmen as to always be an honour to their God, country and fellow Knights! These favours we ask in the name of Jesus Christ, the Klansman's true criterion of character. Amen! "

The prayer ended, the Kludd led the entire assemblage in what was supposed to be a song. The tune I scarcely recognized as " From Greenland's Icy Mountains," but the words were the Klan's own:

> We meet with cordial greetings
>   In this our sacred cave,
> To pledge anew our compact
>   With hearts sincere and brave;
> A band of faithful Klansmen,
>   Knights of the KKK,
> We will stand together
>   For ever and for aye!

" Candidates, kneel! " the Wizard commanded imperiously.

We got down on our knees on the rocky ground.

" Do you solemnly swear to be ever faithful to our God, his son Jesus Christ and the tenets of the Christian religion? "

" I do! " we all chanted.

" Do you solemnly swear to always uphold the flag and constitution of the United States of America? "

" I do! "

" Do you believe that this is a White Man's country, and should so remain, and will you do all in your power to uphold the principles of White Supremacy and the purity of White Womanhood? "

" I do! "

" Do you solemnly swear to be ever faithful to the Klan and each other, and to come to the aid of a Brother Klansman in any extremity—treason, rape and malicious murder alone excepted? "

" I do! "

" Sirs, have each of you, in taking the fourfold oath of a Klansman before this Sacred Altar, done so without mental reservation? "

" I have! "

I looked up, and saw that the Wizard was looking directly at me!

" You! " he cried, pointing to me. " Come forward and kneel before the altar! "

This was so unexpected I wobbled on my way. I must have been discovered, after all! I looked at the ranks of Klansmen, three deep, their arms still interlocked, and knew that escape was utterly impossible. But why had they let me in on all the secret ritual—unless they intended to kill me?

I knelt directly in front of the altar, and noted that the Night Hawk had sprung to fill the vacant spot I had left in the line of other candidates, who were still kneeling.

The Wizard stepped forward and lifted the sword from the altar, its point glowing hot from the flames of the fiery cross.

As he began to speak, I hung on to his every word:

" By virtue of the authority vested in me as Imperial Wizard, Knights of the Ku Klux Klan, I dub thee ' Klansman,' the most honoured title among men! "

As I groaned with relief, the Wizard tapped me on the left shoulder with the flat of the sword blade, and then went on:

" I command you forever to bear in mind that it would be better that this knightly sword which now has touched your shoulder should pass itself through your heart—"

With this the Wizard suddenly plunged the point of the sword at my heart, almost causing me to fall over backward.

" —than that you should ever forget the oath you have just assumed, or prove false to it, or any part of it! "

Replacing the sword upon the altar, the Wizard waved his outstretched palm first over me and then over the rest of the kneeling men.

" Rise, Knights of the Ku Klux Klan, and let your Brother Knights never have cause to regret that they believed you worthy of fellowship! "

We struggled up from our sore knees and brushed the red clay from our trousers. Acting on cue from the Wizard, all the Klansmen suddenly removed their hoods and masks. The Wizard came around in front of the altar and gave my left hand a fish-wiggle handshake. The Klan square broke, and the old and new Klansmen mingled, giving each other this same left-handed shake.

Pulling a wide assortment of whisky bottles from beneath their robes, the Kluxers passed them from one to another, grimacing, coughing and spitting as the fiery raw corn whiskies went down.

" Care fo' a li'l drink, Your Majesty? " a wizened little Klansman asked, holding out a Coca-Cola bottle containing a rich brown liquid. " It's good stuff—I made it myself."

" Much obliged, Brother, but I brought some of my own," the Wizard replied. The little man walked away, and I heard the Wizard mutter to the Klaliff:

" It don't pay to sample the rot-gut liquor some of these poor white trash make up. The last time I tried any I asked the man how he made it, and he said he fed his mule corn and then made the whisky out of the fresh dung! "

I looked around me at the assemblage. Unmasked, the spectacle struck me as even more foreboding than before. Here was naked, brazen power, over and above the law, wielding the power of life and death over every community into which its tentacles reached.

" Well, how does it feel to be a Klansman? "

There was a slap on my back which almost floored me in my shaky condition, and I turned around to find Slim grinning at me.

" Great! " I lied. " That's some show you boys put on! "

" I never get tired of seeing it," Slim agreed reverently.

" I can hardly wait to attend my first Klan meeting," I said.

" Monday night, eight o'clock, at 198½ Whitehall Street," Slim said. " We'll teach you then all the secrets of Klankraft and the Way of the Klavern."

" Do I ride back to town with you and the officers? "

" You'd better go back in one of the buses. We're gonna stop off and do a little Kluxing on our way home." He smacked his lips in anticipation.

" What about this oath against ' rape, malicious murder ' and so on ? " I asked innocently.

" Oh, that don't count against niggers, kikes, Catholics, Reds and suchlike! " Slim laughed.

" When do I get in on the fun? " I felt obliged to ask.

" Easy does it," Slim laughed again. " Your time will come."

CHAPTER FOUR

THE WAY OF THE KLAVERN

At last I was a Klansman!

The big question mark in my campaign to get the goods on the Kluxers—whether I could succeed in penetrating their ranks—had been answered. I was in. It was now up to me to pick my way carefully to take advantages of the opportunities before me. I resolved to keep my identity secret as long as possible, to gather all the evidence I could, and to put that evidence to the best possible use.

During the week that intervened between my initiation and first meeting I acquired a robe.

" I think I can save you five bucks on your robe," Slim said. " There was a Brother banished last month, and he was ordered to turn in his robe. I'm pretty sure I can get it for you for ten bucks, it being second-hand."

" Sounds like a bargain," I agreed, handing him the ten dollars then and there. " He wasn't bumped off, was he? I don't think I'd be comfortable in a dead man's robe."

" Naw! " Slim laughed. " This one was eased out for not paying his dues. I'll give you another little clue on how you can save yourself some money. One of our Brothers has a laundry on the corner of Hemphill Avenue and 10th Street; he launders our robes at a special rate of only thirty cents."

" Good deal! " I said, making a note of the address—and hoping my robe would never be stained by blood.

The following Monday night I made my way at eight o'clock as directed to 198½ Whitehall Street, to a large frame building where Klavern No. 1 held its meetings. A half-dozen men were lolling about the entrance.

" I'm looking for some left-handed Americans! " I said as I approached them, throwing out my left palm in the Klan sign of recognition which Slim had taught me.

" You've come to the right place! " said a big man standing guard at the door. I recognized him immediately as Cliff Carter, Night Hawk and chief of the Klavaliers. " I'm charged with protecting the security of the Klavern, but I remember you from Stone Mountain. Go on up! "

I climbed the stair and found myself in a large room, where there were about fifty men standing about, talking and smoking. Almost all of them, I saw, were like myself, initiates from the mountain ceremony. On the far side of the room there was a closed door, with a wicket peephole in it. After a few minutes the Night Hawk appeared at the head of the stairs.

" All right, Klansmen, gather around me and I will instruct you in the way of the Klavern! " he called out. He took a stand in the centre of the room, and we formed a circle around him.

" There is but one way to gain admission to the Klavern of the Klan in Klonklave assembled," he intoned importantly. " Pay you strict heed, for if at any step you falter or make a false move, you will be immediately challenged and required to prove your identity as a true Klansman! But first, now that you have become citizens of the Invisible Empire, you must know something of its language. In general, the Klan terminology is derived by substituting the letters ' kl ' wherever the letter ' c ' occurs. For instance, instead of ' cavern ' we say ' klavern." Get it? '

There was an assenting chorus, and the Night Hawk continued.

" How many of you know how the Ku Klux Klan got its name? "

" I've heard tell the words ' Ku Klux ' came from the sound of cocking a rifle . . ." one man hesitantly volunteered.

" Haw-haw-haw! " the Night Hawk laughed. " That sounds like something some darky cooked up while on the business end of a Klan rifle! Not a bad idea—but it's not right."

" I've heard it said that the letters ' KKK ' stand for ' Kill! Kill! Kill! ' " another Klansman spoke up.

" That's hot! " the Night Hawk laughed again. " You fellows are teaching me things. But the truth is we get our name from the Greek word *kuklos*, meaning circle. During Reconstruction days after the Civil War the first secret societies were called the White Circle, and the Klan itself was founded in 1865 in Tennessee, with General Forrest as the first Wizard."

" What about the Klan part of the Klan's name? " I asked, thinking it might be a good idea to show an interest.

" That comes from the Scottish clans," the Night Hawk replied. " Our custom of burning fiery crosses comes from the same place. The Scottish clans used to send out riders on horseback with fiery crosses to summon their fellow clansmen to war."

" I had to be drafted into the war against Hitler," a young man declared bitterly, " but when the war of the races comes I'll be one of the first to volunteer! "

"Attaboy! " the Night Hawk nodded his approval. " Now before we go ahead I want to tell you a thing or two about the names of our Klan officers, and so on." From his pocket he pulled a worn small blue book. Fortunately I stood in the front rank, where I was able to read the title page. In large letters on the cover it said:

The Kloran
The Rites of K-Uno—Karacter, Honour, Duty

As the Night Hawk thumbed through the volume I was able to read the further inscription on the cover:

IN WARNING: The Kloran is THE book of the Klan, and is therefore a sacred book with our citizens and its contents MUST be rigidly safeguarded. The book or any part of it MUST not be kept or carried where any person of the alien world may chance to become acquainted with its sacred contents. A penalty sufficient will be speedily enforced for disregarding this decree in the profanation of the Kloran!

I made up my mind that someday, somehow, I would lay hands on *The Kloran* (a resolve in which I eventually succeeded, though I cannot reveal how without endangering another person who is still within reach of the Klan).

"All right, now, pay attention!" the Night Hawk commanded. "I'm going to read off the names of the various Klan officers. You won't be expected to remember all of 'em, but will catch on soon enough. . . .

"I guess you all know we call the geographical jurisdiction of our order 'The Invisible Empire.' A Realm of this Empire consists of a group of several adjoining states. A Province is a sub-division of a Realm, and consists of one or more counties. A Klanton is the area over which a local Klan has jurisdiction.

"We call the meeting of a Klan a Klonklave, a province meeting is called a Klonverse, a Klorero is a meeting of a Realm, and an Imperial Klonvokation is a nationwide meeting of the whole Invisible Empire.

"The government of the Invisible Empire is vested with the Imperial Wizard, the Emperor, assisted by his fifteen Genii—the Imperial Officers constituting his official family. The government of a Realm is vested with a Grand Dragon, assisted by his nine Hydras—the Grand Officers. The government of a Province is vested with a Great Titan, assisted by his twelve Furies—the Great Officers. And a local Klan is governed by an Exalted Cyclops, assisted by his twelve Terrors."

The Night Hawk paused and cleared his throat.

"Now then," he resumed, still reading from *The Kloran*, "our other officers consist of the Klaliff, or vice-president; the Klokard, or lecturer; the Kludd, or chaplain; Kligrapp, or secretary; Klabee, or treasurer; Kladd, or conductor; Klarogo, or inner guard; Klexter, or outer guard; Klokan, a member of the five-man Klokann investigating committee; and the Night Hawk—yours truly—whose job is to protect the sanctity of the Klavern. It's also my job to serve as custodian of the Fiery Cross, which I carry in all ceremonies and parades, and to instruct new members in the Way of the Klavern.

"An organizer of the Klan is called a Kleagle, and a Klavalier is a soldier of the Klan, a member of our Military Department. A Past Exalted Cyclops we call a Giant, a Past Great Titan is called a Great Giant, and a Past Imperial

Wizard is called an Imperial Giant. And that takes care of the officers. . . .

" Now for our secret signs. Some of these I will show you after we enter the Klavern. But right now I want to be sure you know the Klan handshake. Most of you must have learned it on the mountain last week. But try it again among yourselves. Always with the left hand—all Klan signs are executed with the left hand, unless both hands are required. Nothing to the shake except you just wiggle each other's palm back and forth a time or two. . . ."

After we had all shaken hands in the prescribed manner, the Night Hawk spoke up again.

" Another thing you need to know is how to vote. We don't do an awful lot of voting in the Klan—the presiding officer generally makes up his own mind, or carries out the edicts of his superiors without question, and it's our duty to do the same. But anyway, here's how it's done:

" When a vote is called for, the presiding officer will rap once with his gavel. At this signal every man will place his left elbow on his left knee, letting his left arm fall straight. The left thumb is folded across the palm, like this, and the four fingers spread out to symbolize the four principles of Klannishness. The officer will then rap again, and the left hand is then thrown up and out in a salute, which we call the Sign of Recognition, keeping the thumb and fingers as before. At the third rap of the gavel, those voting affirmatively will drop the arm again to its previous position, which, by juncture with the leg, forms a ' K.' Anybody who doesn't go along with the vote keeps his arm upraised—"

The Night Hawk frowned suggestively, and we understood it was not healthy to vote negatively on anything proposed by the hierarchy.

" I think that just about does it," he said, tucking *The Kloran* back into his pocket. " Oh yeah, there's one more thing. The MIOK, or Mystic Insignia of a Klansman. This is a triangular emblem, bearing the letters ' AKAI,' which stands for ' A Klansman Am I." To locate your brethren when visiting in a strange neighbourhood or town, all you have to do is ask ' Do you know a Mr. Ayak around here? ' This means ' Are you a Klansman? ' If the fellow is one, he'll

answer you, ' Yeah, and I also know a Mr. Akai.' Get it? "
We chorused assent, and the Night Hawk pushed his way
toward the door leading to the next room.

" Fall in behind me, single file, and pay strict attention! "
he ordered. " We are standing in what we call the Outer
Den of the Klavern. To gain admission to the Inner Den,
you will approach its outer door, knock once, and scratch
a circle on the door with your thumbnail."

The Night Hawk demonstrated. The wicket opened, and
an eye glared balefully through at us. Then the Night Hawk
gave a long slow whistle.

" Who are you? " demanded a voice from inside.

" That is the Klexter stationed inside," the Night Hawk
said to us over his shoulder. " Give him your name as
Klansman so-and-so, the number of your Klavern, and its
Realm! "

I was first in line, so I answered:

" Klansman Perkins, Nathan Bedford Forrest Klavern
No. 1, Realm of Georgia! "

" Advance and give the countersign! " the Klexter
commanded.

Again the Night Hawk coached us: " The current password of the Klan is ' White Man.' Here you give only the
first half of it—"

" White—" I whispered dutifully into the wicket.

At this the door was thrown open, and the robed and
masked Klexter said, " Pass! "

" Klexter, what of the night? " the Night Hawk
demanded.

" Strangers are near; be prudent! " the Klexter responded.

We had all filed into the Inner Den, which was much like
the Outer Den except that its walls were lined with steel
lockers, each of which was heavily padlocked.

Turning to us, the Night Hawk explained: " When the
Klexter says that, it means there may be non-members or
impostors present, and therefore you must enrobe before
entering the Klavern. Since most of you don't have your
robes yet, you will disregard this for tonight. When you get
your robes, you will keep them in one of these steel lockers.
Now then, if the Klexter says instead, ' All are known,' it

means you may enter without robe. Watch, and I will show you how to gain admittance to the Klavern proper."

Approaching a closed door with wicket on the opposite side of the room, the Night Hawk knocked four times, slowly, and then scratched on the door a cross with his thumbnail. The wicket opened and the Klarogo inside demanded:

" Who is it and what is your business? "

" I am Klansman Carter; I seek entrance to the Klavern to meet with my fellows," the Night Hawk replied.

" Password? "

" Man! "

" Pass, Klansman! " said the Klarogo, throwing open the door.

We filed in behind the Night Hawk. The Klavern presented an awesome spectacle, arranged in much the same manner as the quadrate upon the mountain. Midway along the four walls of the Klavern were the stations of the Klaliff, Kludd, Cyclops, and Klokard. Around the walls, several rows deep, sat well over one hundred and fifty robed and masked Klansmen. The red neon cross at the station of the Cyclops illumined the Klavern with a roseate hue. As the Klarogo slammed and locked the door behind us, the Night Hawk led us forward and arranged us in two rows before the station of the Cyclops.

" Do as I do! " the Night Hawk commanded, throwing out his left arm in the distended finger salute he had shown us outside. " This is called the Sign of Greeting. You will hold it until it is returned as a Sign of Recognition by one of the Kloranic officers stationed at one of the four altars! "

The purple-robed Wizard who served as Cyclops returned the salute himself. The Night Hawk then turned to the American flag which hung from a staff at the side of the Wizard.

" Next you give the National Honours, like this," the Night Hawk said to us.

Stooping, he took the lower hem of the flag in his left hand and raised it to his heart. With his right hand he then gave a military salute in the U.S. Army style (palm inward), then the salute of the Confederate Army (palm outward), and finally, coming back to attention, slowly lowered the hem of the flag.

" Don't forget to lower the flag *slowly*," he cautioned. " If you let it fall you will be challenged! "

Again facing the Wizard, he suddenly threw out both arms horizontally, with fingers distended as in the Sign of Greeting.

" This is known as the Sign of the Fiery Cross," he said. " After that comes the Sign of Secrecy. If your Brothers are wearing masks, you will make the sign like this—"

With his left hand he held a forefinger under his lower lip, then passed the hand over the top of his head, bringing it down in a chopping motion on the back of his neck.

" That signifies the penalty for betraying the Klan's secrets," he said. "—Off with the head! If upon entering the Klavern you see that your Brothers have removed their masks, you will do likewise. And now we come to the final step, the Sign of Klan-Consecration, which is given like this—"

Kneeling before the Wizard on his right knee, the Night Hawk threw out his left hand in the Sign of Greeting, at the same time holding his right hand over his heart. We all did likewise. The Wizard threw out his arm in the Sign of Recognition.

" Klansmen, be seated! " he ordered, waving us to two rows of empty seats along the back wall.

" I forgot to tell you," the Night Hawk whispered as we sat down. " One rap of the gavel calls for attention, two raps to be seated, and three raps to rise to your feet! "

He left us then, and took a seat on the Wizard's left.

" The Kladd of the Klan! " the Wizard said with a rap.

The red-robed Kladd, who was stationed on the Wizard's right, stepped forward and saluted.

" The Kladd, Your Majesty! "

" You will ascertain with care if all present are Klansmen worthy to sit in the Klavern during the deliberations of this Klonklave! "

" I have your orders, Sir! "

With that the Kladd began to file through the rows of seated Klansmen. As he approached each man, the man would rise and whisper the password in his ear, and then sit down again. One man, however, was asked to remain standing.

" Your Majesty, I respectfully report that all present are Klansmen, except the man who stands before you; he presumes to be a Klansman, but he has not the words! "

I wondered if someone else had succeeded in getting into the Klan as an investigator before me, and was about to be captured before my eyes!

" Come forward, and unmask! " the Wizard ordered.

The man did so, and there was a murmur as he was recognized as a delinquent Brother who had not attended a meeting since the current password went into effect. Upon paying his dues in full he was told the password and ordered back to his seat.

There were three raps from the gavel, and we all leapt to our feet.

" You will bow your heads for our opening devotional. . . ."

The blue-robed Kludd then intoned:

" Our Father and our God: We, as Klansmen, acknowledge our dependence upon Thee and Thy loving kindness towards us; may our gratitude be full and constant and inspire us to walk in Thy ways. May each Klansman forsake the bad and choose and strive for the good. We invoke Thy blessing upon our Emperor, the Imperial Wizard, and his official family, in the administration of the affairs pertaining to the Invisible Empire. Oh, God! For Thy glory and our good we humbly ask these things in the name of Him who taught us to serve and sacrifice for the right! Amen! "

" Amen! " we echoed.

There were two raps of the gavel ordering us to our seats.

" I now officially proclaim that this Klonklave of Klavern No. 1, Realm of Georgia, duly opened for the dispatch of business! " the Wizard said. " The Kligrapp will read the names of persons who have applied for membership in the Klan and have been investigated and approved by the Klokann. If any of you know of any reason why any man whose name is called should not be admitted, speak up! "

The Kligrapp, seated at a desk on the Wizard's far left, began to read. Some were up for a first reading, and some were being read for the second—last—time. When the reading was finished without objection, the Wizard spoke again.

" Next, communications. I have here a letter from Brother H. F. Shaffer, E.C. [Exalted Cyclops] of the Franklin County Klan up in Pennsylvania. It seems that some lame-brained pervert by the name of Stetson Kennedy has written a bunch of crap under the title ' We Must Clamp Down Again on the Klan,' and an outfit which calls itself the Fellowship of Southern Churchmen has sent it out to American Legion posts all over the country. Brother Shaffer has already written this outfit a hot letter, warning them to watch their step! "

Turning, the Wizard barked:

" Brother Kligrapp, you will prepare an edict to all Klaverns, calling upon all Klansmen who belong to the American Legion to be on the lookout for this propaganda, and to denounce it as communistic or anything else they can think of! "

Though I was startled to hear my name under attack at my first Klan meeting, it was gratifying to know that the article in question had hit the Klan where it hurt.

" Now for something more pleasant," the Wizard re-sumed. " Brother Kligrapp, you will prepare an official letter of commendation to our esteemed Brother Klansman, Police Officer ' Itchy-Trigger-Finger ' Nash, for killing his thirteenth nigger in line of duty. Brother Nash, take a bow! "

A Klansman arose, the blue trousers of a police uniform protruding from beneath his robe, while everyone clapped, whistled and stamped.

" Thank ya kindly," he said, and sat down.

" Just two more letters, Brother Kligrapp," the Wizard continued. " One to Civil Court Judge Ross McClellan, commending him for jailing a nigger gal who called a white lady ' poor white trash '; and the other to Superior Court Judge Bond Almand for confirming the sentence. Tell 'em their decisions are a victory for white supremacy, and in the best tradition of Klankraft!

" And now for Klan-building! Brother Kleagle, which of

our rival teams, the Bumble Bees or the Yellow Jackets, brought in the most new members last month? "

There was a murmur of anticipation as the Kleagle arose to announce the winner.

" The Yellow Jackets, Your Majesty—they signed up 173, and the Bumble Bees got 146! "

Tumult broke out as the Yellow Jackets slapped each other on the back in congratulation.

" All right! " said the Wizard, rapping for order. " Don't forget—the losers must treat the winners to a steak dinner at Wingo's Café next Saturday night. Now let me tell you something about the Klan-building I've been doing. I've plumb wore out my car in the process. But last week I received requests from the mayor and police chiefs of Waycross and Douglasville for Klan charters, also from the fire chief and city councilmen of Griffin, and officials of McDonough, Sandersville and Blackshear. I took a little spin up into Tennessee, and the Klans in Chattanooga and Maryville are going great guns—but we'll have a more complete report on that later tonight. I've also had word from the Klan in New York, where they're organizing as the ' Circle Club.' In Detroit, the new Klan is calling itself the ' Dreamland Club.' In Chicago, there are already 2,900 active members again. I've taken a nationwide sampling of former Klansmen from our files, and sent them business reply cards asking ' Would you like to rejoin the Klan? ' Ninety-four per cent. have been favourable. There's no doubt about it—the Klan has a great future as well as a great past! "

He paused and looked around the Klavern.

" Anybody else got anything to report before we go on? "

" Your Majesty, Klansman Lanham of Atlanta Cab and Baggage Company," said a Klansman. " I beg to report that we have practically achieved our goal of a Klan closed shop among the cab-drivers of this city. There are only three hold-outs."

" I suggest you get those three signed or fired! " the Wizard barked. " The day may soon come when the Klan will need every cab in Atlanta to do some quick work! "

" All we need is the word," the driver promised.

Nodding, the Wizard rapped again.

" Our next order of business is political action," he said. " I don't need to tell you that the Klan's effectiveness in politics depends on our strength. If we continue to make such good progress with our Klan-building, you can be sure the politicians will come flocking to us. We'll have them eating out of our hand, and can dictate our own terms!

" Now then, I want to remind you that the Klan's No. 1 political job is to elect Talmadge Governor of Georgia! I am happy to announce that our goal of an active Klavern in each of Georgia's 159 counties, to ensure a Talmadge victory at the polls, has already been realized! But we must continue to work hard. I've just spent $8,000 on some campaign literature, and I want you to stuff your pockets with it when you leave, and get it into the hands of your friends and neighbours."

A big Klansman had stood up, and with outstretched arm was asking for the floor. The Wizard threw out his arm in recognition.

" S. W. Roper, E.C. of Klavern 297," the man announced himself. " I thought the Brothers might be interested in a little talk I had with Talmadge last week. I asked him what he thought was the best method of keeping niggers from voting. He didn't say anything, but picked up a scrap of paper and wrote one word on it: ' Pistols '! He also promised me that if elected he would give the Klan a free hand in any race rioting, before calling out the militia! "

Cyclops Roper sat down amidst a flurry of applause.

" Our second most important political job is to see that Judge Jim Davis of Stone Mountain is elected to Congress," the Wizard resumed. " I'm ordering every Klansman to keep both ears open for anything that can be used against his opponent, and to report directly to me! "

The Wizard looked around the Klavern.

" We will now hear a report from our esteemed Kludd, the Reverend Tom Harrison, otherwise known as ' The Railroad Evangelist,' who has just returned from a lobbying expedition to Washington! "

At his station, the blue-clad Kludd arose.

" My chief business," he said importantly, " was to call

on three Senators, Brother Walter George of Georgia, Brother Olin Johnston of South Carolina, and Brother John Bricker of Ohio. We talked about ways and means of getting around the Supreme Court decision against the restrictive covenants whereby we have been keeping the niggers and kikes out of our neighbourhoods. While in Washington I also talked to Senator Dick Russell, and he promised me faithfully he would introduce a Bill in Congress making it a Federal offence for any two people of different race to get married. And I'm proud to say the Senator said he would use some copies of my book to muster support for this Bill! All things considered, things are going our way in Washington! "

" You can say that again! " the Wizard echoed. " At long last the Klan Doctrine has become the Truman Doctrine. Every branch of the Government—executive, legislative and judicial—has finally come around to the programme we have been advocating for so many years. . . .

" Now then, Brother Kligrapp, you will prepare an edict to all Klaverns, calling upon all Klansmen to write their Senators and Congressmen, urging them to filibuster and vote against any and all civil rights legislation—fair employment Bills, anti-lynching Bills, anti-polltax Bills, and anything else the communists cook up. If possible, Klansmen should enclose a dollar or more in their letters to encourage these men in their fight. The letters should also pledge the Klan's all-out support, at the polls and otherwise! "

The Wizard reached under his robe, extracted a small carton, and dumped the contents into his purple hood.

" Now for something a little different," he said. " I have here fifty ·45 calibre Police Special revolver cartridges. I'm putting them up for auction, minimum bid one dollar each! The proceeds will go towards our political action fund. It cost us a lot of money to get rid of that Jew Henry Morgenthau as Secretary of the Treasury, and now we're out to get rid of that Catholic Francis Biddle as Attorney-General! The Klan is applying pressure at the proper places to clean Jews and Catholics out of high Government places. We all feel that Truman will do his best to help us.

He's firing F.D.R.'s Jews and niggers as fast as he can. Now what am I bid? "

The Klavern was filled with shouts as the Klansmen placed their bids, ranging as high as five dollars, and went forward to claim the cartridges. In a short time the Wizard's hood was empty, and he put it back on his head.

" I have a suggestion to make," he said, rapping for order. " Why don't we contribute these cartridges to Brother Itchy-Trigger-Finger Nash? He knows what to do with them! "

Shouting their enthusiasm, the Klansmen who had acquired the cartridges came forward and deposited them in Nash's police cap.

" I'm much obliged," Nash said modestly, " but I hope I don't have to kill all the niggers in the South without getting some help from my Brothers! "

" Don't worry—you'll have plenty of help! " a number of Klansmen shouted.

" In God's sight it's no sin to kill a nigger, for a nigger is no more than a dog! " the Kludd intoned piously from his station.

" I will say one thing," Nash concluded. " Chief Jenkins has put me on the day shift on the police force, so I can devote my nights to riding with the Klan! "

" You have all spoken like true Klansmen," the Wizard said. " But we must get on with our meeting. We come now to complaints—"

There was a roar as the Klavern exploded with Klansmen leaping to their feet to demand the floor.

" Who's first? " the Wizard asked.

" I am! " a dozen cried out at once.

" Take it easy! " the Wizard laughed. " You there—" He pointed to a man who was holding up a hand wrapped in dirty bandage.

" Just look what a no-count nigger done to me! " the man said in an aggrieved tone. " Done cut off my thumb, that's what he done! "

" That nigger's name and address are known, and he will be taken care of! " the Night Hawk spoke up.

" Next case! " commanded the Wizard with a rap of the gavel.

" What about that nigger at the Henry Grady Hotel coffee shop who has been acting up, like I reported last week? " a Klansman demanded.

" Cliff, I turned that case over to you for handling," the Wizard said to the Night Hawk. " What say you? "

" We considered the case very thoroughly, Chief, and finally decided the best thing to do was ask one of our Brothers who is a deputy sheriff to give the nigger two years on the chain-gang."

" Does that answer your question? " the Wizard asked.

" Good enough! " the Klansman said with satisfaction.

" I have something urgent! " another Klansman called out. " I've been told that a family of niggers has moved into an apartment building for whites at 300 Pulliam Street! "

At this the Wizard leapt to his feet.

" Nash! " he ordered. " Take three more of your police officers and go in your police car to that address at once, and report back here! "

Nash got up and peeled out of his Klan robe, revealing his police uniform beneath. He called the names of three other men who did likewise, and the Klarogo unlocked the door to let them leave.

" Grand Titan Ransome," said a man taking the floor. " I have a very serious problem to present. My children keep coming home from school, telling me how their teacher keeps talking about how we must be tolerant of the niggers, Jews and so on. Now just the other day this teacher said something against the Klan. In my opinion, such teachers are the greatest menace to white supremacy, and we ought to do something about it! "

" We will! " said the Wizard. " Brother Kligrapp, you will prepare an edict to all Klaverns, ordering them to activate all Klanspeople to activate their children to report on such teachers to their parents. The names of such teachers should then be sent to me, and I'll take care of the rest! The Klan has many members and friends on school boards. . . ."

" Klansman Joe Wallace, chairman of the Klan's Housing Kommittee," said the next man to gain the floor. " I want to tell about a new strategy we've worked out. Until recently we used to call on niggers who moved into white neighbourhoods, and tell them to " Get out, or else . . . ! " Most of them got. But now we've worked out another method, under the slogan ' Not strife, but psychology.' We've set up a corporation and gotten a charter from the state as the ' West End Co-operative Association.' Our goal is to build a ' Great White Wall ' around West End. Here's how we do it:

" First of all, we've organized about 1,500 watchdogs, and whenever one of them sees a nigger trying to move into West End, they telephone me at Amherst 1000. Then I put some of our ladies to work making chain telephone calls, and in no time at all we mobilize quite a crowd around the house where the nigger is trying to move in. Then I step in and have a little private talk with the nigger. I tell him he has a perfect legal right to move in, and that I will try to protect him. But at the same time I tell him I doubt if I can control more than a small part of the mob, and that if he does move in he'll be endangering his whole family. Ninety-nine times out of a hundred, that ought to do the trick! "

Wallace paused, and the Klansmen chuckled.

" Just to wake the white people up, we're getting out a little paper called *West End Facts*, which we distribute free to the homes," Wallace continued. " Let me read you a sample:

> The danger of a Negro invasion of West End has not passed as yet. The only remedy we have is with a concerted action. Come to our meetings and learn how. The Negroes will have Atlanta lock, stock and barrel in less than ten years if we fail to act. The Negro race multiply so rapidly and then we will again even at the edge of town be forced to live with them or move farther out. You of the middle class, you with that Southern accent, Georgia-born and reared, are you going to stand by and lose your birthright without a struggle? "

" *Nooooo* . . . ! " cried the Klansmen in a roar that shook the Klavern.

" Any of you who are itching for action are welcome to work with us," Wallace said, taking his seat.

" The niggers are getting out of hand! " growled the Night Hawk. " We've got to dish out some more floggings, and if necessary a few lynchings! "

" The time is about ripe for the Klan to show itself in force and strike! " the Wizard agreed. " We've been quiet long enough! "

There was another rap of the gavel.

" And now we come to the most enjoyable part of our meeting—' For the Encouragement and Edification of the Klan.' We are fortunate in having with us tonight two distinguished Klan leaders from neighbouring states. First, I give you the Grand Dragon of the Federated Klans of Alabama, Dr. E. P. Pruitt! "

A pot-bellied Kluxer lumbered to his feet and launched into a violent tirade.

" No, we are not a hate group! " he shouted hoarsely. " The Klan don't hate nobody! In fact, the Klan is the good nigger's best friend. If the nigger will devote his energies to becoming a better, more useful nigger, rather than the dupe of Northern interests who have caused him to misconstrue his social standing, he will reap the rewards of industry, instead of the disappointments of ambition unobtainable!

" Southern whites, occupying that super-position assigned them by the Creator, are justifiably hostile to any race that attempts to drag them down to its own level! Therefore let the nigger be wise in leaving the ballot in the hands of a dominant sympathetic race, since he is far better off as a political eunuch in the house of his friends, than a voter rampant in the halls of his enemies!

" Yes, the Klan loves niggers—in their place. I've delivered many a nigger baby without charging a cent for it. My nigger maid even washes my Klan robe for me. But when I see some of these uppity nigger gals coming down the street, I just stiffen up and stand stock still. I hope none of 'em ever bump into me, because if they do I'll slap 'em flat!

" We keep mighty busy over in Alabama. Last week I had a letter from a woman in Tuscumbia, complaining that her husband was running around with another woman. She said if the Klan would give him a good beating to make him

behave, she would organize a branch of our ladies'
auxiliary! "

There was a roar of laughter.

" Did you straighten him out? " someone asked.

" First I've written a letter to the Governor, asking him
to put the sheriff on the man," Dragon Pruitt replied. " Oh,
I get lots of such letters and phone calls from people who
want the Klan to flog somebody. Know what I always tell
'em?—' Join the Klan! ' "

He sat down, and the Klavern echoed with applause.

" Our next speaker," said the Wizard, " is Brother J. B.
Stoner, Kleagle for Tennessee."

A slight figure beneath his robe, Stoner walked with a
limp. I could tell from his voice that he was still in his
teens.

" In the Tennessee Klan we consider Jews to be America's
No. 1 enemy," he began. " We ought to get all Jews out of
our country—and I don't mean send them to some other
country! I'll never be satisfied as long as there are any Jews
here or anywhere. I think we ought to kill all Jews just to
save their unborn generations from having to go to Hell! "

I sat up on the edge of my chair. This guy must be stark,
raving crazy, I thought to myself.

" We ought to get rid of them legally, of course," he
resumed. " I have already petitioned Congress, urging it to
adopt a resolution recognizing that the Jews are children
of the Devil, and consequently constitute a grave danger to
the United States. Our goal is passage of a Constitutional
Amendment making it illegal to be Jewish in the U.S.A.,
punishable by death! Those pleading guilty would only
need a judge to sentence them. Any who might claim to be
Christians could be given a trial.

" As for the guilty, we ought to just take them out and
kill them. That may sound a little extreme, but other
countries have done it. We ought to be more modern about
it than Hitler.

" During the war I used to listen to Lord Haw Haw
broadcasting from Germany, and one time he said that after
Hitler won German doctors would reward me by operating
on my lame leg. But I supported the American war effort

because I resented the Germans' attempt to get rid of our Jews for us. Every nation has a right to get rid of its own Jews! Only through intolerance do nations become great! I'm intolerant! The so-called Brotherhood of Man is in reality the Brotherhood of the Devil! "

" Ain't J. B. a card? " I heard a Klansman whisper behind me.

" Before we attack Russia," Stoner raved on, " we must first get rid of our Jews and abolish the UNO, which ought to be called the ' JewNO.' We should use our superior force to get from other countries whatever we need, and make them all do business on our terms. American aid should be predicated on anti-Jewishness; no person who is anti-Jew should have to go hungry!

" As for niggers, I haven't anything against them personally, but only as a race. The Klan believes 100 per cent. in white supremacy—social, political, and economic. We are against racial equality in any form, whether with niggers, Japs, Chinese, Filipinos or what have you. I am willing to give niggers just about every so-called right they want—in an African country of their own! I will never be satisfied until all niggers in America are resettled in Africa.

" All we need to carry out this entire programme is money; if I could just get some big Gentile money I could build a fire overnight! "

The applause for Stoner was scattered.

" I don't know that I go along with everything that feller says," the Klansman behind me whispered. " If we send 'em all back to Africa, who's gonna do our dirty work? "

At this point there were four raps on the door. The Klarogo opened it, and the four policemen entered.

" False alarm, Chief! " Nash reported disgustedly.

" Fast work, anyway, men! " the Wizard said. Turning to the Night Hawk he added, " Cliff, you'd better keep an eye on that house!

" Now if there's no further business I will make the final announcements. . . . On the second Thursday in May, Brother Judge Luke Arnold will speak at Klavern 297 on a plan to keep Negroes from voting. I personally urge every Klansman in the city to be there! . . . Next Friday, at ten o'clock in the morning, an important case is coming up in Brother Judge Callaway's court. A streetcar motorman had to kill a nigger out on Mitchell Street for refusing to take a back seat. I want that court-room packed with Klansmen to let Brother Callaway know the white people are with him, and want that motorman to go free! "

Rising suddenly to his feet, the Wizard threw out his arm in salute.

" The crowning glory of a Klansman is to serve—"

" Not Self, but Others! " the Klansmen all chorused, rising to their feet and returning the salute.

" Klansmen: United in the sacred unfailing bond of Klannish fidelity we stand, but divided by selfishness and strife we fall. Shall we stand, or shall we fall? "

" We will stand, for our blood is not pledged in vain! " the answer came in a crescendo.

With a final rap of his gavel, the Wizard said:

" I now officially proclaim this Klonklave closed. To you, Faithful Klansmen, good night! "

" Your Majesty, good night! " we replied.

" The Klan is dismissed. The Kladd and the Night Hawk will make secure the properties of the Klan. Faithful Klarogo, you will open the portal that all Klansmen may pass to the outer world. . . ."

We filed out into the Inner Den, where the Klansmen in robes removed them and put them away in the steel lockers. I wandered about the Den, but came to a sudden halt when I heard someone say " machine guns." Pretending to look for a cigarette, I listened. The Cyclops of 297 was questioning another man.

" How many machine guns? "

" Thousands! "

" Where did you say? "

" You know the place—that big warehouse out on Sylvan Road, run by the War Assets Administration. I'm working there as night watchman."

" What's to prevent us from tying you up one night and making off with some of those machine guns? No telling when we may need 'em! We could even rough you up just a little to make it look good."

The man thought a minute.

" Anything the Government can't prove can't hurt me! " he said finally.

I looked around hurriedly for Slim.

" Who's that guy talking to the E.C.? " I nodded.

" Him—? " Slim answered. " That's Ben Culpepper. Belongs to 297. Wanna meet him? "

" Not specially," I said. " I thought for a minute I had already met him somewhere."

I had had all I could stomach for one night, and hurried out into the cool air. So this was what went on in Klan meetings! What fiendishness the Klan embraced beneath its cloak of " Kristianity "! With such incitement going on in Klaverns all over the country, it is no wonder it is drenched with innocent blood!

(Needless to say, I promptly reported the matter of the machine guns to the authorities. Months later, when I checked, I discovered that Culpepper had been promoted to the office of Regional Director of the War Assets Administration!)

The Sign of Secrecy (TSOS) made by Klansmen exiting a klavern, sealing their lips on all that had transpired (posed by the author). Photograph courtesy Keystone Pictures Inc.

CHAPTER FIVE

OPERATION ANTI-KLAN

" YOU'VE *what?* " exploded my old friend Charlie Pike, Southern director of one of the big unions.

" I've just joined the Klan," I repeated, handing him my membership Kard for inspection.

" What's the big idea? " he demanded. " I always considered you a union man from the ground up."

" That's one of the big reasons I've joined the Klan," I hastened to explain. " I know the Klan has been giving the union fits, and I thought it might help to have a union man inside to keep tabs on them."

" It damned sure would! Those guys are lower than a snake's belly! Here lately they've been waylaying our organizers, catching them one at a time and beating the daylights out of them. They've even tossed bombs at some of our meeting halls. If you could just tip us off when and where they're coming on us next we could set up a reception . . ."

" That's exactly what I had in mind," I assured him. " All I need is a handful of telephone numbers where I can reach you and some of your other leaders at any time of the day or night."

He started scribbling on a scratch pad.

" Here you are," he said. " Call my number first, and if you don't reach me, keep calling right on down the list. They're all top-notch men. I'll get together with them right away and set up a little counter-Klan organization. Just leave it to us. But for gawd's sake watch your step! Those Kluxers are a mean bunch of bastards. If they catch you, they won't do a thing but kill you! "

" They made that clear enough in the initiation," I said. " I'm going to do my best to keep one jump ahead of them."

" Well, I wish you all the luck in the world—you'll probably be needing it! When's the next Klan meeting? I've been waiting to get back at those babies for a long time! "

" You'll have to hold your horses," I said. " I'm brand new in this thing, and I doubt if they'll let me in on any of the rough stuff right away. The first lead I get, you'll hear from me. But in the meantime there is something we can work on. . . ."

" What's that? "

" I've been doing some digging into the records over at Fulton Superior Court. It turns out the Klan holds a corporate charter from the State of Georgia, issued July 1st, 1916, and renewed for twenty more years in 1935. You'd never recognize the Klan from the description that charter gives—says it's a non-profit, charitable, benevolent, eleemosynary society for the promotion of True Americanism! "

" The truth is it's the most damnable, money-making, union-busting, hate-mongering racket on the face of the earth! " Pike declared, his eyes burning. " I knew the Ku Klux lie every time they open their mouths, but I didn't know they were founded on a pack of lies accepted by the state as though it were the gospel truth! "

" It's a rotten business," I agreed. " That charter is what makes it possible for the Kluxers to holler that they're a ' legal, law-abiding ' organization every time somebody attacks them for being the outlaw band they really are. Besides, having a charter as a non-profit corporation keeps the Klan from having to pay any taxes, no matter how many millions it rakes in. . . . But that's not all—having a charter keeps the Klan leaders from being sued personally for damages when the Klan destroys life and property."

" I'm a Georgia boy, but I never knew my own state was a partner to all the Klan's crimes," Pike said, shaking his head. " I knew the Government seldom does anything to check the Klan, but I didn't realize it was actually in cahoots with it! "

" It's not just Georgia," I pointed out. " This charter is for the parent body of the Klan, and authorizes it to set up lodges and conduct its affairs in all of the forty-eight states and territorial possessions of the U.S.A. That's why, if we could persuade the authorities to take away that charter, we could cramp the Kluxers' style considerably! "

" How would you go about it? "

" The state issued the charter and the state can take it away," I explained. " Georgia's Attorney-General could hail the Klan into court under a *quo warranto* proceeding, and force it to show cause why the charter should not be taken from it."

" On what grounds? "

" There are plenty," I assured him. " I could draw up a whole string of them on the basis of the Klan's public record. And after I've looked around inside the Klan a while I'll be able to turn up a lot more."

" Attorney-General Eugene Cook isn't a bad fellow, but I don't believe he'll tackle the Klan unless he's told to. Seems to me the thing to do is to put a bug in Governor Ellis Arnall's ear. He's got real gumption! "

" So I hear," I said. " Anybody who can defeat Talmadgism in Georgia would have to have. But how can we get to him? "

" Leave that to me. I'm in touch with the leaders of a number of community organizations—the National Religion and Labour Foundation, the Ministerial Alliance, the National Conference of Christians and Jews, the National Association for the Advancement of Coloured People, and Anti-Defamation League of B'nai B'rith. When a community-wide problem like the Klan presents itself, we sometimes get together to see what can be done about it. I'll put it to them."

The next thing I knew, I was reading in the *Atlanta Journal* that Governor Arnall had asked Attorney-General Cook to see if he could find any legal grounds for revoking the Klan's charter.

But what would happen if Cook said he couldn't find any?

I promptly sat down and wrote the Governor a letter outlining the following bases for revocation:

1. In violation of its non-profit charter, the Klan had

been found by the U.S. Treasury Department to have been operating for profit.

2. In violation of its non-political charter, the Klan was engaged in political activity.

3. Either the Klan misrepresented its purposes upon being incorporated, or it had exceeded its corporate powers after being incorporated.

4. The Klan had used intimidation and violence to deprive citizens of rights guaranteed them by the state and Federal constitutions, and therefore the Klan was not entitled to the privileges of incorporation, which are intended to cover lawful activities only.

In a few days I had a letter from Arnall thanking me for these suggestions, and saying he was forwarding them to the Attorney-General. The next morning, I was delighted to read the headline in the *Atlanta Constitution*: " ARNALL DECLARES WAR ON KLAN! "

The Governor, it said, had called in the Press to announce that he was instructing (not asking) the Attorney-General to start proceedings immediately to take away the Klan's charter on the grounds I had suggested to him!

" Brother, you're in demand! " Pike exclaimed when I dropped into union headquarters to congratulate him on getting such prompt action from the Governor. " The Attorney-General's office has been calling here and everywhere else in town, trying to locate you! That must have been some letter you wrote Arnall. I have it from inside that your letter hit his desk the same moment as one from the Attorney-General saying there was no way to get at the Klan. If you hadn't written, the whole thing would have been over before it started. No wonder Cook wants to talk to you! "

" Tell me more about Cook, " I said. " I'd like to know what I'm getting into. "

" Nothing to worry about, " Pike chuckled. " He may not do you any good, but he won't do you any harm, either. On the other hand, his assistant, Dan Duke, believes in action and plenty of it—you can always depend on Dan to do *something*, even if it's wrong. My guess is that Cook will drop this whole thing in Duke's lap. As a political potato, it's too hot for Cook to handle. But Duke doesn't much give a damn—he's a Klan-buster from way back! "

" Isn't he the guy who spoke up in opposition when Talmadge tried to pardon a bunch of Klan floggers a few years ago? "

" The same. He was assistant solicitor of Fulton County then, and put a bunch of Ku Klux in the pen after they flogged one of our organizers at Piedmont Mills to death...."

" Sounds like a good man for me to work with," I said. " But now that I've managed to work my way into the Klan, I don't want to stick my neck out too far, too fast. I can't help but feel that walking into the Capitol would be like sticking my head into a hornets' nest—the place must be swarming with Klansmen. If they were to spot ' John Perkins ' hanging around the Attorney-General's office, it wouldn't be very healthy for me."

" You're dead right about that," Pike nodded. " Why don't you let me call Duke and put it to him? I've got a private line phone number for him—doesn't go through any Capitol switchboards. Maybe he can suggest some place where you two can get together and talk over this thing."

" But where? " I asked. " There aren't many spots in the Imperial City that are safe from Klan eyes."

" You've got me there—a restaurant or bar would be as bad as his office...."

" I've got it—ask him if he can pick me up in his car in half an hour at the end of the streetcar line out on Auburn Avenue. That's a Negro neighbourhood, and should be safe enough."

A half an hour later, Duke's car pulled up beside me at the kerb, and I climbed quickly into the front seat with him. There were no other whites in sight, but we continued to drive on out towards the open countryside.

I found Duke to be a big man, a real heavyweight, who looked like he might once have been a fullback in a football team.

" So you're the fellow who started all this! " he said, with a sparkle in his eye. "It's a hellova note when a private citizen has to interpret the law for the Attorney-General!"

"I didn't expect the Governor to let him know it was my idea," I said. "How is he taking it?"

"He's not—he's handed it over to me," Duke grinned. "But the job suits me fine. I managed to tie knots in the tails of some Klan floggers a few years ago, and they've been afraid of me ever since. They'd better be. They know I'm on to their tricks and will out-Klux 'em if I have to! But what's all this secrecy about? Pike wouldn't say anything on the phone except to see that I wasn't being followed."

"Well, I just joined the Klan a couple of weeks ago, and I don't want to be banished anytime soon—"

"Joined the Klan!" Duke said excitedly. "To bust it up?"

"Nothing else but."

"You're just the man I've been looking for! With a set-up like that, we ought to be able to fix those babies for good! How would you like to work with me? If we're going to use your evidence and testimony in court, you ought to be on our staff in some capacity."

"I've been feeling a little lonesome," I admitted. "Some solid backing wouldn't hurt."

"I could put you on as a special agent of the G.B.I.," he said.

"What's that?"

"Georgia Bureau of Investigation—the fact-finding arm of the Georgia Department of Law."

"No connection with the F.B.I.?"

"No, we're a state agency."

"But what are the chances of my running into some Brother Klansmen among my brother G.B.I. agents?" I asked.

"That is the question. . . ." Duke frowned. "Quite a few of them are hangovers from the Talmadge régime, and you never know."

"If there were some way for me to be a secret agent among secret agents—" I suggested. "In other words, if my being an agent of the G.B.I. could be kept secret from other G.B.I. agents, it might be safe enough."

" I don't see why that couldn't be arranged. You could report directly to me. I'll take all this up with the Governor. There'll also be a problem of the payment—there's been a lot of stuff in the newspapers in the past to the effect that the state treasurer is an old-time Klansman."

" Maybe you could get an anonymous appropriation somehow under the heading of ' special research '—"

" That's probably the answer," Duke agreed, turning back towards the city. " I'll be able to let you know tomorrow. You ought to have some sort of protection, too—do you have a gun? "

" No—but I'd feel better if I did."

" I'll try to have a licence for you tomorrow. Now where can we meet? "

" Riding around like this couldn't last long, and we're not going to bust the Klan in a day. The hotter we get on their trail, the closer they're going to be watching you and your visitors."

" I've got an idea," Duke said. " There's a friend of mine, who doesn't like the Klan any better than I do, who has a law office in the Smith Building. We could meet there as often as we like. Just see that no one sees you go into the office, and I'll do the same. How about meeting me there at two-thirty tomorrow afternoon? "

" I'll be there," I promised, making a mental note of the office number he gave me. " You can put me out at the end of the car line where you picked me up."

" It's all settled! " Duke said happily when we met the next day. " You can go to work immediately, and report to me here anytime you have anything. Just give me a ring on my private line at the office. If you need to call at night, you can get me on the private line to my home out in Fairburn. I'll draw the money to pay you, and give it to you in cash so there won't be any trip-up over cheques. And here's your pistol-toter's permit."

He handed me a slip of white paper. It actually said " Pistol Toter's Permit (Law of 1916)." Reading on, I found it said: " It appears that *John S. Perkins* is a proper person to carry a pistol, and he is hereby authorized to

tote one —— calibre —— for a period of four years from
this date."

" When you get the gun, you can fill in the calibre and
make yourself," Duke said, " but let me know what you get
so I can make a record of it."

" Good deal," I agreed. " Now what's our next step?
I suppose you'll want me to report right after each weekly
Klan meeting? "

" By phone the same night if there is any immediate Klan
action planned that I might be able to stop! " he said. " If
not, then meet me here at ten the following morning, with a
written report on every blessed thing you can remember! "

" What about documentary stuff? I've already got my
membership Kard, a couple of application blanks, and a
few pieces of propaganda. I'd like to keep the originals for
my own files, if you can have photostatic copies made."

" Good enough," he agreed. " But I don't want to take
a chance having copies made in the Capitol photostat room.
I think the N.A.A.C.P. and Anti-Defamation League have
photostat machines. I'll farm the stuff out to them, where it
will be in good hands."

" That sounds good," I agreed, " but there's the further
problem of how to handle these." Reaching into my pocket,
I extracted a small object closely resembling a cigarette
lighter. Actually, it was a tiny camera, specially made for
detective work. Entirely automatic, it could be concealed in
the palm of the hand, and, simply by touching a small button
with the thumb, scores of pictures could be taken on negatives no larger than a fingernail.

" Quite a gadget," Duke said admiringly, turning it over
in his hand.

" I've been practising with it, and by holding it over
letters or other documents spread over a guy's desk, I can
take photos of them without his knowing it. But where can
we get the negatives developed? "

" Just bring them to me. I've got a small darkroom out
at my home."

" Well, I think that takes care of everything. When do I
see you again—next Tuesday morning? "

" No, as a matter of fact I was wondering if you could get

together with me here in the morning to go over some notes for the *quo warranto* brief for taking away the Klan's charter. I'm outlining it along the lines you proposed in your letter to Arnall, but I could use all the specifics you have at hand."

" The first thing I need to know," Duke began when we got together again the next morning, " is who is running the Klan now. I intend to name names in this suit! "

" I'll give you what I can," I assured him. " You know of course that Dr. Samuel Green has been heading up the Klan ever since the war as Grand Dragon, and sometimes even calls himself Imperial Wizard. His chief assistant is a guy named Brown—G. T. Brown. I have his signature on a Klan summons, listing him as Grand Titan of the Georgia Realm. Then there's Roper, who is Exalted Cyclops out at Oakland City Klavern No. 297—"

" Sam Roper? " Duke interrupted.

" That's right. The boys all call him Sam, and I have his signature on another summons, as S. W. Roper."

" I know Roper all right! He used to be head of the Georgia Highway Patrol under Gene Talmadge, and served as Gene's personal bodyguard. Who else? "

" I know one other leader—the Cyclops out at the East Atlanta Klan on Crooked Road is B. G. Otwell."

" That'll do. I'm going to name the Knights of the Ku Klux Klan Inc. as defendant, and throw in these birds as co-defendants."

" They may try to wriggle out of it by arguing that they have nothing to do with the old Klan corporation, but are an entirely new outfit," I warned. " But I see no reason to let them get away with it. I can prove that they're using the Klan's copyrighted name and rituals, its patented insignias, and everything else."

" That's more than enough! They aren't going to get away with any of their Ku Klux doubletalk with me. Now listen to some of these charges I've lined out, and tell me if you don't agree we can make them stick. . . ."

Pulling a sheaf of notes from his briefcase, Duke began to read:

" ' The Ku Klux Klan has knowingly abused its corporate

privileges and powers, has committed acts which are contrary to law and to the public policy of the state, and has carried on its business and conducted its affairs in such a way as to bring contempt and disrespect upon the state, to break down the orderly process of legal justice, to invade the private rights of Georgia citizens and to create confusion, discord and discontent.' "

" You said a mouthful," I nodded. " That hits the Klan nail squarely on the head."

" That's only the beginning," Duke went on. " Listen to this ":

" ' The Ku Klux Klan has arrogated unto itself the power of a court and substituted a trial by ordeal for a trial by jury. By the inculcation and dissemination of racial and religious prejudice, intolerance and hatred, and by means of secret propaganda, it seeks to enforce its principles and doctrines upon the State of Georgia by force, violence, terrorism and hate.' "

There was more, in which Duke lined out the exact provisions of the Georgia and U.S. constitutions which the Klan is dedicated to subverting.

" I suppose you know the Klan was tied up with the Nazi German-American Bund before the war," I said.

" Hell, no! How was that? Where? "

" The Klan and the Bund held a joint rally at the Bund's Camp Nordland in New Jersey. I have a copy of the Bund's propaganda paper, *Weckruf und Beobachter*, advertising the affair. Grand Dragon Arthur Bell and Bundesfuehrer August Klapprott spoke. Klapprott said: ' The principles of the Bund and the principles of the Klan are the same.' "

" That stuff has got to go in our suit! It would have to be in documentary form, though. I'd like to have a copy of that Bund newspaper. Do you suppose if I were to take a quick trip north I could get depositions from the attorney-generals up that way on this kind of thing? "

" No doubt about it," I said. " They'd be glad to help."

Some weeks later the *quo warranto* suit of the State of Georgia versus the Knights of the Ku Klux Klan Inc. was duly filed in court.

Morgan Belser, the Klan's attorney, promptly filed a

sixteen-page reply to the state's suit, saying " each and every allegation therein contained is denied."

More specifically, the Klan asserted, " The KKK denies that at any time it has ever followed a designed policy that violated any rights of Georgia citizens." It asked that all charges against it be dropped, and that the state be required to pay all court costs and lawyers' fees! The case was not dropped, of course, but the Klan attorney pleaded illness, and so won repeated postponements of the trial. . . .

" I know that the court action is only one of the incidents of a bigger and broader job to be done," Duke told the Press. " A thing that is un-American and that violates the civil rights of persons must be fought in the court of American public opinion. It is my hope that the newspapers will carry the story we will unfold in court to every corner of the nation so the American people can see that the Klan harbours the seeds of a future American Gestapo! "

The news of Georgia's action against the Klan soon led to similar action in other states where the Klan still held corporate charters. Less than two months after the filing of the Georgia suit, Attorney-General Nathaniel Goldstein of New York succeeded in revoking the Klan's charter on very similar grounds. Investigations by his office established that there were fifteen active Klaverns in the metropolitan New York area.

A month later, Kentucky followed suit.

Shortly after I first made connections with Duke, I walked into the Atlanta headquarters of the F.B.I.

Having studied the Klan's record of the past couple of decades I knew the F.B.I. had taken precious little action against it. Still, I felt it to be my duty to turn over to it any information having to do with the violation of Federal law. And I wanted to set the machinery for this in motion before rather than after something broke.

" I want to speak to someone about the Klan," I said to the young lady who served as the F.B.I.'s receptionist.

" The Klan? " she said, showing an un-F.B.I. surprise.

" That's right."

" Just one moment, please."

She left her desk, and disappeared down the hallway. After some minutes she returned with a well-dressed young man in his middle thirties.

" This is Mr. Phillips," she said. " He will take care of you."

" Won't you come into my office? " Phillips said, leading me down the hall.

When we were seated at his desk he pulled out a large pad of note-paper.

" And what was it you wanted to see us about? " he asked.

" The Klan," I repeated. " I have just recently become a member of the Headquarters Klan here in Atlanta, for the purpose of gathering evidence against the organization. My reports on the Klan's weekly meetings are being turned over to Mr. Dan Duke, the Assistant Attorney-General of Georgia, for use in the state's revocation proceedings against the Klan's charter, and also with a view to criminal prosecutions. If the F.B.I. does not have an agent inside the Headquarters Klan, I thought it might like to obtain copies of my report from Duke's office."

" H'm . . . hah . . . yes, I see," Mr. Phillips said thoughtfully. " And what did you say your name was—"

" Stetson Kennedy," I said. " But as far as the Klan is concerned, my name is John Perkins." I pulled out my Klan Kard and showed it to him.

" Very interesting," he said, like a kid with a toy. " Do you mind if I show it to some of the boys? "

" Not at all," I said, trying to conceal my shock that a KKK Kard should be such a curiosity in the F.B.I. office in the city which was the focal point of Klan activity.

Phillips punched some buzzers on his desk, and in a moment several other agents appeared, to hum and haw over the Kard.

When they finally disappeared, Phillips handed the Kard back to me.

" And where are you living now, Mr. Kennedy? " he asked.

I told him.

" But please don't ever pay me a visit there and ask for Kennedy," I warned, " or my name will be mud."

He went on to ask me a number of other questions—
where I was from, how long I had been in Atlanta, and so
on. I soon lost patience with this line of questioning.

"Is there anything in particular you would like for me to
be on the lookout for in the Klan?" I asked abruptly.

"What? Er . . . I don't know of anything just now," he
said in some confusion. "Can you tell us where they are
meeting, who their leaders are, and that sort of thing?"

I had heard enough.

"If you don't already have that information in your files,
you can get it from my reports in Duke's office," I said. "I
haven't time to go into such details now. Would you care
to give me a telephone number where I can reach you at
any hour, in case I get a lead on some Klan plan to violate
Federal law?"

"You can call here and ask for Phillips," he said.

"But what about at night?" I persisted. "I get most of
my information at Klan meetings at night, and if they start
out on a job that same night, I'd like to be able to get in
touch with you."

"Ah, yes, I see. Well, in that case I will also give you
another number for use after 5 p.m."

In the months and years that followed, I was to call that
number many times. And each time there was a pause while
they switched on recording equipment to make a record of
everything I had to report.

But somehow I always had a feeling that I was speaking
to a machine that could not respond. . . .

I had not been long in the Klan when the Dragon said
something at a meeting one night which made me sit up and
take notice.

"The Kligrapp will please note in the records that I have
sent a Klan cheque for twenty dollars to the Wildwood
Orphanage, and two weeks ago one for fifteen dollars to the
Peachtree Church for playground equipment," he said. "I
will of course hang on to the stubs and cancelled cheques,
but I also want it to appear in the minutes. There's no
telling when the Revenuers may take a notion to knock on
our door and try to collect on that tax lien that put us out

of business during the war. When that day comes I want to be in a position to open our books and show them we're a bona fide charitable order and ought not to be taxed! Every Klavern in the Invisible Empire is being sent orders to do the same! "

Kicking myself mentally for not having thought of this angle sooner, I remembered where I had first heard of the Klan's tax troubles. Before leaving Miami I had a little chat with the Klan's retired Wizard, James A. Colescott, and he had let the cat out of the bag.

" It was that nigger-lover Roosevelt and that Jew Morgenthau who was his Secretary of the Treasury who did it! " the ex-Wizard said bitterly. " I was sitting there in my office in the Imperial Palace in Atlanta one day, just as pretty as you please, when the Revenuers knocked on my door and said they had come to collect three-quarters of a million dollars the Government had just figgered out the Klan owed as taxes on profits earned during the 1920s! "

" What did you do? " I asked with feigned sympathy, but smiling inwardly at the picture.

" What *could* we do? " the Wizard replied indignantly. " We had to sell all our assets and hand over the proceeds to the Government and go out of business. Maybe the Government can make something out of the Klan—I never could! "

Looking at his comfortable home and the Packard limousine in which he went fishing every day, I just nodded.

And now Dragon Green, who had taken over and revived the Klan, was losing sleep over the prospect that the Revenuers might come calling again!

What had become of that three-quarter-million-dollar lien? To what extent had the Klan paid it off? Had the balance been cancelled by the Government? If not, why didn't the Bureau of Internal Revenue use it to put the Klan out of business again, as it had under Roosevelt ?

The next morning I went to see Charlie Pike at union headquarters.

" Charlie, I just might have the Kluxers by their shirt-tails," I said.

" Yeah? " he said. " How's that? "

I told him the whole story, so far as I knew it.

" Sort of like having a pack of hounds baying at the bottom of a hollow tree," Pike observed. " Maybe if we build a fire in the bottom of it we can smoke out whatever's in there. . . ."

" Just what I've been thinking. There's nothing like publicity to generate smoke and heat too, sometimes. But how can we get a story into the papers calling attention to the tax lien, if any? "

" We've got a meeting of the Georgia Legislative Council coming up in a couple of days," Pike suggested. " Maybe it could do something."

" What is this Council? "

" A joint labour group—the C.I.O., A.F.L. and independent unions all have representation in it."

" Seems to me it might well concern itself with the KKK," I said. " A resolution from the Council would be sure to get some attention."

" If you'll draft one, I'll introduce it," Pike promised.

We went to work and drew up a strong resolution, condemning the Klan for using " cross-burning, flogging and terrorism to try to deprive workers of their right to organize freely into unions of their choice," and concluding with a declaration that " the Klan's programme of stirring up religious and racial hatreds is in opposition to the fundamental principles of union brotherhood."

In the body of the resolution we included a demand that the Bureau of Internal Revenue do something about that three-quarter-million-dollar tax lien.

The Council adopted the resolution unanimously, and the Press gave it considerable prominence. Intrigued by the reference to a tax lien, reporters called on Collector of Internal Revenue Marion Allen in Atlanta, who had jurisdiction over the entire south-eastern states where the Klan does most of its business.

" Why yes," Allen admitted, " I do have in my files a lien outstanding against the Knights of the Ku Klux Klan Inc., but it is my understanding that this organization is no longer in existence."

" There's some kind of Klan kicking up sand all over the South," a reporter retorted. " Can we see that lien? "

" My files are confidential, and are not open for public inspection unless a lien is filed in Federal court for collection."

" Then how about filing the Klan lien? " the reporter insisted. " It's delinquent, isn't it? "

" Why, yes; yes, it is—perhaps I will file it," Allen demurred.

And so he did. When the reporters trooped over to U.S. District Court to have a look at it, they discovered that the KKK still owed the U.S.A. a balance of $685,305.08.

" If anyone knows of any assets owned by the Klan corporation, I shall be glad to levy against them," Collector Allen said dutifully.

A few days later, I noticed in the newspapers that Frank J. Wilson, Chief of the U.S. Secret Service, had been " detailed to direct a small army of Treasury Department agents in running down tax evaders."

Wilson, I knew, had once upon a time put the notorious Chicago gangster Al Capone behind bars for income-tax evasion, and it seemed to me he might be inclined to put some of the big-time race racketeers in the Klan's hierarchy in jail too.

So back I went to the Georgia Legislative Council, and we got off a letter to Wilson urging him to help Collector Allen in Atlanta prove " that it is impossible for anyone to dodge taxes by donning a bedsheet and buying a rubber stamp."

Wilson turned the letter over to the chief of the U.S. Bureau of Internal Revenue, Commissioner Joseph D. Nunan, Jr.

" Needless to say, the collector at Atlanta is exercising due diligence in locating assets of the subject taxpayer," Nunan replied lamely. But he added an invitation for us to help the collector if we could, so we did.

I went to work and put together sixteen documents which I procured from the Klan in various ways. This evidence, marked Exhibits A through P, showed that the Klansmen who were kicking up their heels all over the place were using all of the old money-making properties of the Klan corporation, including its name, copyrighted rituals, patented insignia, membership applications and reinstatement forms.

It is a basic principle of law that a lien follows the property, and I couldn't believe that Uncle Sam would let the Klan wriggle out of a three-quarter-million-dollar tax debt.

The Georgia Legislative Council had photostatic copies made of all these documents, and we sent one set to Collector Allen at Atlanta and another to Commissioner Nunan in Washington.

Some weeks went by before we had the Commissioner's answer:

" The Bureau has no information with respect to the organization or organizations which you refer to as ' the operating Klan.' "

The newspapers had of course been filled with accounts of the Klan's periodic outrages ever since the end of the war. However, I promptly prepared a list of a couple of dozen Klan offices of which I had first-hand knowledge, giving the addresses, the night on which meetings were held, and in most cases the names and addresses of the officers, including their phone numbers and places of employment. Copies of this list were then sent by registered mail to Commissioner Nunan, with a copy to Collector Allen.

Another month passed before we had Nunan's final answer:

" The Bureau has reached the conclusion that there is no basis upon which the case could be referred to the Department of Justice with a view to instituting legal proceedings for the collection of the taxes."

That, I feared, was the end of this road.

However, I continued to keep my eyes open and ears peeled for information which might eventually come in handy if the Government were to change its mind about making the Klan pay up—or the voters were to change the Government. . . .

A partial victory was scored, though, when I got wind that a Mr. and Mrs. Ball, who had belonged to Philadelphia's William Penn Klan No. 350, had willed $1,200.00 to the KKK. The Exalted Cyclops of the Philadelphia Klan,

A. W. Johnson, had written the Klan's attorney in Atlanta, Morgan Belser, about the matter, and Wizard Colescott had called a special meeting of the Klan's five-man Imperial Kloncilium to authorize Belser to accept the money.

By telegram I tipped off the Revenuers in Washington and Atlanta that this money was being transferred to the Klan. A few days later I checked with Collector Allen by phone.

" We got the twelve hundred dollars," he said. But I think I was happier about it than he was.

The chief of Atlanta's Associated Press Bureau had the Grand Dragon of the Klan on the phone.

" This is A.P. calling," the newsman said. " You don't happen to be listening to the Superman radio programme, do you? "

" No! " the Dragon spluttered. " Why the hell should I? "

" You'd better tune him in," the A.P. chief chuckled, "—he's after you! "

" What is this—a gag? " the Dragon demanded.

" Nope—Superman's really on your trail. They just announced it. On the air coast to coast every day for the next four weeks. The kids who are Superman's helpers are rattling off your secret passwords a mile a minute! "

" Just a bunch of junk some hack radio writer made up," the Dragon said confidently.

" I dunno—sounds like it might be the real thing. Your secret password right now wouldn't happen to be ' Red Blooded,' would it? "

" Did they say that? Where the hell— "

" Then it is straight stuff, after all? "

" I didn't say it was," the Dragon said glumly.

" Sounds to me like Superman's got a pipeline into your Klaverns somehow," the A.P. man said. " You'd better watch your step! "

" I smell a rat! " the Dragon said bitterly. " Just wait till I get my hands on him! "

" You'd better make it snappy—Superman just flew over your Imperial Palace to case the joint! "

" Nuts! " the Dragon said, and hung up.

This marked the beginning—as I read about it in the papers the next morning—of one of the most rewarding phases of Operation Anti-Klan. But the case of Superman after the Grand Dragon also started the chase of the Dragon after me.

The Superman idea came one day when I saw a group of small boys playing with secret passwords in much the same way that grown men played with them in the Klan. Why not get the Klan's secret password into the mouths of kids? It would make a laughing stock out of the Klan's gobbledygook rigmarole! But to do any good this would have to be done all across the country.

It was then that I thought of Superman. The radio version of this fabulous, jet-propelled character, who was capable of performing any feat and impervious to even atomic attack, had already won national recognition for going after real villains, including hate-mongers.

I got in touch with the creators of the radio Superman script, and they jumped at the idea of having him beard the Grand Dragon in his den. Armed with complete information about the Klan's set-up, ritual and the roles played by Cyclopses, Terrors, Ghouls and Titans they wrote a series of programmes. I also gave them the Klan's current password, and promised to keep them informed every time it was changed.

Things happened fast after that first broadcast went on the air. The Dragon came to the next meeting breathing fire, and every Kluxer in the place was just as sore. I had visions of how they must have all huddled around their radios at six o'clock every day to hear what new Klan secrets Superman would expose.

" Brother Grand Dragon! " a rank-and-filer stood up and shouted as soon as the meeting was called to order. " I say to hell with the agenda! We've got a rat in our midst, and we ought to make that our first order of business! You all know what I'm talking about. When I came home from work the other night, there was my kid and a bunch of others, some with towels tied around their necks like capes and some with pillow cases over their heads. The ones with capes was chasing the ones with pillow cases all over the lot.

When I asked them what they were doing, they said they was playing a new kind of Cops and Robbers called ' Superman against the Klan.' Gangbusting they called it! Knew all our secret passwords and everything: I never felt so ridiculous in all my life! Suppose my own kid finds my Klan robe some day? Men, are we going to let ourselves be made fools of like this? "

" Nooooh! . . .! " the Klansmen all chorused, stamping their feet.

" Dragons have been impeached for letting such secrets get out . . ." a Kluxer named John Perkins muttered in a familiar voice.

" Order in the Klavern! " the Dragon rapped. " You men are not any more wrought up over this Superman thing than I am! But don't try to pin the blame on me! There's a Judas among us, probably sitting right here tonight, and we've got to weed him out or he'll wreck the Klan! God knows I've exercised due caution. As you know, I've appointed the best city detectives in Atlanta to our Klokann investigating committee. I'm ordering the Klokann to reopen its investigation of every man who has been naturalized in the last three months. But every man in the Klan has got to help trap the rat. If any one of you has any suspicions at all as to who he is, don't lose any time telling me! "

" The damage has already been done," a Klansman said. " Superman has spilled the beans from coast to coast! "

" Our sacred ritual being profaned by a bunch of kids on the radio! " the Kladd of the Klan moaned. " I'll never feel the same about putting on an initiation again."

" They didn't put it *all* on the air," the Dragon ventured weakly. " We could make some changes. . . ."

" What they didn't broadcast wasn't worth broadcasting," the Kladd said bitterly.

" They didn't give our top-secret final oath," the Dragon persisted. " From now on I'm going to administer that privately in the back room."

" We've got to have a new password right away," a Klansman pointed out. " Anybody could have walked in here with our password tonight."

"How about 'Death to Traitors!'?" the Dragon suggested. "That's all I can think of."

As soon as the meeting was over I put in a call to Superman's authors in New York. I gave them the new password, and urged them to work in the Klan's final oath.

"That's coming up!" they assured me. "We're really going to turn on the heat next week!"

When Headquarters Klan was again called to order the following Monday night, attendance was at rock bottom, and there were no new applications for membership. The Dragon looked sick.

"I know," he said before anyone could begin to berate him, "we need a new password. It's 'Damn Superman!' I'll bet they won't put that on the air!"

"Very funny," the Klansman sitting next to me said sourly. "Here we are a secret organization without a secret left, and all the Dragon does is crack jokes!"

Superman pursued his month-long chase of the Dragon, lambasting the Kluxers for the cowards, bums and bullies that they are. In the end Superman cornered the Dragon, knocked him out, and brought the whole gang to justice.

From inside and outside the Klan I could see that a real victory had been won. Never again would the hooded hoodlums be able to face the American public with their old air of self-importance. Equally important, I knew that the millions of kids who had listened to Superman were not likely to grow up to be Klansmen.

CHAPTER SIX

I WORK MY WAY INTO
THE FLOG SQUAD

I WAS having a beer in the bar where I first made contact with the Klan when Slim walked in, and without any greeting slipped a small card into my hand and walked out again. I looked at it. Crudely hand-lettered in black ink, it said:

Are You Ready To Meet—
DEATH?
Wednesday Night at 8
in Klavern No. 1
Be There!

At the bottom of the card there was a crude skull, with two curved cavalry swords as crossbones. It was signed " Brothers of the Sword."

I've been discovered, and this is the Klan's way of inviting me to my own funeral, I thought. There would be a mock trial in the Inner Den, followed by a mock burial symbolizing my banishment as a citizen of the Invisible Empire—and then perhaps the " Death, death, at the hands of a Brother " which I was sworn to accept if I betrayed the Klan's secrets!

Or could this be the Klan's way of inviting me to join its Klavalier flog squad, which I had been trying to penetrate for so long?

There was only one way to find out. I would be expected to keep the appointment—and ask no questions in the meantime. The more I thought about the two possible prospects, the more I was convinced that the odds were no better than fifty-fifty. If this were indeed the opening of the door to the flog squad, it was the long-awaited goal of my

Klan probe. I felt that at last I had reached the front line, and the hour of attack had come. I was determined to press forward. . . .

It was about five minutes before eight o'clock when I arrived at Klavern No. 1 on Wednesday night. A single light was burning in the entrance, but there was no one in sight. An ominous quiet prevailed as I walked up to the door of the Klavern. Taking a deep breath, I scratched the Klan's sign of the cross on the door with my fingernail.

An eye glared at me through the peephole wicket, and the Klarogo inside said, " Save—"

" —America," I replied, completing the current Klan password.

" Pass, Klansman," the Klarogo said, throwing open the door.

Accustomed as I was to Klan spectacles by that time, I was nevertheless taken aback by what I saw inside. The red neon cross was glowing behind the altar of the Grand Dragon, and about thirty-five men were seated about, robed in the deathly black of the Klavalier Klub. The effect was so foreboding I must have taken a step backward.

" Advance, Klansman! " the figure seated at the station of the Grand Dragon ordered. I recognized the huge bulk and grating voice as belonging to Cliff Carter, the Night Hawk of the Klan. I walked slowly towards him, and stood at attention with arms folded across my chest, Klan-style, in front of the altar. The altar, I noticed, was draped as usual with the Confederate flag, with a cavalry sword lying diagonally across it and a ceremonial bowl in the centre. But the customary Bible was lacking, and the bowl, ordinarily filled with water, was empty. . . .

Very soon now I would know whether I was coming or going.

" Klansman Perkins," Carter began to intone in his best ritual manner, " for some time you have been under investigation—"

I braced myself for his next words.

" —to find out whether you are worthy of the highest honour and trust that can be bestowed by the Klan—

elevation to the Order of the Knights of the Great Forest, otherwise known as the Klavalier Klub. . . ."

My breathing returned to normal. I felt like a tight-rope walker who had just made a safe crossing.

"The *Kloran* of the Klan," Carter continued, "defines a Klavalier as the soldier of the Klan. We take our name from the cavalier—a courtly, polite, cultured and very courageous and skilful soldier of the seventeenth and eighteenth centuries. . . . Do you think you can measure up to this description?"

"I do!" I said as fervently as I could.

"As the Military Department of the Invisible Empire, we Klavaliers also serve as the secret police of the KKK and are entrusted with carrying out all 'direct-line' activity. Do you understand what I mean?"

"Absolutely!"

"In various Realms of the Invisible Empire the Klavaliers go by various names—in Detroit, the Black Legion; in New Jersey, the Legion of Death. We are a militant army, serving our country in peacetime as the U.S. Army does in wartime! Our country was founded as a white Protestant nation, and we intend to maintain it as such! Any attempt to influence its affairs by inferior racial minorities or persons owing allegiance to foreign prelates or potentates will not be tolerated!"

Carter pounded on the altar with such force that the ceremonial bowl leapt into the air and almost fell on the floor. In the light of the red neon cross his eyes seemed to flash fire through the slits in his black mask.

"All hyphenated groups—whether they be Negro-Americans, Jewish - Americans, Catholic - Americans, Italian-Americans or what-have-you—must become American-Americans, or leave the country! The Ku Klux Klan is an American-American organization. As the Army of the Klan we Klavaliers are dedicated to saving America for Americans! Do you subscribe wholeheartedly to these principles?"

"I do!" I said.

"To be a Klavalier, you must be able and willing to respond to a call to duty at any hour of the day or night, dropping instantly whatever else you may be doing. The only excuse tolerated for not mobilizing in response to a Fiery Summons is for you to be bedridden by severe illness! Do you still wish to join our ranks? Consider well, and if you are fainthearted, retire now before it is too late! "

" I wish to proceed . . ." I replied grimly.

There was a silence, which was broken by the sound of someone scratching the sign of the cross outside the door. The Klarogo sprang to the wicket. The countersign was exchanged, and an unrobed man entered excitedly, holding a small white envelope in his hand. He stood just inside the door, and gave the extended-arm sign of greeting.

" Advance, Klansman, and state your business! " Carter said, returning the salute as a sign of recognition.

The man walked forward and handed Carter the envelope. Carter opened it deliberately, then read slowly:

> *At least twenty good men needed at once to come to the aid of their brethren in Klavern 066! There is important work to be tended to, putting down armed rioting by Negroes!*

" I call for volunteers! " Carter cried.

There was a chorus as every Klavalier present raised his hand.

Suddenly I realized that Carter was glaring at me.

" What about you? " he roared. " Are you afraid of being hurt or killed? What are you anyway—a coward? "

" Throw the yellow bastard out of the window! " a Klavalier called out, and the others echoed approval. I decided the time had come to do some fast talking.

" Your Excellency and Brothers," I said as loudly as I could, " I did not understand that I was already privileged to take part in your activities. Had I known that, I assure you I would have been among the first to volunteer! "

This quieted them, and after a moment Carter said:

" Spoken like a true Klansman! You are to be congratulated upon passing your first test. There's not really any emergency at Klavern 066—this is only one of the ways we have of testing whether or not a candidate is worthy. . . ."

The plain-clothed brother, having done his job, slipped on his black robe and hood and took a seat with the rest.

"As a Klansman you are already sworn to secrecy,"
Carter went on. "As a Klavalier you must be doubly
sworn! Our operations are such that we must keep them
secret not only from the prying eyes of the public but even
from our own Brothers in the Klan. In the event that something should go wrong, it is the duty of the Klavalier to
accept whatever fine, imprisonment or other punishment
may be meted out to him, without revealing his identity as
a Klansman. The good name of the Klan must be shielded
at all costs! You know the penalty for betraying the secrets
of the Klan—' Death, death, at the hands of a Brother.' To
become a Klavalier you must seal that oath with your own
blood! Do you still wish to proceed? "

"I do . . ." I replied, trying to tell myself I was lucky not
to be having my throat cut!

"Advance, then, and take your position before the altar! "

I stepped closer to the table.

"This is the Confederate flag for which the South fought,"
Carter intoned. "Red, symbolizing the blood shed for the
South; white, for the purity of its womanhood; and blue
for God's blue canopy that covers us. . . . The blood oath
you are about to take is the same as that taken by our
illustrious forbears, the Knights of the Ku Klux Klan of
old. Extend your left hand! "

Reaching under his robe, Carter brought forth a large
jack-knife. He pressed a button on the handle, and a long
blade leapt out. Grasping my hand, Carter made a quick
slash at my wrist. I was hoping he knew what he was doing,
and that the result would not be fatal. A veteran no doubt
of many such blood-lettings, he inflicted a gash which missed
the principal veins and arteries, but produced a steady flow
of blood. Holding my hand over the bowl, Carter let it drip
in silence for a minute. Finally he released me and said,
"Bind up your wrist! "

When I had tied it in my handkerchief, Carter
ordered:

"Klansman, you will now give the Sign of Consecration! "

I knelt in front of the altar on my right knee, placed my
right hand over my heart, and raised my left hand in
outstretched salute. . . .

With great solemnity, Carter administered the blood oath of the Klavaliers:

"Klansman, do you solemnly swear by God and the Devil never to betray secrets entrusted to you as a Klavalier of the Klan?"

"I swear."

"Do you swear to provide yourself with a good gun and plenty of ammunition, so as to be ready when the nigger starts trouble to give him plenty?"

"I do...."

"Do you further swear to do all in your power to increase the white birth-rate?"

Despite the seriousness of the moment, I almost laughed. So the Klavaliers were a menace to white Southern womanhood as well as to everybody else!

"I do!" I blurted out with more gusto than I had thus far been able to muster.

Carter dipped his forefinger into the bowl of blood, and smeared the Klan's sign of the cross on my forehead. Taking up the sword, he tapped me alternately on each shoulder with the flat of the blade.

"Klansman, I dub you Knight of the Klavaliers! Live up to your oath! Be you ever ready to fight for your Honour, your Home, the Klan, and White Supremacy! Arise!"

"Congratulations!" Carter added as I stood up. He pulled off his hood and mask, and wiped the perspiration from his jowls. As he gave me the Klan handshake, he said, "Unmask, men, so Perkins can see who his new brothers are. After we've cooled off a bit, I'll explain to Perkins how we work."

I looked around the den. I had seen many of the faces before, in various Klaverns around Atlanta. There was Randal, Grand Kligrapp of the Georgia Realm, my old "buddy" Slim Pickett, and a tough little Kluxer named Ira Jett (who was eventually to save my life, for reasons of his own). I had found Kluxers to be an ugly lot, but this hand-picked gang of strong-arm Klansmen were the meanest I had ever seen under one roof. They were capable, I felt sure, of every conceivable form of violence. Frustration, cruelty and alcoholism showed in every face. I resolved to

take a look into a mirror at the first opportunity, to reassure
myself that I did not look like a Klavalier.

I took a seat among the ranks of the Klavaliers, and
Carter resumed his station behind the altar.

" Perkins," he began, " the Klectoken fee for joining the
Klavaliers is ten dollars. In addition to your regular Klan
dues, we charge one dollar a month just to meet expenses.
Every fifth Wednesday we get together for a steak dinner
at Wingo's Café over in West End; the cost of that is one
dollar fifty. We reserve a private dining-room there, and
that's where we transact most of our business, unless something urgent comes up at a Klan meeting, in which case we
meet here in the Inner Den right afterwards. You'll be
expected to provide yourself with another robe immediately,
and to dye it black."

I must have winced visibly at all these expenses.

" If it's action you crave, you'll get your money's worth,
I promise you," Carter continued. " Now if you'll come
forward I'll issue your membership Kard in the Klavaliers,
and explain its secret symbolism."

I walked up to the altar, and he handed me a small
wallet-size card, white, with various cabalistic-looking
symbols hand-drawn on it in heavy black ink.

" The question mark," he said, " stands for secrecy, and
the corkscrew for crookedness—"

There was an appreciative titter from the Klavaliers.

" What about the letters ' A.T.'? " I asked.

" They stand for Ass-Tearer," Carter replied, and the
Klavaliers roared at their " joke." Such kid stuff, I thought
to myself—if it weren't so deadly serious! " My title is
Chief Ass-Tearer," Carter continued, " and I hold Klavalier
Kard No. 1. We are organized along military lines, and I
serve as Chief of Staff to the Grand Dragon, who holds
Klavalier Kard No. 0. The line of authority is there—we
don't make a move except on the Dragon's orders or O.K.
But if trouble comes, I take the rap for the Dragon, to keep
the Klan's name clear. That number in the corner of
the Kard, seventy-three, is your identification. The Kard
is your passport to all Klavalier functions — guard it
well! "

With that, I slipped the Kard into my wallet and resumed my seat.

"There are certain precautions we take in telephone conversations among ourselves about Klavalier business. You must never address me by name on the phone—call me 'Clearwater.' My office is to be referred to only as 'Hole in the Wall.' For mobilization, we've set aside two principal points with code names—Five Points, which we call 'Chinatown,' and Buckhead, which we call 'Black Rock.' Think you can remember all that?"

"Clearwater, Hole-in-the-Wall, Chinatown, Black Rock . . ." I repeated.

"Good man! Now I'll tell you about one of the jobs we pulled lately, just to let you know how we work. You remember a complaint that came up in the Klavern a couple of weeks ago about a nigger who had a habit of jostling white ladies at the bus stop in front of Davison-Paxon's department store?"

"Sure," I replied. "The Dragon said he was turning it over to the Klavaliers for handling."

"Well, we handled it all right! I'll bet that nigger won't never get within six feet of no white lady as long as he lives!"

"Let me tell him how we did it, Chief," Randal broke in. "You've done talked yourself hoarse."

Carter nodded, and sat back while Randal related the sordid tale. . . .

"Our calendar has been so full it took us a while to get around to this case, Perkins, but when we did, we set it up like this. The nigger always showed up there at six o'clock rush in the evening. First, a couple of our boys staged a fake fist-fight down the street a ways, to attract everybody's attention. While that was going on, a bunch of us pulled up in a car to the bus stop, right beside the nigger. I was already there, standing in back of him, and when they opened the door I pressed a gun in his back and told him to get in. He got in without making any fuss and we drove on down Ivy Street to the Grand Theatre. You know where that is. It's been abandoned a long time, and there's a parking lot in back of it, real dark. After looking to make sure we weren't being followed, we turned in there and changed cars. The idea is that if anybody had noticed the gun and given the cops a description of the car, we'd be in the clear."

" Every job pulled around town here calls for the same routine," Carter interjected.

" Soon as we had switched cars we drove out of town and over into Rockledge County," Randal went on.

" The idea there," Carter cut in again, " is to do our work among friends. We've got Rockledge County completely Kluxed—police, sheriff's office, prosecutor, judges, fire department, even the dog-catcher. If anything was to go wrong, we wouldn't have a thing to worry about so far as being prosecuted is concerned. That's why we take all our cases, if at all possible, into Rockledge County for handling. . . ."

" We'd already planned to meet another carload of our boys at a certain wooded hummock over the county line," Randal went on. " They were supposed to bring the whip with them—we've got one made out of a piece of sawmill belt nailed on to a sawed-off baseball bat handle—but they had a flat tyre and was late getting there. So we cut some pine branches off a tree and went to work on the nigger.

" He was the stubbornest one I ever beat on! No matter how hard we hit him, we couldn't make him holler. Said he hadn't never jostled no white ladies. Kept talkin' about how he had fought for democracy and all that stuff during the war, and hadn't ought to be treated that way. I told him that was probably what was wrong with him—rubbin' up against them French women and comin' home with all kinds of crazy notions about equality! "

While Randal chuckled at his own brand of humour, Carter again put in his oar:

" I sent 'em down to the creek to dip their switches in branchwater—makes 'em heavier, and you can do a better job! "

" The rest of the boys finally got there with the whip, and we all gave the nigger three licks apiece with it for good measure," Randal added.

" In the Klavalier Klub," Carter said pointedly, " every man takes his turn with the whip on every job. That way, there's less chance of anybody ever doing any talking.

There's a certain knack to using that bullwhip. A time or two we killed men with it when we wasn't aimin' to. You'll catch on to it soon enough! "

" When we finished with this nigger we drove him back to nigger town and dumped him out," Randal finished, eager to get another word in. " Told him if he ever said one word to anybody about being beaten, he'd be a dead one! "

" That reminds me—" Carter said, looking around the room. " Slim, what'd you do with that whip? "

" Don't worry, Chief, it's perfectly safe. I throwed it way up under my brother's house. I can fetch it anytime at a moment's notice."

" You should've brought it with you tonight! It's still early yet, and there's a little job I want taken care of—"

" Are we going to ride tonight, Chief? What's cooking? " the Klavaliers broke in.

" Hold your horses! " Carter shouted, not displeased by their blood-lust. " Slim, we'll let the whip go tonight, but next Wednesday when we get together at Wingo's you be damned sure you bring it with you! The Dragon has a rush call for us to take care of some damyankee nigger-lovin' union organizers who are causing trouble out in Chinquapin Mill Village. Our most important job is to run union carpetbaggers back across the Mason-Dixon Line where they come from! "

" I happen to know a couple of them union organizers, and they is Georgy boys, born and bred right around here," a Klavalier sitting next to me ventured. " It ain't going to be easy to run them off nowhere. . . ."

" Are you takin' up for the nigger-lovin' sonsabitches? " Carter barked. " I don't care who they are! It ain't the old-time honest-to-god unions for white folks we're after, it's these new-fangled outfits that don't care who they take in! They're run by a bunch of no-good Catholics, Jews and foreigners up North, and don't know what's good for the South! The Dragon has a whole stack of requests from mill-owners all over the South begging us to send men to chase those babies away from their gates! All expenses paid, and plenty of drinkin' liquor for all hands! "

The Klavalier who had dared question Carter's union-busting leaned over and whispered in my ear.

"You can bet your bottom dollar ole Cliff and Doc Green rakes in a heap more than expenses on these deals!" he said. "Them mill-owners pay plenty for our services. Green and Carter pocket it, and all we get for doin' the dirty work is a slug of rot-gut liquor!"

"Before we get going on such serious business, I want to clear our docket of all these little piddling cases," Carter resumed. "You can get along without the bullwhip tonight —cut yourselves some more switches, or do whatever you want with the rascal. I'm goin' to let you boys handle this one yourselves, as I've got some important business of my own to 'tend to."

"Yeah, I know," the Klavalier next to me whispered again. "Cliff pulls most of these cases out of his hat to get away from his wife once a week so he can get in the pants of a lil ole gal he knows out in East Point. . . ."

Author (*right*) and colleague Elizabeth Gardner showing Klan "trophies" to Dr. James Shelton, director, Non-Sectarian Anti-Nazi League, where Kennedy worked as director of covert operations (New York City, 1948). Photograph courtesy Llewellyn Ransom.

CHAPTER SEVEN

THE KLAVALIERS RIDE TO A FALL

" This job for tonight is a cinch," Carter declared. " As y'all know, there's a law against coloured cab-drivers carrying white folks. But near 'bout every week we get reports that the law ain't being enforced. When the law fails, it's time for the Klan to step in. . . ."

He paused, and there was a supercharged silence in the den as the Klavaliers waited for their briefing to continue.

" One nigger cab-driver especially, who operates out of the bus station, is in the habit of pickin' up white ladies. Tonight we're going to put a stop to it. I've got it all set up. There's a Klanswoman down at the bus station right now. She's going to get in his cab, throw a gun on him, and hold him for us."

Then he looked directly at me. " Perkins, I'm going to give you your first chance to show us what you're made of. I want you to report to the bus station right away, and relieve Brother Jim Meeks, who's on duty there. Keep an eye on a woman in a canary yellow blouse with a silver spider breast-pin. When she gets in the cab, you come out the side door of the station and give a long, low whistle. Then stand by for the boys to pick you up!"

"Just watch my smoke!" I said, starting for the door. I wanted to get to a phone as fast as I could to put in a riot call for Duke's men.

"Hold on!" Carter shouted. "No need to charge off like a bull moose going to crap! Brother Randal here will drive you over to the station. He's got a fast car, and I want it to be on hand."

Just my luck, I thought, to get sent out on a flog party and not even be able to try to stop it. I resolved to make every effort to put in the call to Duke after I got to the station.

When we got there, Randal put me out, and drove off into the dark side street leading up to the side entrance. I soon spotted Meeks, who threw out his left palm in the Klan's secret sign of recognition.

" Clearwater gave me instructions to relieve you, and to give the signal when our girl friend climbs into the cab," I said to him.

" There she is, right over there—" Meeks indicated with a jerk of his head. I looked, and saw a buxom peroxide blonde of the sort generally found in third-rate bars. She gave me a wink, and I winked back. She's a Klanswoman, all right, I said to myself, and I'll bet she knows how to use the pistol in her purse.

" The nigger's cab is parked in the taxi stand out front right now," Meeks went on. " How long do you reckon it'll be before the rest of the boys get here? "

" Clearwater didn't say—he must've given our girl friend some kind of cue. My orders are to follow her lead."

" O.K.—I think I'll duck out the side door and see if I can spot the boys when they drive up."

This, I thought, would give me a chance to phone Duke! As soon as Meeks disappeared through the side door, I headed for the phone booths. Just before stepping into one, something told me to look back. Meeks was watching me like a hawk through the window! Instead of entering the booth, I cocked one leg against it and pretended to tie my shoelace.

So Clearwater was testing me in more ways than one. . . . I wondered if every new recruit into the Klavaliers was given the same treatment, or whether I was under suspicion. Of course, I could claim I was phoning a girl friend—but I would need a far better excuse than that if Duke's men pounced and caught them in the act. For a moment I debated with myself—was this the time for a showdown—or should I hold my fire for some more serious occasion? Remembering what Carter had said about getting along without the bullwhip, I decided that relatively minor

" punishment " was to be meted out. I had no way of knowing that the night would end with murder. . . .

I straightened up and walked back to the centre of the waiting room. About fifteen minutes went by before the woman in the canary blouse suddenly went into action. I watched as she walked quickly through the front door and climbed into the Negro's cab. Hurrying to the side door, I walked over to the darkness of the side street and whistled. . . .

The Klavaliers must have been waiting with motors running—in a matter of seconds they pulled up beside me in two cars.

" Get in! " I heard Randal bark.

I climbed into the back seat of his car, and we drove around in front of the station. The cab had already disappeared. There must have been a prearranged plan, however, for the woman to direct the cab to a certain spot, for we had scarcely driven a half-mile before we pulled into a deserted street to find the cab parked at the kerb. Cutting our lights, we coasted up behind it, climbed out and walked up to the cab.

The Klanswoman was sitting on the edge of the back seat, pressing a huge pearl-handled Police Special ·45 revolver into the back of the driver's neck! Her chubby hands with their long red fingernails held the baby cannon firmly.

" Here's your meat, boys! " she said with a grin.

" Good girl! " Randal said, taking the pistol from her.

" You've done a good night's work—you can run along now, and we'll take care of the rest! "

He opened the front door of the cab, shoved the Negro aside, and climbed in behind the steering wheel.

" Let's get going! " he ordered. We piled into the back seat, and Randal handed Slim the ·45. Without being told, Slim stuck the barrel back into the Negro's neck.

" White folks, what y'all want with me? " he said with dignity. " I ain't done nothing to be treated like this. . . . You must be got the wrong man. . . ."

" You're wrong, but we're goin' to set you right! " Slim said, jabbing him savagely with the gun barrel.

" Meanwhile, keep your mouth shut or I'll blow your head off! "

We drove off, followed by the other carload of Klavaliers.

" Pass the whisky," Slim said. " Nigger-killin' is hard work, and a man needs a little nip now and then. . . ."

The other Klavalier on the back seat fished out a bottle of cheap blended whisky and handed it to Slim. Slim tilted it to his mouth and let it gurgle.

" Don't kill it! " the Klavalier said.

" Hell, ain't I doin' all the work so far? " Slim asked, handing the bottle to Randal. Randal took a short pull, and passed it to us in the back seat again. It was my turn next, and I pretended to drink deeply. The keeper of the bottle drank last.

" Damn' thing's 'most empty! " he complained bitterly. " You'd think Clearwater would come across with a bigger bottle."

" We just crossed the county line," Randal said. " You can put on your robes now."

The man with the bottle had a robe for me. As we got into them, the Negro man watched out of the corner of his eye. But the fear he must have felt upon discovering he was in the hands of the Klan did not show in his face.

We turned off the highway and on to a clay road that threaded off through the pine flatwoods. When we came to a clump of hardwood trees at the head of a branch, Randal stopped the cab. Reaching over and opening the door, he gave the Negro a shove that sent him sprawling face first on to the ground. Almost before I knew what was happening, both carloads of Klavaliers had swarmed around him, and were kicking at his prostrated form amid a torrent of profanity. The Negro groaned and doubled over to protect his groin, but he made no plea for mercy. I felt like vomiting, and was glad my face was masked to hide my disgust. With great effort I kicked in the direction of the Negro, missing deliberately. Randal, meanwhile, was standing on the sidelines, calmly putting on his robe. That done, he stepped up, and the kicking subsided.

" You'd better say your prayers, nigger! " he said. " Your time has come."

" I don't know why y'all are treating me like this," he groaned.

" You know better than to pick up a white woman! " Randal said. " And now you're going to pay the penalty. Are you going to pray or not? "

" I never was no prayin' man . . ." the Negro replied, with more hatred than fear showing in his eyes.

" Let's stop foolin' around and get on with the killin'," Slim said, emptying the whisky bottle and heaving it off into the woods. The bottle struck a tree and broke with a loud smash.

" We got to change this nigger's attitude first," Randal said. " We got to put the fear of the Klan and God both in him! Get up! " He kicked the man fiercely in the ribs.

The Negro groaned and struggled painfully to his feet.

" We're callin' the tune, and you're goin' to dance! " Randal said. " Get goin'! " He took the ·45 from Slim's hand and began firing at the Negro's feet, kicking up puffs of red dust. " Come on, boys, help me provide the music! "

All of the Klavaliers pulled pistols from beneath their robes and began firing at his feet. I was glad I was just a novice, and, as far as the Klavaliers knew, unarmed.

" Dance, damn you! " Randal cried in a rage.

Mechanically, but still not showing the fear the Klavaliers longed to see, the man began to jog up and down. Suddenly he stopped.

" If you're aimin' to kill me, you'll just have to kill me," he said.

" I'm givin' you one more chance! " Randal snarled. " Start running down that road—but don't dare leave the road, or your running days will be over! "

Randal climbed back into the cab and motioned for us to get in. The Negro started on a slow, painful lope down the road, and Randal began to follow. Leaning out of the window, he fired at the Negro's heels.

" Step on it! " he yelled, increasing the speed of the car. Slim and the others followed suit, leaning out of the windows, firing and cursing. We kept going faster and faster, and the distance between the cab and the fleeing form grew perilously shorter. The Negro had been running in the centre of the road, between the ruts, when suddenly he started to cross the road and head for the woods. He stumbled in the rut and fell. Randal jammed on the brakes, but there was a sickening thud and the car passed over the Negro's body. I turned away, sick. Without looking, I knew he was dead.

"The black bastard had it comin' to him!" Randal said bitterly. "He wouldn't pay no attention to nothin' we said. We'd better get out of here!"

I looked through the rear window. The other Klavaliers in the car behind us, seeing what had happened, made a wide detour around the body. Together we raced back to Atlanta, and abandoned the cab where we had first commandeered it.

"Disperse, and keep a tight lip!" Randal ordered.

It was after 1 a.m. I hurried to Atlanta's only all-night drug store and put in a call to Duke's home. His wife answered the phone.

"Dan's not here," she said sleepily. "He's down in Macon on business, and won't get back until tomorrow...."

"Thanks," was all I could say.

I felt completely frustrated. I had seen a murder committed, and yet there was no one to whom I could turn. There was not even any point in reporting the matter to the F.B.I., which has no jurisdiction over murder. For the first time in my life, I had a real insight into how it must feel to be a Negro in a part of the country where there is no authority to whom one can appeal for justice.

After a restless night reliving the tragedy, I was awakened by the thud of the morning paper being delivered. I brought it in and scanned it hurriedly, Just as I was about to give up, I found what I was looking for. It was a one-inch notice buried on a back page:

Body Found

The body of a Negro man, with head and chest crushed, apparently the victim of a hit-and-run driver, was found in the early morning hours on Pryor Road by Rockledge County Police. From papers on the man's body he was identified as James Martin, a driver for the Lincoln Cab Company.

So that was how it was being written off! I wondered how many Negroes' had died similarly violent deaths in the South, only to have one-inch obituaries bury the atrocities as " accidents." James Martin, I swore to myself, was not going to be buried that way.

The next morning I was at the State Capitol building bright and early, and slipped into Duke's office while the hall was clear. I was sitting there when Duke arrived a little later.

" What kind of devilry have they been up to now? " he asked, studying my face.

I told him the whole story. When I had finished, he snubbed out his cigarette.

" Rockledge County! " he said bitterlv. " First, I'd play hell getting the prosecutor to issue wa.rants. Then if we ever got the case into court, every Ku Kluxer you named would trot a dozen of his lying Brothers across the stand to perjure themselves by swearing he was somewhere else that night. The judge would be against us, and I doubt if we could scrape together a jury without at least one Kluxer on it to hang the jury and cause a mistrial. The killers would go free—and your days of usefulness inside the Klan would be over! "

" But we can't let them get away with this kind of thing, Dan! " I pleaded. " What about the big union-busting drive they're going to launch next Wednesday? We've got to do something! "

Duke lit another cigarette. " This Rockledge County routine can keep us stymied indefinitely," he admitted. " And the counties where the mill workers are organizing are just as bad. I'd like to put the Klavaliers behind bars for a long time, but if we can't do that, maybe the next best thing is to put them out of business."

" I'd settle for that," I said. " But how? "

" What's this about a bullwhip? "

" I spent all morning tracking it down. I didn't want to ask any questions, so I called nearly every Pickett in the phone book before I found Slim's brother. His name is

Frank, and the house where the whip's hidden is at 3664
Watson Street."

" You never can tell what a Kluxer will do when you turn
on the heat," Duke said. " They act tough when they're in
a gang, with their faces covered up and holding the whip
hand, but if you unmask 'em, take the whip away, and
turn the heat on 'em one at a time . . ."

He picked up the phone and dialled a number.

" Hello . . . Is Hawkins around? . . . Hello, Hawkins—
Duke! I've got a little job for you on our special project.
Take Evans with you and run out tomorrow morning about
seven-thirty to 3664 Watson Street. You'll find a guy named
Frank Pickett there; take him into custody. Under his
house somewhere you'll find a whip; bring it in. You may
need a flashlight. After that, pick up Frank's brother Slim,
who lives at 167½ Pulliam. Then on the way in, go by the
Carter Trucking Company and pick up Cliff Carter. Don't
get into conversation with them; just bring 'em all to my
office! "

" Can't I get in on the fun? " I asked as he hung up.

" You can hang out in my secretary's office and watch
through a crack in the door if you want to. . . ."

Needless to say, I was doing just that when Duke's agents
brought in the three Klavaliers the next morning.

" Here you are, Chief," Hawkins said, tossing the whip
on to Duke's desk. He was still covered with dirt from
crawling under the house.

The Pickett brothers were slouching against the wall,
their hats in their hands, but Carter was chewing on a cigar
and trying to look tough.

" You haven't got a thing on us, Duke! " he muttered.

Duke turned on him, cracking the whip in his face.

" Whadaya call this? " he bellowed. " You could kill a
bull elephant with a whip like that! If I weren't an officer
of the law I'd be tempted to turn it on every one of you
bullies who ever used it! "

For a moment the two men stood toe to toe. Finally
Carter's gaze broke, and he shrank back.

" You can't prove nothin'," he said lamely.

" Take 'em down the hall and hold 'em in separate
rooms," Duke ordered Hawkins, waving his hand at Carter
and Slim. " Frank, you stay here! "

When the room was clear, Duke went to work.

" You're in a hot spot, son," he told Frank grimly. " I
don't need to tell you this whip we found under your house
was used just last week to beat a man within an inch of his
life! "

" Honest to God, Mister Duke, I don't know nothing
about it! I never seen that whip before in my life—didn't
even know it was under my house! "

" Don't hand me that crap—it's too soft to plough! You
know damned well your brother chucked it under there for
safe keeping until you yellow-bellies were ready to go out on
another raiding party! "

" No, sir! I never did join the Ku Klux, and don't know
nothing about their doin's! I told Slim he was going to get
in trouble messin' around with them."

" I happen to know you're telling the truth about not
being a Klansman. But you'd better come clean about this
whip."

" Mister Duke, I swear on a stack of Bibles a mile high
I don't know the first thing about it! "

Duke studied him in silence, watching him twist his hat,
before he finally spoke.

" O.K., Frank—I'm going to let you go for the time
being. But don't get lost, because I'll be calling for you
again."

Frank clapped on his hat and scuttled through the door.
Through a window I could see him hurrying down the
street to a bar on the corner.

Duke raked Slim over the coals next. It was a sight to see,
and several times Slim was obviously on the verge of breaking down and talking. But each time he glanced at the door
and clamped his mouth shut, with the muscles of his jaw
twitching and sweat pouring from his forehead. I knew that,
afraid as he was of Duke, he was still more afraid of Carter.
Even when Duke threatened him with the electric chair for
his part in the killing of James Martin, Slim remained silent,

knowing that if he talked, retribution from the Klavaliers
would be swift and certain.

" You'll talk when I pop you on the stand and the hot
seat stares you in the face! " Duke predicted. " Now get
out! "

Like his brother, Slim beat it for the bar on the corner.
I could imagine the family reunion that must have taken
place there.

At last it was Carter's turn. Duke pushed him down in a
chair, and the two men glared at each other—two Georgia
giants, one dedicated to enforcing the law, the other to
violating it.

" I've got the goods on you, Clearwater! " Duke said, as
Carter recoiled at hearing his " secret " code name. " Your
days of sending out flogging and lynching parties from your
hole-in-the-wall are over! Yes, and I'm going to nail the
Grand Dragon to a fiery cross along with you! "

" This ain't got nothin' to do with the Klan . . ." Carter
mumbled.

" It hasn't, huh? Just wait till I show this to a jury."
Duke reached in the top drawer of his desk and pulled out
the copy of the Klan's *Kloran* that I had turned in to him.
Carter paled with the knowledge that Duke held in his hands
the Klan's innermost secrets. Deliberately, Duke proceeded
to read the section providing for the Klavalier Klub as the
Military Department of the Klan.

" Hell, I know you're Chief Ass-Tearer of the outfit, and
hold Kard No. 1, and that the Dragon holds Kard No. 0
and gives all the orders! I've had men in your outfit ever
since you went back into action after the war. I've known
every move you made, even before you made it. I've just
been giving you rope, that's all, and now you've come to the
end of it. . . ."

" You can't scare me, Duke," Carter said, but he seemed
to shrink in size as Duke talked. " You'd better turn me
loose—"

" I'm gonna turn you every way but loose! " Duke
shouted. " Damn your cowardly hide—crawl on back to
your hole-in-the-wall. Just as soon as I'm ready I'm going
to stage a last round-up of your whole bloody gang! "

Carter lost no time in leaving, obviously relieved not to be clapped behind bars then and there. As he went through the door he spat at the brass spittoon in the corner—and missed.

Duke had no sooner slammed the door on him when I re-entered his office.

" That was worth seeing," I said.

" It hurts like hell not to be able to lock 'em up," he said, toying with the bullwhip.

" I've been doing some thinking in the next room, Dan. Sometimes when you can't get such crooks before a court of law, you can try them in the court of public opinion. The results can be just as good, maybe even better."

" What's your idea? " Duke asked.

" These cockroaches can't stand the light of day. Rip the mask from them and turn on the spotlight, and they'll crawl back into their cracks and stay there. . . . How about letting me call in the Press? You can show 'em the bullwhip and tell 'em you've had the Klan's Chief Ass-Tearer and a couple of his buddies on the carpet, and are just biding your time for a round-up."

Duke thought for a moment.

" O.K.—call 'em," he said grimly.

The next day, both the *Atlanta Journal* and the *Atlanta Constitution* carried front-page stories, with a photograph of Duke brandishing the bullwhip. " The symbol of fascism in America! " he was quoted as calling it. I checked with the news services—the story and photo had gone out not just on the Southern wires but the national ones as well. The impact, I felt sure, would be felt far through the Invisible Empire.

Repercussions came thick and fast. During the night someone slipped up in the dark, doused Carter's six moving vans with petrol and applied a torch! All that was left of the Carter Trucking Company next morning were the twisted, smouldering steel skeletons. This was Ku Kluxery in reverse—and something I had not anticipated. Undoubtedly one of Carter's victims—someone who had been flogged or dynamited or burned out of his home—had, upon learning the identity of his persecutors by reading the papers, resorted to fighting fire with fire. With the roads to justice in the courts closed, the development was not too surprising.

But this was only the beginning. Heartened by the news of Duke's drive against the Klan, a host of victims of the Klavaliers—who had previously been afraid to talk—began to trek into Duke's office to tell their tales of beatings, torture and arson.

A white revivalist minister displayed scars on his back which the Klavaliers had inflicted eight months earlier. At my suggestion, Duke again called in the news photographers, and this story too was spread throughout the land. Next came Lemon and Mary Gates, an elderly Negro couple who drove up from South Georgia in their mule wagon to tell Duke how the Klavaliers had beaten them for urging their Negro neighbours to vote. There were many others, and they all had the same ending: the victims had been warned that if they talked the Klan would descend upon them again and " seal their lips for ever."

We released every word of it to the Press. Our initial spotlight had uncovered one of the worst reigns of terror ever to be inflicted upon any land at any time. The effect upon public opinion—even among those persons with an inculcated predilection for Ku Kluxery—was highly constructive, judging from street-corner conversation and the letters which poured in to newspaper editors. The Klan, nearly everyone agreed, had " gone too far."

It was then that Carter sent out his Fiery Summons in a desperate effort to " catch the rat."

" As long as he is in our midst," Carter said, " our hands are tied. Catch him, and I promise you we'll light up the skies with fiery crosses! There'll be something doing every night! "

But the exposé had done its work. At the next meeting of Headquarters Klan No. 1 the infuriated Dragon pounced, bellowing like a bull.

" Cliff, you're busted from Night Hawk to a Ghoul! You and your Klavalier Klub have made such a hellova mess the whole future of the Klan is imperilled! Your job was to keep the heat off the Klan, and now the whole world knows everything there is to know about our Military Department. If anybody ever publishes that *Kloran* we'll be ruined."

"Duke didn't get the *Kloran* from me . . ." Carter countered morosely.

"Silence, Klansman! One more word from you without permission, and I'll have you up for banishment!"

Carter collapsed like a pricked balloon. What Duke and I had begun, the Dragon was finishing. The ex-Night Hawk was a broken man.

"Just look at this meeting," the Dragon growled. "Not more than a couple of dozen men with guts enough to attend, all because Duke sounded off in the newspapers. I'm going to keep close tabs on attendance, and those who stand by the Klan in her hour of need will have their reward. We've got well over a hundred policemen in Klavern No. 1, but not one of them is here tonight. God knows when we'll ever be able to get our Brothers who are public officials to stick their heads in the door again. . . .

"This thing has not only knocked attendance on the head, but has stopped our organizing drive in its tracks. The week before Duke turned on the heat we had one hundred and sixty-seven applications and sixty-four renewals pending, but last week there wasn't a blessed one! A whole flock of applicants have phoned or written in, cancelling their applications. It's not just happening here in Atlanta, either; from all over the Invisible Empire Klansmen are sending in resignations. It's going to take years of lying low for this mess to die down to a point where we can hope to make headway again. . . ."

Turning to the Grand Kligrapp, the Dragon ordered:

"Randal, you will prepare immediately for my signature an edict to be sent to every Exalted Cyclops in the Empire, as follows. Number one: All activities of Klavalier Klubs are hereby suspended until further notice from me. No direct-line activity whatsoever is to be undertaken without my prior written consent. Number two: All Klan robes are to be called in immediately from the homes of individual members, and henceforth kept under lock and key inside the Klaverns. Number three: The office of the Grand

Dragon hereby offers a reward of one thousand dollars per pound for the traitor's ass, f.o.b. Atlanta.   That's all. Klavern adjourned! "

On the way out, I passed Slim in the hallway.

" This thing's gettin' too hot to suit me," he whispered. " I'm goin' straight home and burn my Klavalier robe and Kard too! "

" Same here! " I replied.

Assistant solicitor Dan Duke (*left*), Fulton County, shows Georgia's Governor Eugene Talmadge the type of whip allegedly used by the six Klan members serving sentences for lashing pro-union mill workers in 1938. Duke and a number of others were urging denial of clemency at a hearing called by the governor in 1941. Photograph courtesy UPI/Bettman Newsphotos.

CHAPTER EIGHT

JUVENILE DELINQUENTS OF THE KKK

ONE hot August day while on my way to report to Duke on the previous night's Klan meeting, I turned a corner to be confronted by the " Stars and Bars " of the Confederacy— an enormous battle flag floating from the second-story window of a dilapidated office building.

The Confederate banner is by no means an uncommon sight in the South. In fact, the United Daughters of the Confederacy encourage its display on every possible occasion. But this was no ordinary Confederate flag. Superimposed on its centre was a large circle containing a thunderbolt!

Painted on the window itself, I read:

Columbian Workers Movement
" Race, Nation, Faith "

This, I said to myself, deserves to be looked into. . . .

The thunderbolt, I knew, was the most widely used of fascist symbols. It was first adopted by the *Auditi*, who were the nucleus of Mussolini's Italian Blackshirts, and later formed the core of his O.V.R.A. secret police. In Nazi Germany the thunderbolt became the insignia of both the Hitler Youth and the S.S. Elite Guard. The emblem of the flag above me I recognized as an almost exact replica of the " Flash and Circle " used by Sir Oswald Mosley's British Union of Fascists and its adjunct in Canada. Not only that, I knew that much the same thunderbolt was worn by the Youth Division of the German-American Bund and by the Blackshirts of the American Fascist Party!

It was with such thoughts as these running through my head that I looked around for the entrance to the place. Finally I found it—82 Bartow Street. Climbing the rickety stairs, I knocked on a door which also sported a thunderbolt.

The door was opened cautiously—just a crack at first. Then it was thrown wide, and a sallow-faced youth about seventeen years old, wearing a surplus G.I. officer's khaki shirt with a thunderbolt shoulder patch, threw out his left arm in a Nazi salute.

" *Heil Columbia!* " he said with a sheepish grin.

Needless to say, I was somewhat taken aback. This was postwar Georgia, not prewar Germany. These guys must be crazy or joking, I thought to myself—and resolved to find out.

" My name is John Perkins, Atlanta representative of the *Southern Outlook*," I said, fishing a copy out of my briefcase and handing it to him. The issue had a headline which said " Elinor [Roosevelt] Shakes Nigger's Hand." This seemed to appeal, for he grinned broadly.

" Come right in, Mr. Perkins," he said, introducing himself as " Jimmy Akin, secretary of the Columbians."

I looked around, and noted that the Columbians actually had three adjoining rooms. There were desks, filing cabinets, chairs, and a large portrait of Confederate General Robert E. Lee. On one desk I spotted a copy of *Mein Kampf*, in German, by A. Hitler.

Akin invited me to sit down, then disappeared into the next room. In a few moments he emerged with another man, likewise dressed in a brown shirt with thunderbolt shoulder patch. This fellow was, I judged, about thirty-two. With medium but athletic build, his hair was close cropped, Prussian style, and his eyes and smile had a Satanical look about them.

" Mr. Perkins, meet our leader, Homer Loomis," Akin said.

" Glad to know you, Mr. Perkins," Loomis said delightedly. " This seems to be quite a paper you have here. It's almost incredible—an openly anti-Semitic paper in the South! "

His fancy had been caught by another front-page story in the copy of the *Southern Outlook* I had presented to Akin— a rehash of a forged anti-Semitic letter attributed to Benjamin Franklin.

" I'd be glad to present you folks with a complimentary subscription," I offered.

" Wonderful," Loomis replied. " In return we can issue you a complimentary membership in the Columbians, if you'd care to join our ranks. There are just three requirements: Number one: Do you hate niggers? Number two: Do you hate Jews? And three: Have you got three dollars? We can pass over the last one in your case."

" It's a deal," I said. " But I'll have to ask you to keep my name secret, because of my business connections."

" Don't worry," Loomis assured me.

" What's it all about? " I asked as he typed out my membership card.

" Briefly, the mission of the Columbians is to separate the white man from the nigger, and the Jew from his money," Loomis snickered.

This guy is just slick enough in his perverse way to be dangerous, I thought.

He handed my Columbian card over to me, emblazoned with a thunderbolt.

" I see I've got card number 5101—do you really have that many members? " I asked.

" No," he confessed. " We jumped from card number 15 to 5101 to impress newcomers. Actually you're the sixteenth to join."

From his desk drawer Loomis fished out a small news clipping, which had appeared in the *Atlanta Journal* several days before but had escaped my attention. It was headed: " *Group Chartered for Moral Revival.*" Needless to say, it put the aims of the Columbians in very different terms from those Loomis had just voiced.

A corporate charter as a non-profit, tax-free, charitable and fraternal order had been granted by the State of Georgia to the Columbians Inc., the news story revealed. In this charter, the Columbians declared their purposes to be " To encourage our people to think in terms of Race, Nation and Faith, and to work for a national moral awakening in order to build a progressive white community that is bound together by a deep spiritual consciousness of a common past and determination to share a common future."

" Isn't it ridiculous for the state to grant us a charter just when it's trying to revoke the Klan's charter, when we're forty times worse than the Klan? " Loomis gloated.

" How did you manage it? " I asked.

" One of our founding members, Mr. Vester Ownby, is a lawyer and he got it for us," Loomis explained.

" I know Ownby well," I said. " For a long time he was Exalted Cyclops of the East Atlanta Klan."

" That's right," Loomis admitted with a grin. " A lot of our people are prominent in the Klan. The relations between the two organizations are very good indeed."

" I'm pretty well acquainted in Klan circles myself," I said. Little did I realize that my efforts to break up the Columbians were eventually to force me to bow out of the Klan!

" Glad to hear it," Loomis countered. " I'm expecting our President, Emory Burke, to come in anytime, and I'd like for you to meet him. He's also a member of the East Atlanta Klan—joined up while Ownby was Cyclops."

" I thought Akin said you were the real leader? " I said pointedly.

" Oh, that," Loomis laughed, slightly taken aback. " Burke is president, but I sort of look after things as secretary."

Pretty soon other Columbians began to arrive in a steady stream.

The first to knock was a shapely blonde girl, with a pretty face to match. She also wore a khaki shirt, like the others, with the thunderbolt shoulder patch. She came in swiftly, giving Akin a hug, while Loomis looked on enviously.

" Mr. Perkins, this is Miss Betty Penland, who is one of our most valuable members. Betty hails from Texas, and does all our stenographic work."

" Nice," I observed. " But how can you afford a secretary with only sixteen members? "

" Oh, Betty is a volunteer," Loomis laughed. " She believes in the Columbian cause like the rest of us. Besides, we all live here at headquarters—got some cots and a small kerosene cooking stove in the next room—so we don't need much money."

"Sounds cosy," I said, wondering whether Betty slept behind a screen, or what.

Betty and Jimmy Akin went out shopping, arm in arm, for some crackers, canned beans and sardines.

As they went out, they crossed trails with a couple more brown-shirted Columbians on the way in. These turned out to be Lanier Waller and Ralph Childers, who seemed like rough-and-ready shock troopers. Waller, it developed, was also from Texas. He had joined the U.S. Marines at the age of fourteen, and had seen service during World War II in the Pacific area. As for Childers, he had been working as a short-order cook in a "Hamburger Heaven" establishment when his eye had been caught by the snappy officers' shirts worn by the Columbians. Such shirts may be bought by any civilian at Army surplus stores.

When Betty came back she had her shirt sleeves rolled up, and inside her right forearm I noticed that she had the Columbian thunderbolt tattooed in red ink—in much the same manner as Hitler's S.S. Elite Guard.

"That's to symbolize that Betty is a member of our inner circle Legion of Loyalty," Loomis explained, noting my interest. "The penalty for any member of the Legion who betrays the Columbians is to have their tattooed arm burned off up to the elbow."

Betty's manifest charms, I thought to myself, would not be enhanced by such an operation.

At last Burke came in. Loomis sat back and let him do most of the talking, except when the discussion turned to action. It soon became apparent that Burke served as theoretician of the Columbians, while Loomis held the actual reins of leadership with a firm hand.

Burke turned out to be, like Loomis, in his early thirties. Considerably more frail than Loomis, he worked as a draughtsman for a small Georgia railroad—and looked it. Also like Loomis, Burke was on the verge of continual hysteria. As they talked they both paced up and down like caged tigers, consumed by a lust to be free to kill. Carried away by their own rantings, their voices frequently broke and became shrill.

"Maybe I can get you fellows some publicity in the

Southern Outlook," I intimated, thinking this might be a short
cut to finding out more about their personal backgrounds.

Loomis leaped at this idea, and proceeded to tell me some
things about himself.

" I'm a native of New York City," he began.

"—we had to teach him how to say ' nigger,' " Burke
interjected with a smile.

" I've come a long way from the old homestead at 815
Park Avenue," Loomis conceded, " and from such schools as
St. Paul's, Groton, and Princeton too. I guess it's to my
credit that they kicked me out of Princeton. My old man
is an Admiralty lawyer, 60 Wall Street, and used to represent
the Italian-American Steamship Line up until the war. He
never has liked Jews since a Jewish lawyer beat him in an
important case.

" You may remember reading something about me in the
papers once before," he went on. " When the C.I.O. was
staging sit-down strikes in factories all over the country, I
thought it would be a good protest if I staged a sit-down
strike in a New York City night club, demanding ' taller
drinks and longer drinking hours.' I stayed on strike for
four days and four nights, and after a while the club thought
it was such good publicity for them they brought me a pair
of pyjamas and called in the photographers. My picture
was on front pages all over the country."

" Where were you during the war? " I asked.

" I volunteered and served in Germany in the 2nd
Armoured Division," Loomis said. " What I saw and heard
in Germany made me decide to devote the rest of my life
to the counter-revolution in America. Atlanta is the logical
place to start something—the South comes by its racial
convictions instinctively."

" But how in the dickens do you fellows manage to keep
eating? " I asked, anxious to find out who was back of the
Columbians financially.

" Oh, I'm drawing twenty dollars a week from the
Government as my veteran's unemployment pension,"
Loomis laughed, " and several of the other boys are too.
We put it all into the pot, and manage well enough. Things
ought to begin to hum for us as soon as Gene Talmadge

takes over as Governor of Georgia. We'll eat better then."

At that point there was a vigorous knock on the door. Loomis opened it.

In walked Ira Jett, my Brother Klansman and Klavalier! With him was James Shipp, known to me as chieftain of the Commoner Party and American Gentile Army down at Conyers, Georgia. Both wore silver Columbian thunderbolts in their coat lapels.

" I see you already know each other," Loomis remarked, noting the Klan handshake that passed between us. Turning to Jett, he added:

" That was a first-rate job last night! "

" Not bad," Jett replied.

I was itching to know what sort of " job " they were referring to, but decided not to be too inquisitive, and to bide my time. But I wondered if it had anything to do with the bombing of a Negro home the night before. I knew this had taken place at 3.30 a.m., when the house of Goldsmith Sibley, who had moved on to the " white " side of Ashby Street, had been bombed. Sibley, his grandmother, sister and niece were sleeping inside, but had miraculously escaped serious injury.

My curiosity about what made the Columbians tick financially was at least partly satisfied when a middle-aged man came in, not wearing the Columbian shirt but equipped with a silver thunderbolt in his lapel.

" This is Bill Storey, the leading anti-union organizer around here," Loomis said in introducing him to me.

Storey knew all about the *Southern Outlook*. It developed he was employed by Exposition Cotton Mills, where a strike was then in progress. The company had refused to comply with a National Labour Relations Board order to recognize the union, had evicted striking workers from their company-owned homes, and employed goons with baseball bats in an effort to break the strike. At one point a number of pickets, both men and women, had to be hospitalized as a result of burns suffered from an acid which had been sprayed on the company hedge where they marched up and down.

" They've been very generous out at Exposition Mills, helping us get started," Loomis confided to me.

Some of the Columbians' first meetings were held in the company-owned Exposition ball park, with the company's permission, he added. Loomis and Storey joked of having held a Columbian meeting on the second floor of a building out in the Exposition Mill neighbourhood, to discuss ways and means of breaking the strike, at the very time the union's strike committee was meeting downstairs.

" We don't regard any C.I.O. union, and very few A.F.L. unions, as being legitimate," Loomis explained.

A final caller was a big fellow wearing an Army lieutenant's uniform, who introduced himself as William H. Couch, Jr. Couch said he was on terminal leave from the Army, and was interested in working with the Columbians. He, Loomis and I had quite a conversation.

Couch kept talking about " we intellectuals," but Loomis insisted that the rank-and-file of the Columbians would have to be drawn from the working class " because they have nothing to lose."

" We're going to the masses and putting on a show," he said. " We're telling them stuff they want to hear—that they, the white Anglo-Saxons, are the best people on earth, and that they're entitled to more than they're getting. We're trying to show them they have power in their grasp if they'll just organize and assert themselves! We're going to show the white Anglo-Saxons how to take control of the Government. First a neighbourhood, then the whole city, then the state Government, and finally the national Government! "

Couch, like Loomis and Burke, spoke German. He learned the language, it developed, in a German prisoner-of-war camp, where he was confined after being shot down while serving as a bombardier in the 8th Air Force. Couch said he had eventually taught German to incoming British and American prisoners, and was granted many special privileges. " Life in camp wasn't half bad," he said.

" We have the worst men in the world at the head of the American Army," Couch went on. " Of course you know Eisenhower is a Jew."

" The man who ought to have Eisenhower's job is Major-General George Van Horn Mosely," Loomis declared.

" You know who he is—he was selected to head up the American Nationalist movement before the war. He lives out at the Atlanta Biltmore Hotel."

Our little gab-fast was broken up suddenly when the chair on which Loomis was sitting collapsed. Pulling himself together with what dignity he could muster, Loomis gave the remains of the chair a kick and said, " Probably a damned Jew chair! "

" I'd better be running along," I said. " Mighty glad I came across you fellows."

" How about coming out to our meeting tonight? " Loomis suggested. " Out at Exposition Mills at eight o'clock."

" I'll try to make it," I promised. " See you later."

With that I hurried off to Duke's office, and told him everything I had learned about these strange new birds. Duke listened intently. When I had finished he exclaimed with conviction:

" The Ku Klux and Gene Talmadge hatched this biddy! "

" Do you think anything will come of it? " I asked.

" Come of it? Looks to me like something's come of it already. I'll bet you anything it was these Columbians who tossed that dynamite at Goldsmith Sibley's house last night. And that was the seventh bombing of Negro homes we've had in three weeks. This could explain why you haven't been able to pin anything on the Klan's Housing Kommittee lately—maybe they've set up the Columbian outfit as their dynamite detail! "

" So far we're just guessing."

" You never can tell," Duke replied. " You'd better stick with them—drop into their headquarters at least once a day. And by all means cover that meeting tonight! "

" You mean that besides riding with the Klan I've got to march with the Columbians? "

" That seems to be the size of it," Duke said.

CHAPTER NINE

ASSORTED NUTS

THAT night as I approached the Exposition Mill Village I could hear, from several blocks away, the phonographic blaring of the " Confederate national anthem," *Dixie*, together with *Hail, Columbia*, as the Columbians turned the amplifiers on their sound-truck up to full volume.

Attracted by the prospect of any free and lively affair, the textile workers had turned out in numbers, and were waiting for the speaking to get under way. Meanwhile, I found Columbians Akin and Waller busily distributing anti-union leaflets among the spectators.

Ex-Cyclops Ownby opened the ceremonies, speaking from the back of a truck draped with the Columbian battle-flag. The Columbians, he claimed, were not affiliated with the Ku Klux Klan, " although I understand the Klan is a group with members of sterling character and a history and tradition that is beautiful. We are proud to be for Talmadge, and if being fascist means being anti-communist, we don't mind being called fascist! "

The next speaker, I was startled to see, was none other than Hoke Gewinner, chairman of the Klan's Committee to investigate Un-American Activities. Gewinner charged that the " nigger block vote " was backing Helen Douglas Mankin for Congress. He called upon the audience to join the Columbians and organize on a ward and precinct basis to defeat Mrs. Mankin in the general election.

" There are just two ways to fight these things—with ballots and with bullets. We are going to try ballots first! " Gewinner concluded.

I walked around among the spectators, watching their expressions and listening for comments, with a view to

129

finding out whether the talks were going over. I decided that they were.

Burke was then introduced as president of the Columbians. In a voice even more hysterical than when I had listened to him earlier that day at Columbian headquarters, Burke shouted:

" The Columbians are the long-awaited movement which is destined to save first the South and then the nation! We fight for our race and civilization! The voices of our dead and unborn millions cry out to us not to bow down."

A child in its mother's arms, frightened by Burke's voice and cavorting, let out a loud wail, and several other infants joined in.

Loomis spoke last.

" Our movement is not based upon hate, but upon logic! " he proclaimed. " We offer the masses leadership, and are willing to die if necessary! If you will just listen to us, you can control America completely in six months! We don't want anybody to join who's not ready to get out and kill niggers and Jews! "

This, I thought, is far more than anything the Klan ever dared call for in public under its own name!

" There is no end to what we can do through the ballot," Loomis cried. " If we want to bury all niggers in the sand, once we come to power we can pass laws enabling us to bury all niggers in the sand! "

When the meeting ended, everyone present was invited to join. A long line formed as both men and women waited their turn to sign their names on application blanks—and plank down $3.

The Columbian movement, I reported to Duke the following morning, was definitely on the move and was destined to go places—unless strong measures were taken against it.

" On the basis of what Loomis said last night, can't we nail him on a charge of inciting to riot? " I asked.

" It may sound funny," Duke replied, " but until we can actually pin the blame for some rioting or similar violence on them, it will be difficult to get a conviction. There's no doubt now in my mind that these Columbians are responsible for the new wave of bombings of Negro homes during the past few weeks. But how are we going to prove it? No, we mustn't jump the gun. When I take out warrants against these birds, I intend to make them stick. That means you'll have to stick with them until we get the evidence we need."

So I stuck, spending many hours daily at Columbian headquarters, keeping my eyes peeled and ears open for what lawyers call " actionable evidence "—the stuff jail sentences are made of. Loomis was very cautious about letting me in on things, despite my Klan connections. While he didn't mind talking to me about the theory of Columbianism, when it came to letting me in on future " direct action " I was brushed aside. When I hinted that I might like to take a hand, Loomis replied airily, " Oh, our Legion of Loyalty takes care of that kind of stuff! " It was difficult sometimes not to ask too many questions, but I clung to the faith that " all things come to him who waits."

Of course I didn't just wait—I tracked down every lead I could think of.

For one thing, I dropped in to see my old acquaintance, ex-Cyclops Ownby. While he didn't tell me anything I didn't already know about the Columbians, I did learn something about his own machinations—by glancing over his secretary's shoulder.

She was busy going through a city directory, addressing postcards from the listings of residences on Formwalt and Ashby Streets—the " borderline " between white and Negro neighbourhoods. All names which did not have a " c " after them to indicate that they were " coloured " were being mailed cards saying their property was bound to decrease rapidly in value because of the " nigger invasion." These white home-owners were advised to sell out as fast as possible—with Ownby offering to handle the sales!

In other words, the old Cyclops was on the one hand offering to sell these home-owners " protection " at $3 per head by roping them into the Columbians—and at the same time, through a dummy real estate outfit, was cashing in on the very fears the Columbians stirred up!

From Ownby I also got one of my most fruitful leads.

Although he had served as the Columbians' attorney in obtaining their charter, he said a Miss Mary Lane, Atlanta's only "female lawyer," had taken over the organization's legal affairs. I had met Miss Lane casually in my perambulations around the Capitol, and knew her to be close to both Talmadge and Congressman John S. Wood. So I decided I ought to get closer to Miss Lane.

One afternoon I dropped into her law office, around closing time.

"I just happened to be in the building, and thought I would look in," I said. "I understand we're fellow Columbians."

"I didn't know you were a member," she said, coming from behind her desk to shake hands. "And I don't know whether you can call me a fellow or not—I definitely belong in a ladies' auxiliary."

She wasn't kidding. Blonde, in her early thirties, she was about as charming as a Talmadgite can get.

"If you're through for the day, why don't we drop into the Owl Room and toast the Brotherhood, or whatever you want to call it?" I suggested.

"A wonderful idea!" she agreed. "I'm so glad you came by."

So began a not unpleasant relationship. One cocktail led to another, and at the end of each day we tended to gravitate toward the Owl Room, which became our regular hangout. As we became better acquainted, I found her to be a strange mixture of prejudices and sympathies—one moment inveighing against some minority group, and the next moment planning a project to improve conditions at the State Insane Asylum! But despite her split personality in this respect, she was very well co-ordinated on the dance floor.

Little by little, I was able to get her to warm up and spill some very interesting facts about the Columbians' background.

"It all began in Germany after VE Day," she confided one evening when we were both feeling mellow. "Homer told me he bribed some American officers, and they gave him free time and even free travel by Army plane to go around the country to contact important Nazis whose financial assets had been frozen by the occupation. Homer said he used his old man's financial connections in America to help these Nazis, and they in turn gave him advice on how to launch a fascist movement in America. They suggested that he begin in the South, and concentrate on anti-Negro propaganda first."

" I'll be damned! " I said, giving her hand a squeeze.

" When Homer got back to the States he headed South, stopping off in Washington to confer with Senator Bilbo," she went on.

" That probably explains why the Columbians' first leaflet, *Separation or Amalgamation?* has the same title as Bilbo's book, which hadn't even been published then," I remarked.

" Could be," she agreed. " Anyway, Homer's next stop was Richmond, Virginia, where he went to see a man named Ernest Sevier Cox. You know his book, *White America?* That's the one Bilbo reads into the *Congressional Record* every time he filibusters. It was Cox who put Homer in touch with James Shipp of the Commoner Party.

" They first set up something called ' The Citizen's Forum'," she went on. " Shipp was a brains-truster for the group, and so was Mrs. Nettie Meredith Stewart. You know her, don't you? She heads up the Republican Women's Study Club in Atlanta. Homer got kind of impatient with all this running around. About all they did was send him to talk to Congressman John Wood, who was acting chairman of the House Committee on Un-American Activities."

" And what did they talk about? " I asked, playing knees with her under the table.

" Oh, something about an article by Stetson Kennedy in a magazine called *Common Ground.* Homer told Wood the article advocated social equality with Negroes, and Wood promised to investigate."

" But who actually cooked up the idea of the Columbians? " I pressed her.

" Homer did. By this time he wanted to get started by himself. But first he met with a secret Imperial Kloncilium of the Klan's leaders out at the East Point Klavern. The Ku Klux liked Homer's ideas about stirring up people with sound-trucks and street meetings: but he almost queered the deal by proposing that all Jews be sent to gas chambers and all Negroes be re-colonized in Africa—' with time bombs on board the ships as an economy measure,' he said! After hearing that, the Klan decided Homer's boys ought to have a name of their own—and that's how the Columbians were born."

" Pretty damned clever," I said, clinking glasses with her.

In time, Mary and I became such close friends that she even put away the silver Columbian ear-rings Homer had given her as a token of affection. . . .

Meanwhile, Betty Penland's star had been rising in the Columbian firmament. First, she gave up Jimmy Akin and became Ralph Childers' girl, while Loomis continued to look envious. Then one day Loomis assembled his entire crew and made a dramatic announcement.

" Men," he said, " I'm going to ask each and every one of you to make certain sacrifices—we're all going to have to give up drinking, smoking and women. This is a test of loyalty to the Cause! "

There was a great deal of grumbling—especially by Childers.

It was not until about a week later, when some of the boys returned unexpectedly from a patrol on which Loomis had sent them . . . and walked into the Columbians' inner bedroom without knocking, that the real reason for Loomis' " New Order " became apparent. . . . From that time on, Betty was Loomis' girl, and no one else dared do more than look at her.

After a while, even the looks made Loomis jealous, so he installed Betty in an hotel room.

I thought very little about this change of residence, but reported it casually to Duke. The next thing I knew, Betty and Loomis were in jail on a morals charge. Georgia law, it seems, is quite strict about such things. " When two persons of opposite sex occupy the same room at night, it shall be considered prima facie evidence of cohabitation," is the way the law reads.

As a " loyal Columbian," I went along when the two were

haled before Judge A. W. Callaway. It developed from the testimony that Loomis had been tailed at night. Officer W. J. Nelms testified that in short order he spied Loomis entering Betty's hotel at 2 a.m. Officer Nelms knocked sharply on the door, and ordered it opened " in the name of the law! "

When there was no response other than some strange sounds, Officer Nelms forced open the door.

Betty was sitting up in bed, clad only in a slip.

" Is anybody in here with you? " he asked her.

" No, there isn't—can't you see? " she replied.

" Well, I'll just have a look."

Looking into the bathroom, he caught Loomis barefooted.

" Your Honour, there was two in there when there ought to have been one," Officer Nelms concluded his testimony.

" Young man, what have you to say for yourself? " Judge Callaway asked Loomis.

" Your Honour, I had just dropped in to wash my feet," Loomis said solemnly.

The court-room roared with laughter, while the judge rapped for order.

" Young lady, was there any act of immorality between you and Homer? " Judge Callaway asked, turning to Betty.

" None whatsoever in any shape, form or fashion! " Betty replied, her eyes flashing.

The court-room roared again.

" I find you both guilty," Judge Callaway declared. " You know that Georgia law forbids the occupancy of hotel rooms by unmarried couples. Fifty dollars or thirty days! "

Loomis promptly coughed up the $100, and he and Betty walked out, arm in arm.

I noticed Homer had appeared in court with a large knot on his head.

" What hit you? " I whispered. " Did the cops rough you up? "

" No," he replied somewhat sheepishly. " Betty's brother Clarence came raving into the office, saying I had ruined his sister's reputation. We were slugging it out until he reached for his pocket. I thought he was going for a gun, so I jumped out of the window without waiting to see."

The Press, of course, reported all the lurid details of Homer's and Betty's arrest and conviction with great glee. From my vantage point inside the Columbians I was able to observe the after-effects, which were considerable. Many Columbians—especially women and older members— promptly resigned because of the " disgraceful affair." Some even wrote in and reminded the Columbians of their professed purpose, as stated in their charter, of bringing about a " moral revival." Hard-shell Baptists of the Deep South's " Bible Belt " felt that the Columbian leader had committed an unpardonable sin. . . .

While Loomis was thus busy getting himself into hot water, I continued to scout about for fuel to add to the fire.

My conversations with Mary Lane had been so rewarding that I decided to pay a visit to the other girl friend of the Columbians she had mentioned—Mrs. Nettie Meredith Stewart. I found Mrs. Stewart, a frenzied middle-aged woman, at her home in the suburbs. In introducing myself as Perkins of the *Southern Outlook*, I intimated that Burke and I were collaborating on an article.

" I can tell you a lot more about the Columbians than he can! " she shrieked. " I was the one who helped them get started. Homer Loomis is the real leader—he's a great patriot, the equivalent of Patrick Henry! "

" I understand you are also head of the Republican Women's Study Club," I said.

" Oh, yes," she replied. " The Republican National Committee refers to me all applications for affiliation with the Republican Party that come in from Georgia women. We have a very nice group here in Atlanta where we have social teas and discuss burning issues of the day. I'm so glad that a Republican, that nice J. Parnell Thomas, is about to take over the House Committee Investigating Un-American Activities. Let me show you a copy of a letter I've just written to him."

Her letter, it turned out, consisted largely of a list of people and organizations she wanted Thomas to investigate. I noted with interest that along with such people as Drew Pearson, Walter Winchell, Ellis Arnall and Dan Duke,

Stetson Kennedy was also recommended for investigation.

But my big discovery concerning Mrs. Stewart was that she was very much involved in a series of pro-Columbian columns which Westbrook Pegler had just begun to dish out to the newspapers of the country.

"I called Loomis and read him the first Pegler column over the phone," Mrs. Stewart said. "He said he wanted to get in touch with Pegler, so I gave him Pegler's home address. The Columbians' attorney, Vester Ownby, wrote Pegler, thanking him for the column and asking permission to reprint it. Pegler gave the Columbians permission, and added, 'You ain't seen nothing yet!'"

With some further questioning, I learned that Mrs. Stewart's principal pipeline to Pegler was a woman in New York City named Pear Bussey Phinney. This dame, I knew, was one of the best friends of the totalitarian-minded groups throughout the country. I had already come across her name in the Columbians' ledger where they listed their financial contributors.

But I was most anxious to verify Mrs. Stewart's assertion that the link between the Columbians and Westbrook Pegler was more than just a meeting of minds.

"Old lady Stewart tells me Pegler wrote 'you ain't seen nothing yet' when Ownby thanked him for his columns defending the Columbians," I said one afternoon when Jimmy Akin and I were alone at headquarters.

"Those were his very words!" Akin grinned. "I've got his letter right here on file. I'll show it to you."

And so he did.

The Columbian file cabinet was kept locked, and I wondered if I would ever find it left open so I could delve into its contents. Even if I were left alone in the office, I knew it would be quite a chance to take, what with Columbians always popping in unexpectedly.

Meanwhile, I resolved to latch on to the next best thing—the contents of the Columbians' waste-baskets. I had watched everyone from Loomis on down toss all sorts of intriguing things into these receptacles. Incoming mail, first drafts of outgoing mail, memos to themselves and one another, all had a way of ending up in the waste-baskets.

Once or twice I drove by late at night, dumped the contents of the Columbian ashcan standing on the kerb into the back of my car, and sped off. But I knew I could not get away with that procedure for any length of time. For one thing, the Columbians never seemed to go to bed—no matter how late I drove by, they were burning the after-midnight oil plotting fascism for America. " Operation Ashcan," I knew, would have to be carried out by a Negro in broad daylight, since only Negroes are employed to collect garbage in the South.

I scouted around until I found a Negro man with a horse and wagon. Explaining what it was all about, I offered to pay him if he would drive by Columbian headquarters early every morning, dump the contents of their trash can into his wagon, and deliver it to me. It was a risky business, and he knew it. If the Columbians took notice of him and demanded an explanation, he would be hard put to concoct one. But he undertook the job, even though I could pay him very little.

While this meant many hours of painstaking work for me every day, sorting out the scraps, piecing together the jig-saw puzzle bits of torn-up letters, tossing out the sardine tins and cigarette butts, the net results were very good indeed. It was in this way that I was able to keep tabs on the Columbians' connections with fascists elsewhere in the country.

One of my " finds " was a letter from the Reverend A. C. Shuler of Jacksonville, Florida, who had long served as Kludd (chaplain) of the Klan in that state. Kludd Shuler congratulated the Columbians on " weathering the storm," and opined that they had a " great opportunity at this time." He invited them to come down to Jacksonville and stage a rally in his church. By sending this lead to church people in Jacksonville, I was able to nip this project in the bud.

From Porter R. Mitchell, Jr., of Bridgeport, Ohio, I pieced together the following:

The time has come to spread the cause to Ohio! I and some of my most trusted friends have sent out a call and over 200 are ready. It would be very easy for the Columbians to absorb the former Ku Klux Klan and Black Legion in this area. It is estimated that the Black Legion had 7,000 members in this county alone. Several former Klan leaders have agreed to assist in establishing the order.

Edward James Smythe—who had arranged the prewar Klan-Bund rally in New Jersey—dashed down to Atlanta to find out how the Columbians, being such newcomers to the race-hate racket, managed to get so much front-page publicity. Later, Loomis complained to me:

" That bum Smythe is running all over the North collecting money for a ' Columbian defence fund,' and pocketing every cent of it himself! "

Letters poured in, not just from all over the United States, but from other countries as well. For instance, I discovered that the Columbians were in close touch with an old geezer named Einar Aberg of Sweden, one of the most active of the international fascist conspirators. (Aberg was very much involved in the conspiracy of former Hitler generals to re-establish Nazism in West Germany uncovered but not prosecuted by the British occupation forces in 1953.)

A branch of the Columbians was being set up, I learned from the ashcan, in Indianapolis, Indiana, by one Raymond Vick. I sent word to the authorities and newspapers in Indianapolis, and Vick's career as a Columbian organizer was brought to an end when it was revealed that he had a police record of thirteen arrests on such charges as drunkenness, vagrancy, disorderly conduct and assault and battery, and had served a year in the penitentiary for robbery!

Another Columbian correspondent I was able to put the finger on was twenty-three-year-old Maynard Nelson, a student at the University of Minnesota. It seems that Nelson's chief extra-curricular activity was plastering the campus with posters saying " Kill Jews " and " Dead Niggers Make Good Fertilizer." Nelson also wrote a letter to Congressman John E. Rankin of Mississippi, commending him on his anti-Negro and anti-Semitic remarks in Congress. Rankin replied:

> I cannot tell you how grateful I am for your expressions of confidence; and I need not tell you that I agree thoroughly with every statement you make of your own views on these matters. I assure you that I will stand by my guns and continue to do my best to save America for Americans.

To the Columbians Nelson wrote:

> We are beginning an offensive that will justify our claim to being the anti-Semitic capital of the U.S.A. We are all sick and tired of hearing the whining of the racial scum about equal rights, when in reality they have no rights whatsoever. We shall exterminate this Jew-Negro-Communist pestilence.

When the authorities raided Nelson's room they found a formidable arsenal, and a map Nelson had prepared outlining the conquest of the world by the U.S. in " World War III."

Although I am still not at liberty to say how, I gained access to a voluminous file of Burke's personal correspondence with assorted fascists the world over. Much of this was written during the war years, when Burke was holding down a job at the Bell Bomber Plant in Marietta, Georgia!

Here are some sample extracts from these confidential letters:

> I am not willing to shed my blood in a fight against the Germans. . . . In the event of a Russian victory in Europe our first task here in America will be the heavy one of destroying the Jewish peril here in our own land. I do hate. I hate deeply. . . . What the Germans have done to the Jews will be a mere tea-party compared to what we are going to do with them. . . .

> I would even consider an alliance with the Japanese if I could be convinced that we would be the masters of the peace. . . . As for the British Empire, I advocate

merging it into the greater United States. If the mighty power of the Red armies is defeated it will be the heroic arms of the Germans that will accomplish this historic task for Western civilization. . . . I have a deep and comforting faith that the German Wall of Iron will not be broken.

Southerners generally, of all classes, are really at heart followers of the National Socialist creed far more than they are of the world democracy (racial equality) doctrine. . . . The time for speaking has not yet arrived. We must, even yet, continue to mark time. The ground is being perfectly prepared for our movement of the future.

The Columbians, obviously, had turned out to be Burke's "movement of the future."

As I delved deeper into the Columbians' ashcan and Burke's personal files, I began to have recurrent nightmares that somewhere in the past I had come across Burke's name in connection with big-time prewar Nazis. Driven by this subconscious conviction, I finally began rummaging through my " obsolete " files. At length I opened a folder marked " White Front "—and there it was!

The White Front was to the prewar South what the Columbians were in the postwar South. One of their leaders, a lad named Raymond J. Healey, who called himself " The Irish Hitler," landed in jail. Instead of helping him get out, his fascist friends all over the country sent him appeals for financial contributions. Embittered, Healey began to talk about the Nazis he knew. My notes, based upon what Healey said in his Miami jail cell, included the following:

Emory Burke, of Birmingham, Ala., worked during the middle '30s in New York City as associate editor of the *American Bulletin*, published by Mrs. Ann Tellian, a Nazi agent and correspondent for Julius Streicher's *Der Sturmer*. The *American Bulletin* was financed in part by Hubert Schmuederrich, who participated in the early Nazi street fighting in Germany, and came to the U.S.

in 1926 to organize the Grey Shirts of America, which used the swastika and worked for a Hitler victory. Co-worker on the *American Bulletin* with Burke was William Bishop, co-chairman of the Christian Front.

Of the above-mentioned, Bishop was later arrested by the F.B.I. as a Nazi agent, and Streicher was eventually hanged as a war criminal in Nürnberg, Germany.

My notes were passed along to Eugene Segal of the Scripps-Howard newspapers, who was in a position to track down the various leads. He did, and came up with a series of sensational stories, giving complete details of Burke's past associations with notorious Nazis. These revelations did much to deprive the Columbians of their following. The Georgians who had rallied beneath the Columbian banner were white supremacists, to be sure, but they had no liking for German " supermen."

" Perkins, you're our public relations expert," Loomis said to me bitterly after reading the final instalment of these newspaper exposés. " Can't you figure out some way to get us some good publicity for a change? This stuff is hurting us like hell! "

Columbian storm troopers wait their turn on the witness stand in Atlanta's Fulton County Superior Court. Photograph by Marion Palfi, courtesy Center for Creative Photography, University of Arizona.

CHAPTER TEN

IN DANIEL'S DEN

" WE'VE got to fix this guy Dan Duke somehow! " Loomis exploded at Columbian headquarters next morning, shaking the latest news story in our faces. " It's his snoopers who are feeding all this dope to the newspapers, and we've got to put a stop to it! Why don't we stage a meeting in Fairburn—where Duke is Mayor of the town! That would beard Daniel in his den! "

" Damned good idea! " the boys chorused.

So Loomis set the date and ordered a sound-truck to go to beat the bush—to proclaim that the Columbians were coming to " challenge Dan Duke's racial views " in a public meeting on the court-house lawn of his own town.

" Let 'em come! " Duke barked when I told him the news. " I'll grant 'em free speech and even light up the court-house square for the occasion! I know how to handle these brats! They'll get a reception they won't soon forget! "

" Loomis has more or less ordered me to come along and help hand out Columbian leaflets to the crowd," I said.

" You'd better stick fairly close to me, then," Duke said. " You never can tell how a thing like this will turn out. If a scrap breaks out, my friends might rough you up along with the other Columbians."

" That would be a hell of a note," I said.

" Well, it won't do for you to duck out, or the Columbians would be through with you. Stay where I can spot you. If trouble comes, I'll have a cop arrest you, and turn you loose later. That way your stock with the Columbians would actually go up, and at the same time I won't have to let any of my people know who you are."

And so it was arranged.

Several hundred countrymen turned out for the Fairburn

affair. I noted the total absence of women and children in the audience, and decided the crowd had come prepared for action.

Burke spoke first.

" Eighty-two years ago on this very court-house lawn," he began, " our valiant forefathers fought with bullets and bayonets for a noble cause. . . . We Columbians represent the idealism and racial pride of those warriors of the Confederacy; we aim to carry on the glorious fight. Our aim is to save the South for the white man! "

The first indication that the audience was hostile to the Columbians came when Burke said, looking pointedly at Duke:

" When a man shakes hands with a nigger, we can assume he is in sympathy with the nigger point of view—isn't that right? "

The audience remained ominously silent. Burke repeated his question. The audience still didn't answer, so Burke hurried on.

After Burke, P. M. Adams, one of the Columbians' grey-beard adherents, an ex-Shakespearean ham actor currently engaged in peddling baby shoes from door to door, took over the microphone.

The reception given him was even colder than that accorded Burke.

" We don't need you half as much as you need us," Adams told his audience. " Ninety-five per cent. of the white people in America today are nothing but whited sepulchres who sit idly by while our racial integrity is threatened! What this country needs is a resurrection! We Columbians stand ready to die to crush the damnable filth! My poor dead father, who at the age of sixteen fought for the Confederacy, would turn over in his grave if he could see conditions as they are today. You are cowards, otherwise you would join hands with us to protect the white race! Pass out the membership cards! "

While a number of Columbians—myself included—were handing out cards, Duke climbed the court-house stairs and took hold of the microphone. By sheer physical bulk and personality he dominated the scene.

" Fellow citizens," Duke began, " as Mayor of Fairburn I've granted these Columbians free speech, and now I want to say a few words myself!

" You have heard nothing but craven, bald-faced false-hoods! " he went on. " This young dodo, frothing at the mouth like an epileptic, and that decrepit old fossil are lower than yellow dogs trailing behind a chicken thief! They are like the Gad-paw. Do you know what a Gad-paw is? A Gad-paw is one of those long-necked birds you see down around the mill-ponds of South Georgia, who do nothing but wallow in the mud all day, until somebody comes by, and then they set up a squawk just to get attention. Well, these Columbians are nothing in the world but a flock of Gad-paws in human flesh!

" I speak to you as the Mayor of Fairburn. We have a quiet little law-abiding town here. We don't want the peace broken by these irresponsible adventurers who try to tell you somebody is about to slip up on you, and then offer you protection for three dollars apiece. All they want is your money! Furthermore, I resent their inference that you good people are unintelligent cowards! "

At this point Duke began waving a copy of a thunderbolt as worn by Hitler's S.S. men.

" This is the symbol of the Nazis whose defeat cost so many American lives," he declared. " Just compare it with the Columbian thunderbolt on that propaganda they're handing out, and you'll see what they stand for! "

This created quite a stir, with everyone picking up the Columbian leaflets to have a look at them.

To counteract this, Loomis pulled a copy of the *Pittsburgh Courier* from his pocket and began dashing through the audience shouting, " Look at it! Duke's picture in a nigger paper! "

The audience seemed as perturbed about this evident link between Duke and Negroes as the link between the Columbians and Nazis. But Duke soon recaptured their attention.

" This young man, who contorted and cavorted like a maniac at a circus, intimated that I had shaken hands with a Negro. Well, it so happens that the reporter the

Pittsburgh Courier sent to my Press conference was an Irish Catholic!

" Burke is a slimy little man who can't look an honest man in the eye. These Columbians haven't even got their diapers in the ring! I defy them to define my racial views! As a public official entrusted with the enforcement of the law, it is my conviction that everyone who lives under our system of law is entitled to its equal protection! "

The audience was in high glee over Duke's strong language. " I'd sure hate to have him prosecuting me in court," I heard one man remark.

Burke—who had been trembling over on one side of the court-house steps—came forward to offer a rebuttal. When he repeated his question to the audience of " what they thought of a man who called in a nigger paper to his Press conferences," Duke peeled off his coat and charged up the steps demanding, " Did you say I *called in* the *Pittsburgh Courier*? "

Burke hastily retreated from the microphone, uttering a retraction, and Duke returned to his place in the audience.

He had scarcely descended to the bottom of the stairs, however, when Burke asked the audience again what they thought of a " man who would shake hands with a nigger." Duke whirled back up the stairs demanding, " What did you say? "

This time Burke attempted to read the caption under the photograph in the *Courier*, but his hands shook so he could not hold the paper still.

" It doesn't matter anyhow," he said, " that's all water over the hill—I mean dam."

By this time the audience was restless.

" Let's run 'em out of town! " one man yelled.

" String 'em up! " cried another, and others joined in the chorus.

This had an immediate effect upon the Columbians—me included. If there was going to be any lynching, I had no desire to be among the victims. With a Columbian thunderbolt in my lapel, and my arms full of Columbian propaganda, I felt altogether too conspicuous. I began to push my way through the crowd to be sure I was within sight of Duke.

One man reached out and knocked all the Columbian handouts I was carrying into the air. I didn't try to pick them up, but pressed on through the crowd. The next thing I knew, someone had tripped me, and I was lying flat on my face on the ground. All this was doubtless glorifying me in the eyes of the Columbians, but I had no taste for it. The crowd converged on me, but the Columbians, instead of coming to my rescue, scattered in all directions.

Struggling to my feet, I saw that Duke had his hands full, too. Loomis had finally lost his temper, and was charging Duke, cursing as he went. This fracas diverted the crowd's attention from me, and fists started flying in Loomis' direction. Duke motioned for his cops to move in, and they broke it up, ushering Loomis over to the Columbian sound-truck. The rest of the Columbians had already piled in. I decided I ought to join them, despite the excellent possibilities that we might be waylaid *en route* back to Atlanta.

As he clambered into the truck, Burke mustered the courage to yell:

" Does anybody want to join? "

" Nooooh! " roared the audience in one voice.

With that we sped off, not even waiting to unhook the extension line we had rigged to the court-house for lighting.

" We'll be back! " Burke called out lamely, amid the jeers.

But no one ever even suggested that we re-enter Daniel's den again.

CHAPTER ELEVEN

DYNAMITE

A few days later the Columbians were sitting around their own den, licking the wounds they had sustained in Daniel's den, when a riot call came in.

"Just stand your ground!" Loomis bellowed excitedly into the phone. "Don't budge an inch! Stand on the nigger's doorstep, and if he tries to move in, tell him he'll be blown out! Stir up all the white people in sight! Ira Jett just walked in—he and I will be right over! Meanwhile, I'll put Akin on the phone to send you all the reinforcements he can muster!"

Slamming down the receiver, Loomis shouted:

"It's the house we've been watching out on Garibaldi Street! That Frank Jones nigger has finally decided to try to move in. Childers is out there on patrol all by himself. Akin, take this card file and start phoning every man in it! We've got to have man-power. Tell 'em to hurry! Perkins, you might as well be in on this—want to come along and join the fun?"

I knew I had to go telephone Duke about this, so I stalled Loomis.

"I'll go pick up my own car," I said. "We may need it to bring more of the boys over. See you at Garibaldi Street!"

Before Loomis could say anything, I was out of the door. I saw Loomis and Jett pile into Jett's car, and dash off to the scene of action. Just as fast, I dashed off to phone Duke. That done, I got in my own car and headed for Garibaldi Street myself.

When I arrived I found the Columbians had already succeeded in rounding up a mob, which was drawn up threateningly on the "white" side of the street. On the other sidewalk, an equally large crowd of Negroes had gathered spontaneously to defend the Negro home-owner, Frank Jones. In the middle of the street, Loomis and other Columbians were literally doing a war dance and letting out blood-curdling whoops and curses, trying to provoke the whites into action.

" If the cops are coming, they'd better hurry! " I thought to myself. The street threatened to explode into a free-for-all at any moment.

When I finally heard the sirens above the tumult of the mob, I sighed with relief. Three squad cars roared up.

" What's going on here? " Police Chief Hornsby demanded.

" We figured the police had their hands full with nigger troubles elsewhere in the city," Loomis replied. " So we thought we'd help protect this white neighbourhood from invasion! "

" Lock 'em up! " Hornsby ordered, pointing to Loomis, Jett and two other Columbians named Jack Price and Roy Whitman, who were wearing their brownshirt uniforms.

I trailed along to police headquarters, where the four Columbians posed happily for photographers, Burke soon arrived in a great huff, and posted bond for the arrested men.

" What the hell do you Columbians think you're doing? " a chief of detectives asked Burke in the hallway.

" Protecting the integrity of white neighbourhoods," Burke replied grandiloquently. " Here's a copy of a petition we've just started to circulate."

This was news even to me. Looking over the detective's shoulder, I read the leaflet Burke handed him. After a highly inflammatory prelude it concluded:

" We therefore petition the City Council to pass the necessary ordinances setting up residential zones for Negroes and Whites, separate and apart one from the other, in order that our rights as citizens and tax-payers will be protected and in order that bloodshed may be averted."

" I don't know," I said, " but I seem to remember somewhere that way back about 1917 the U.S. Supreme Court ruled residential segregation laws unconstitutional."

" To hell with the Constitution, and to hell with the Supreme Court! " Burke screamed, his voice echoing throughout police headquarters.

" Well, all I've got to say," the detective said frankly, " is that you boys ought to take it easy. We all know a race war is coming, but if you aren't mighty careful you Columbians are going to touch it off before the whites are ready. The niggers' homes are armed to the teeth, and the whites' are not. If you fellows keep on, you're going to get all the whites around the nigger sections killed before we can bring things under control! "

This propaganda to the effect that the Negroes were heavily armed I had heard many times in Klan Klaverns, when of course the very opposite was true.

I was not too surprised when, a few days later, the charges against the Columbians were dropped because of " insufficient evidence."

" We've got some good friends in the police department," Loomis gloated.

Police Chief Hornsby, while saying he would keep close watch on " secret societies," suggested that the way to get at the Columbians was for Duke to revoke their charter.

Duke agreed to take action against the Columbian charter, but in a fiery statement to the Press declared:

" If the Atlanta police really want to investigate secret societies, they could do some investigating right in their own department—and find out about Patrolman Sam Roper, head of Klan 297 in Oakland City. Then they'd have an investigation! The Columbians are nothing but the juvenile delinquents of the KKK. They are one and the same, and ought to be tarred with the same tar! "

Privately, Duke said to me, " Well, now you know what we're up against. We've got to build a fire under the police as well as under the Columbians."

It was a discouraging prospect—not being able to obtain prosecutions after all our fact-finding—but I stayed on the job.

However, new avenues of approach began to open up sooner than I had expected. Evidently feeling I was " one of the boys " after I turned out for the near-riot on Garibaldi

Street, Loomis proceeded to let me in on the master plan which the Columbians were operating.

Taking a large street map of the City of Atlanta from his desk, he pointed to a heavy red line drawn along Garibaldi and Formwalt Streets.

" We've drawn the colour line here," Loomis said, pointing, " and that's the line we're going to hold! We've put up posters on the front of every house on the white side of those streets, reading: *Zoned as a White Community*. We're also visiting the niggers, and explaining that they're not wanted. We're organized to the *n*th degree. You just saw the other day that we can shoot a squad out anywhere anytime we get a call. On top of that, we're maintaining armed patrols, with orders to keep the niggers where they belong. Everything is set up on a strictly military basis. Each neighbourhood has a captain, each captain has five lieutenants, and each lieutenant has ten sergeants, making a total complement of fifty-six men in a company."

" No privates? " I asked.

" Every man an officer," he replied with a grin. " You know—Kingfish Huey Long's idea—' every man a king.' They love it."

With this to go on, I started pumping some of the rank-and-filers for more specific information. Columbians Carlos Allen and Bill Huggins, both teen-agers, told me Jett had " issued " them each a ·38 calibre pistol. Loomis had then handed Allen a blackjack, and the two were ordered to patrol Garibaldi Street at thirty-minute intervals.

" If you see any niggers so much as walking on the wrong side of the street, stop 'em and whip 'em within an inch of their lives! " Loomis ordered. " *After* you've whipped them, tell them what you whipped them for. Tell them that this is a white neighbourhood, and they must not pass through it! If one sasses you and you have to kill him, that's what you've got a gun for! Shoot him and drag him on somebody's back porch and tell them he was trying to break in. The people are afraid, and will believe you. Just tell them to call the police, and when the police arrive, you know what to say! "

With a bit more digging, I verified my suspicion that the

pistols issued to the Columbians were not licensed, and none of the Columbians had permits to carry concealed weapons.

I hurried to Duke with this information, thinking it was enough to clap the Columbians in jail.

"It's no good," he said. "To run them in now on charges of carrying concealed weapons would make martyrs of them and a laughing stock of me. This thing has grown too big for that. To break up the Columbians we're going to have to put the leaders behind bars for a long time."

"But in the meantime a lot of people might get hurt," I protested.

"I know it," Duke conceded, "but far more people are likely to get hurt if we act too soon. Keep after them, and we'll hope for the best."

What happened next, however, was rough.

Clifford Hines, a young Negro boy about the same age as the Columbians, was walking down Formwalt Street one night, whistling, with a portable radio playing under his arm. He and his family had been living on that side of the street for four years. Three Columbians, on patrol, were hiding in a parked car, lying in wait. . . .

"Here comes a damned nigger now!" Childers whispered upon sighting the approaching Hines.

They crept out and threw a gun on the terrified Hines. Forcing him into the back of the car, Childers and Betty's brother, Clarence, proceeded to blackjack him into a state of hysterical semi-consciousness.

When the police finally arrived, they arrested not only Childers but also Hines on charges of assault and battery!

To the Columbians, this looked like an opportunity to set Childers up as a martyr. So they sent out sound-trucks inviting the public to a special meeting — to be held in the Klan's Imperial Palace at 198½ Whitehall Street! I made some inquiries about this startling development, and learned that the Columbians had actually leased the Palace for a meeting one night each week for a period of six months.

The meeting was well attended—including about 200 members of Atlanta's Jewish War Veterans, who said they had come as "observers." There were about an equal number of assorted Columbians, Kluxers and their sympathizers. . . . I took my seat with the latter. The familiar Klan altars stood in each corner of the room. I sat back to await developments.

They came thick and fast.

First, Burke stood up, and while news cameras flashed he pinned a " medal of honour " on Childers for having acted as a " true-hearted member of the white race."

Next, Burke proceeded to rip the Columbians' corporate charter into shreds. This idea, I knew from digging in the ashcan, had come from Klan Kleagle J. B. Stoner of Tennessee. The scraps were then swept into a large manila envelope, and addressed to Dan Duke " to show him what we think of his revocation proceedings."

Loomis spoke next.

" Every nation which has ever amounted to anything has first had to expel the Jews," he said, glaring at the Jewish war veterans. " Too many Jews are going around under Christian aliases; we're going to track down such cases. Another thing we're going to do is see to it that no Jew gets on any ballot. Furthermore, Christians ought to always buy Christian. Rich's department store may be the biggest in the South, but we're going to launch a boycott and picket line against it and put it out of business! "

Taking the floor once more, Burke deliberately set out to provoke the Jewish war veterans to violence.

" The Columbians have fired a shot that has been heard around the world! " he shrieked. " At long last the Jew has met his master in this organization! The fight is on, and we are going to make it hotter and hotter until you go back to the Bronx where you came from! And I say one day we are going to march into the Bronx! "

I looked at the Jewish veterans. They were obviously very hot under the collar, and kept looking at their leader, as though for permission to retaliate.

Then Burke suddenly announced: " All non-members must now withdraw from the meeting! "

" Just a minute," protested the leader of the Jewish vets, rising to his feet. " I'd like to have a chance to answer the charges you've made."

" Throw the Jews out! " Burke yelled in reply.

" You've been spouting nothing but lies! " the vet cried out.

There was an angry roar as the Columbians charged him. One Columbian drew a pistol. Four policemen rushed in, but were submerged in a mêlée of swinging fists. There was a shattering of glass, and a bomb came hurtling through the window.

It was tear gas! Almostly instantly the room filled with choking, blinding fumes and the fight was off.

There was a rush for the door—and the hall was soon empty. I hung around outside, and when the air had cleared inside the hall, re-entered and picked up the tear-gas container.

" No doubt about it," Duke said when I showed it to him the‾ next morning. " This thing came from the Atlanta police department. One of the Columbians' pals on the police force must have slipped it to them, and they tossed it through the window themselves, just to make more head-lines and give them something they could blame on the Jews. Good thing it came through the window when it did, though; otherwise there would've been a real battle up there! "

The first real crack in the Columbian case began to open up when Lanier Waller sickened at their brutality and began to talk about a night ride he had taken with Ira Jett.

" Jett asked me if I wanted to go out and ride around with him," Waller said. " He asked Homer if it would be all right. Homer looked sort of undecided and then said, ' Yes, I think so.' So I went with Jett and we started driving towards out-of-town.

" ' These damned niggers around here won't listen to what we tell them,' Jett said to me. ' We're going to have to show them what we mean! What we need is a bunch of guys who aren't scared of anything, who'll stick together and do what we tell them and not say nothing about it.'

" ' How do you mean? ' I asked him.

" ' I mean if some nigger house got blowed up or burnt down, nobody would know anything about it,' Jett answered.

" By that time we had come to a little shack. Jett cut off the lights of the car and told me to keep quiet. We went around to the side of the shack where there was an old barrel. It looked like it was full of chicken nests. Jett reached inside and pulled out a handful of dynamite sticks.

" Then we went around to the front and knocked on the door. An old man opened it and Jett told him there was something else he wanted. So the old guy brought us about four or five ·45 and ·38 pistols. Jett handed them to me and said, ' Take these out to the car and put them in the glove compartment, and be sure to lock it up! '

" When I came back Jett said, ' Waller, you know how to keep your mouth shut—look in here! ' He showed me a whole mess of guns and ammunition. At a glance I would say there was about twenty-five rifles and shotguns.

" While we drove back to town Jett said, ' Waller, there is going to be some big money in this for all of us, but we've got to stick together and keep our mouths shut.'

" I don't know how you feel about this, Perkins, but it's too much for me—I'm getting out! " Waller finished.

" Who was the old codger at the shack? " I asked him.

" I don't know his name," Waller said. " He lives way out yonder on Grist Mill Road. He's a well-digger by trade, and only got one arm."

That should do it, I thought to myself—and hurried off to Duke with the big news.

The next morning I was sitting in the office of Duke's secretary and was looking and listening through a crack in the door when his agents brought the man in. His name was Jess Johnson, he said—but that's all he would say.

Duke went to work on him. He talked for a long time, trying to make the old man understand what a bad lot the Columbians were. But Johnson just looked at him.

" Mr. Johnson," Duke went on in a friendly tone, " I can't believe a hard-working man like you would be mixed up with the likes of these Columbians if you knew what they were up to. They are nothing but trouble-makers. They are trying to rook people out of their hard-earned cash."

Johnson just looked at him, obviously unmoved.

" I wish you would help us out in this thing," Duke said. " We know that Jett got some dynamite from you two nights ago, and that you've been storing guns out there for him. We could put you in jail, but we don't want to. It's Jett and the rest of his Columbian gang we're after."

Still Johnson would say nothing.

Duke talked on, to no avail.

Then he showed Johnson some of the Columbians' hate propaganda. But Johnson couldn't read.

Just when I was about to abandon hope, Duke had an inspiration. Pulling the Columbians' copy of Hitler's *Mein Kampf* from his desk, he explained to Johnson that it had been picked up in a raid on Columbian headquarters. Flipping open the book, he showed Johnson Hitler's picture on the frontispiece. Turning the pages, he pointed to a photograph of one of Hitler's S.S. Elite Guards, wearing the thunderbolt emblem. Beside it, Duke placed the Columbian thunderbolt.

Johnson looked at the two. The muscles in his jaws twitched. And then he spoke for the first time.

" Mr. Duke," he said, " if that's what these Columbians stand for, I'll tell you everything I know, even if I do have to go to jail. I lost a boy in the fight against Hitler."

With a sigh of relief, Duke rang for his secretary. In short order the affidavit was ready and Johnson signed. He confirmed everything Waller had said, and added the information that Jett had " paid " him for the dynamite with two free application blanks to the Klan, which ordinarily cost $10 each!

" That ought to do it, don't you think? " I asked Duke after everyone else had left the office.

" We should be able to stick them on a charge of illegal possession of dynamite," Duke agreed. " That's a serious charge—especially with all the bombings that have been going on. But I wish we could lay hands on the dynamite."

" I wouldn't know where to start looking," I said.

" Oh, well," Duke shrugged, picking up his telephone. " Miss Wade," he said to his secretary in the next room, " will you please inform Solicitor E. E. Andrews that if he will come to my office tomorrow morning at ten o'clock I

will be happy to present him with certain evidence on which
to bring the Columbians to trial? "

The news leaked out that the Columbian case was about
to be broken wide open, and newsmen came flying in from
all over the U.S. At ten the next morning Duke's office
was crowded with reporters and photographers. Solicitor
Andrews was there too. I joined the journalists in my
capacity as a reporter for the *Southern Outlook.*
" Bring in the Columbians! " Duke ordered.
From the next room, a deputy ushered in Loomis, Burke
and Jett, and stood them against the wall. Then Duke
proceeded to read the affidavit of the one-armed well-digger,
Jess Johnson.
The Columbians listened in stony silence, their faces
betraying nothing.
When Duke had finished reading, he handed the affidavit
to Solicitor Andrews.
" Now," he said, " I have something else here I want to
show you."
Going to his safe, Duke brought out a parcel wrapped in
old newspaper, and laid it gingerly on his desk. Unwrapping
it slowly and with great care he brought forth five sticks of
dynamite!
" Godammit! " Burke exploded. " We three were the only
ones who knew where that dynamite was hidden! Which
one of you dirty rats sold out? "
Loomis and Jett both jumped him—and the flash cameras
banged away.
Deputies moved in quickly and pinioned the Columbians'
arms behind their backs.
" Take 'em away! " Duke ordered with a grin.
" Well, well," Solicitor Andrews said grimly, " I'll trot
them before a grand jury in a hurry! I only wish we had
what it takes to nail them for inciting to riot, too! "
" What do you need? " I asked him.
" Just *one* statement made by one of them at one of their
public meetings that a jury would agree was a direct call
for violent action."
The last of the reporters and cameramen were filing out

of the office, and I signalled Andrews that I had something to say as soon as they were gone. When the room was clear, I asked him:

" I once heard Loomis say from a sound-truck, ' We don't want anybody to join who's not ready to get out and kill niggers and Jews! ' "

" *You did?* " Andrews exclaimed. " When? Where? "

" At one of their first meetings—August 27th it was—at Exposition Mill Village."

" Why didn't you report this before? "

" I did, but at the time the Columbians hadn't actually pulled any rough stuff, and Duke seemed to think we should bide our time."

" Well, he was probably right, but the time has come to wrap all these charges up in one package! Are you willing to testify as to that statement by Loomis? "

I looked at Duke. The minute I stepped into a court-room my career as an undercover agent working on Klan elements would be over.

" I think it's worth it," he said, reading my thoughts. " If we don't succeed in putting these Columbians on ice for a considerable spell, all hell is likely to break loose in Georgia, and there's no telling where it would end. Maybe we can find someone to carry on where you leave off."

" I think you're right," I said. Turning to Andrews, I told him:

" I'll be ready whenever you are."

" Good," he said, shaking hands. " I'm going right to work on this thing."

When he had gone, I turned to Duke.

" Where in hell did you find their dynamite? "

" I didn't say it was *their* dynamite," he replied coyly. " I went out and bought those sticks this morning."

" If Your Honour please, as attorney for the Columbians I wish to ask for a sixty-day postponement of the date of their trial," Homer Loomis, Sr., was pleading before the Atlanta judge. Homer's father had flown down from his Wall Street law office to defend his son in the Columbian trial.

"Your Honour," Duke spoke up, "these people have already had two extensions of time. Their whole record shows nothing but the utmost contempt for our courts and legal processes. In my opinion, the Columbians have had all the consideration they are entitled to from the State of Georgia!"

"I can understand your point of view, Mr. Duke," the judge replied slowly. "But I'm going to grant them this one more extension. Their claim is that they haven't had adequate time to prepare, and I do not want to give them any excuse whatever for asserting that they have not received even-handed justice."

Duke turned on his heel with a shrug.

Burke, who was standing before the bar with Old Man Loomis, opened his mouth.

"Your Honour," he said, "As President of the Columbians I want to express our appreciation for your just decision. Thank God there is at least one honest public official in the State of Georgia!"

Duke whirled, and with a haymaker to the head, floored Burke for considerably more than the count!

As this was a preliminary hearing, the court-room was deserted, except that I had dropped in as a "token of loyalty" to the Columbian cause.

Deputies rushed in and revived Burke, who was led away shaking his head in a dazed fashion, and glaring back over his shoulder at Duke.

"We'll put *you* in jail for this!" Loomis, Sr., threatened Duke, and stalked out of the court-room.

The judge looked at Duke reprovingly.

"Mr. Duke, this is a serious matter! It casts reflection upon not just my court but all the courts of Georgia. Here you are entrusted with the job of stamping out violence which defies the law, and you yourself resort to violence in a court-room!"

"Your Honour," Duke said, thoroughly abashed. "Every word you say is true. I don't know what came over me. But I've been subjected to more abuse and vilification from these Columbians than I could stand. I hope you'll understand that what happened was not without provocation, both immediate and over a long period. I apologize to Your Honour for having lost my temper in your court."

" Mr. Duke," the judge replied, " I accept your explanation and apology."

" Of course, they may very well take out a warrant against me," Duke said.

" There wasn't anyone else in the court-room, except that one man back there."

" You don't have to worry about him," Duke said, giving me a wink. " He's going to be a witness for the State."

" Well," said the judge, " you don't have to worry about me either—my head was turned at the time, and I didn't see a thing! "

And so everything seemed settled. However, during the sixty days of grace given the Columbians another drama began to unfold on the Atlanta stage, which was to have far-reaching consequences for all. . . .

Out from under cover, Kennedy shows secret Klan signs at a news conference at the New York headquarters of the Anti-Defamation League. The sign is TSOG, The Sign of Greeting. Photograph by *New York Post*.

CHAPTER TWELVE

THE WOOL-HAT PUTSCH

I WAS walking along Atlanta's famed Peachtree Street when I came upon a small gathering of people on the sidewalk, listening intently to a news broadcast coming from a radio shop. Obviously, it was big news.

" What's up? " I asked one of the bystanders.

" Ole Gene's dead," he replied, with a face as forlorn as a long-eared coon dog.

" Dead? " I repeated, rightly or wrongly feeling much the same as I had when I heard the news of Mussolini's and Hitler's passing—but trying not to show it.

" Yep," the man said. " Ole Gene's gone. No telling what will become of Georgia without him."

" Oh, I imagine we'll get along," ventured a man who evidently shared my sentiments.

Talmadge had been elected Governor of Georgia after a whirlwind campaign of Klan terror aimed at keeping Negroes from going to the polls. On the eve of the election, fiery crosses had flamed on court-house lawns all over Georgia. Notices signed " KKK " were tacked on to Negro churches, warning, " The first nigger who votes in Georgia will be a dead one." Other warnings were sent to Negroes through the U.S. mails (sometimes enclosing a pistol cartridge), and others were dropped from airplanes over Negro neighbourhoods. On election day, thousands of Negroes awoke to find miniature coffins on their doorsteps. Duke had done what he could to stem this terror, but his hands were tied by the Klan sympathies of the local officials. My union friend Charlie Pike led his locals, white and Negro alike, to march to the polls and vote in a body. And though many thousands of Negroes defied the Klan and voted for the first time, in the end the forces of hate carried the

161

day, Talmadge was elected, and the liberal supported by
Governor Arnall was defeated. With such thoughts as these
running through my mind, I listened as the radio announcer
went on to discuss the possible consequences of the Governor-
elect's death.

The radio announcer, having predicted that the Talmadge funeral procession would be the longest in the history
of the state, went on to a discussion of the consequences of
the Governor-elect's death.

" Eugene Talmadge has passed on just twenty-one days
before he was scheduled to take his seat in the Governor's
chair," the broadcaster said. " Speculation is already rife
as to the future. During the last few days, persistent rumours
have spread through the Capitol that in the event of Ole
Gene's death the Talmadge forces would attempt to give the
governorship to his son Herman—or ' Hummon ' as he is
called by his followers."

" Sort of a ' Talmadge is dead; long live Talmadge! '
proposition, isn't it? " my kindred spirit in the crowd
whispered.

" Just how this might be accomplished is not altogether
clear," the radio commentator went on.   " Under the
state's new constitution adopted during Governor Ellis
Arnall's administration, Georgia for the first time has a
Lieutenant-Governor.   Arnall's former secretary, M. E.
Thompson, has just been elected to that post. However, the
talk is that the Talmadge-dominated legislature will take
the position that Ole Gene didn't really win in the recent
election, because the legislature never had a chance to
declare him winner. Though the fact is not widely known,
during the final days of the campaign the Talmadge camp
conducted a last-minute write-in campaign for Herman—
with the result that he polled 697 votes. The Republican
nominee received several thousand votes, but the legislature
under the constitution can choose between the two top men.
So the idea is to count Ole Gene out, and young Herman
in. Thompson is to be by-passed by a refusal of the legislature to swear him in as Lieutenant-Governor until after
Herman is named Governor."

" I'll be hanged! " my friend muttered. " Governor of Georgia by the grace of 697 votes! "

" Governor Arnall, however, has already let it be known that he will refuse to turn over his office to anyone but Lieutenant-Governor Thompson. . . . Yes, folks, the Georgia political pot is boiling, and what will come out of it is anybody's guess! "

" He can say that again! " my friend said vehemently. " Georgia has already had more than enough of Talmadgism! This scheme is some more of Roy Harris' doings. He's always been the power behind the Talmadge throne, you know. Harris would like to grab the governorship himself, but I guess he's banking on the magic of the Talmadge name to put Herman in."

" Sounds more like voodoo," I remarked, studying the faces of the crowd that had gathered outside the radio shop. I fancied I could tell the Talmadgites among them by the expressions on their faces. Walking down Peachtree Street, I could see that the news was travelling fast, judging from the mixture of glum looks and half smiles I encountered. I decided to walk on down to Auburn Avenue, and over to the Negro section. There I found that the " Black Despatch " grapevine had carried the word everywhere and jubilation was unrestrained. I never saw Georgia Negroes so happy— not even after a Joe Louis victory.

Georgia, I decided, was fast turning into a powder keg —and sparks would soon be flying from all directions.

The next Monday night, Dragon Green called Klavern No. 1 to order with more than usual solemnity.

" With the passing of Ole Gene the Klan has lost one of the best friends it ever had," he pronounced mournfully. " All honest-to-God white Georgians want Hummon to take Gene's place. Hummon has already assured me he will keep all of his father's promises to the Klan, and will go all the way down the road in giving us protection. I'm sending out a Fiery Summons to every Klavern in the Georgia realm, calling upon all true Klansmen to converge on the Capitol to strengthen the hands of the legislators and let them know they have the backing of the people in naming Hummon Governor! "

So, the wool-hat and bed-sheet boys were going to march on Atlanta! I wondered whether this Georgia-style putsch would turn into a violent drive to power such as those staged by Mussolini's Blackshirts and Hitler's Brownshirts. Or would it follow the pattern established by the Louisiana dictator, " Kingfish " Huey Long, who sent out sound-trucks into the hinterlands to foment marches on his Capitol every time he needed mob pressure to bend the legislature to his will?

As it turned out, Georgia's wool-hat putsch had many of the earmarks of both.

The wool-hat horde began to arrive several days before the legislature opened on January 12th. They poured in on foot, by horse and buggy, Model T Fords, buses and trains. There were no actual processions—just a steady infiltration, until the entire business district of Atlanta thronged with them. In the neighbourhood of the Capitol the wool-hatters were so thick I found it difficult to travel on the sidewalks. Many were dressed in overalls, and practically every man was " chewin' black and spittin' red "—as they say of tobacco-chewers in Georgia. In effect, the city was overrun with a vast lynch-mob that was literally ready to roar into action at the drop of a hat.

Using my " John Perkins " Press card as representative of the pro-Klan *Southern Outlook*, I gained admission to the floor of the legislature. The marble columns in the corridors —and the doors to Governor Arnall's office—were plastered with gummed red stickers depicting a Klansman on horseback, and the slogan " Here Yesterday, Today, Forever! " Wool-hatters jammed the halls and galleries, spattering the walls around the brass spittoons with tobacco spittle. As I mingled with the legislators on the floor I spotted many a fishtail-wiggle handshake between them, and even heard one old codger whisper to another by way of introduction, " Klavern 066."

When the session was called to order, one of the few sane heads called for adjournment until a court ruling could be had on the legal aspects of the controversy. But Talmadge's steam-roller politicos would have none of this.

" We are not going to turn Georgia over to niggers, Rosenwalds and Wallaces! " shouted Representative Jewel Crowe.

In a tumultuous voice vote, the motion to adjourn was tabled.

Then the debate was on. Anti-Talmadge legislators were seldom able to gain the floor, and the session turned into a wild harangue that surpassed any Klan Klonklave I had ever attended in its rabid fulminations against Negroes, Jews, unionists and other minority groups, as though this had anything to do with the constitutional question involved. On and on the session rumbled, the hysteria of the legislators and their wool-hat cohorts rising to fever pitch.

Downstairs, meanwhile, Governor Arnall sat staunchly in his office, surrounded by a handful of loyal departmental heads, while the wool-hatters milled outside shouting insults. I milled with them, keeping both ears open with the hope of learning what plans they might have—if any.

It was not until 2 a.m. that the doors of the legislature burst open. Hummon had been declared Governor! Legislators and wool-hatters, with Hummon riding triumphantly on their shoulders, poured in a cheering, singing torrent down the stairway and headed straight for Arnall's office! Duke and several other Arnall lieutenants stood in the door, while he remained firm at his desk. When the first of the wool-hatters reached the door, Duke barred their way, and the slugging and cursing began.

For a few minutes it looked like a free-for-all would break out. Duke was striking out in all directions, bellowing like a bull.

Taken aback by this determined resistance, the Talmadge leaders went into a huddle. Coming out of the confab, Hummon addressed his flock.

" My friends," he said, " we have accomplished enough for one day. We can settle this little matter tomorrow. Let's all go home and get some sleep, content to know that justice has triumphed! "

The wool-hatters, deprived of their prey, cheered with what spirit they could muster, and went off to look for all-night bars where they could toast their " victory " in corn liquor.

The next morning I arrived at the Capitol bright and early, long before any of its offices normally opened.

But when I approached Arnall's office, I found a grinning throng of wool-hatters, backed up by a number of armed state militiamen, standing outside the door. Hummon had been installed in the Governor's chair inside! I didn't have to ask—I could tell from the looks and smells outside.

" How did Hummon manage it? " I asked Ira Jett, my Brother Klavalier who was very much on hand.

" Hey, Perkins," Jett said with a triumphant grin. " Seems as how somebody switched locks on the door during the night! We're just waiting now for Arnall to show up. I want to see his face when he finds Hummon is in there— bet he'll be as mad as a bee in a tar-bucket! "

Taking Jett aside for a private " klonversation "—as confidential talks between Klansmen are called—I learned that the locksmith brigade had been led by Roy Harris, together with Marvin Griffin. (Griffin had served as Arnall's adjutant in charge of the state militia, but had been defeated for the post of Lieutenant-Governor by Arnall's friend Thompson.) Together Harris and Griffin had roused a locksmith from his bed, and under cover of darkness had switched locks and presented Hummon with the key. In return, Hummon had named Griffin to serve as adjutant under him.

Now I understood why the Talmadge chieftains had been willing to call off their mob without a show-down struggle the night before!

" I'm going in to congratulate our new Governor," Jett said, pushing his way through the wool-hatters. " I done a lot of work for Ole Gene, and for Hummon too."

Meanwhile, the temperature outside the Governor's office rose rapidly in anticipation of Arnall's arrival. According to the grapevine, word had already reached Arnall that Talmadge had broken in. The question in everyone's mind was whether or not Arnall would call upon units of the state militia to escort him back into his office and eject Hummon. No one was more confused than the militia itself—the junior officers and rank and file did not know whether to obey the orders of Talmadge's "adjutant" Griffin or Arnall.

The hour of Arnall's usual arrival approached.

"I don't think he's got the guts," one wool-hatter said.

"Don't be too sure," said another.

"I'll bet he's busy rounding up a military escort," a third man predicted.

Meanwhile, more militiamen and State highway patrolmen—some of whom I recognized as Brother Klansmen—trickled in to reinforce Talmadge.

At last the electric word came, "Here comes Arnall!"

The door to the Governor's office was hastily slammed shut and locked. Militiamen and wool-hatters merged to form a solid mass before it.

Then short, stocky Ellis Arnall came steadily up the Capitol steps, alone. He marched straight into the mob as though it did not exist. It hesitated, then gave way before him, opening a path. Arnall walked up to the office door and turned the knob as he would on any other morning. Finding it locked, he knocked loudly.

There was a titter from the wool-hatters.

No response came from within (where the excitement must have also been considerable).

Arnall knocked again, and rattled the door-knob.

The mob and troopers closed in around him.

"Governor Talmadge is busy, and you'll have to wait your turn in the reception room like other private citizens," Hummon's suave aide, Benton Odum, told Arnall.

"I demand admittance to my office!" Arnall said.

Odum repeated himself, and twice more Arnall demanded that he stand aside.

Several troopers unbuttoned their pistols, and one was half drawn.

Finally Governor Arnall turned on his heel and said to the crowd:

"You are all witnesses to the fact that I have been forcibly deprived of admission to my office!"

With that he pushed his way out into the rotunda of the Capitol, and proceeded to set up an "emergency office" in the information booth.

Asked for a statement by newsmen, Arnall said:

" Last night, under cover of darkness, the military forces of the pretender, with the aid of a locksmith, executed a *panzer* movement and removed the locks from the door to my office! " He went on to say that Hummon's claim was based " purely on inheritance," and added, " but Georgia is not a monarchy." From time to time he referred to Talmadge as a " usurper, pretender, imposter and interloper."

" I stand alone, without the military, bodyguard, thugs or bruisers, to defend the constitution of Georgia! " he thundered.

I was in the thick of the encircling mob, and heard one wool-hatter thug mutter to another, " If he calls us thugs one more time, I'm going after him! "

There is no doubt that Arnall actually took his life in his hands. The wool-hat Ku Klux tribe will kill first and worry about it afterwards—especially when the intoxication of hate is heightened by alcohol, as it was that morning.

The rest of the day was like a Roman holiday, with fire-crackers and tear-gas bombs being aimed at Arnall's booth at intervals. To celebrate their successful putsch, the wool-hatters danced a hoe-down in the Capitol, with " Fiddlin' John " Carson providing the music. Thirty years earlier, Carson had fiddled at a similar celebration, over the prostrate body of Leo Frank, innocent victim of a lynch mob. Fiddlin' John's tune, the anti-Semitic " Ballad of Mary Phagan," is still to be heard. Years later, Carson had helped elect Ole Gene Governor by composing the tune:

> Farmer in the cornfield
> Hollerin' Whoa, gee, haw!
> Can't put no thirty-dollar tag
> On a three-dollar car!

Many of the celebrants sported Klan Kards in their hat-bands and willingly posed for photographers.

Needless to say, the affairs of the State of Georgia were soon in high disorder, with both Talmadge and Arnall issuing orders as Governor. One Atlanta newspaper quipped, " They've got a two-headed calf in a tent out on the edge of town and charging two bits to see it—why not throw some canvas over the Capitol and charge two bucks to see the two-headed state?"

Among other things, the crisis proved that Hummon was a real chip off the Ole Gene block when it came to repartee. Referring on a state-wide radio hook-up to Arnall's "claim" to the governorship, Hummon said wryly, "There's a nigger named Father Divine in New York City who thinks he's God, but that don't make him God."

Meanwhile, as the wool-hat coup consolidated itself, a widespread revulsion swept Georgia. Negroes aptly paraphrased the advertising gimmick "LS/MFT" (Lucky Strike Means Fine Tobacco) to "Lord Save Me From Talmadge." Students from all sections of the state marched on the Capitol and protested the Talmadge dictatorship. An organization calling itself the "Aroused Citizens of Georgia" began staging protest meetings, and the Talmadgites countered with an "Aroused White Citizens of Georgia." Dragon Green ordered his Kluxers to attend the anti-Talmadge meetings, and "be prepared for trouble."

By this time Arnall had appointed another adjutant to take the place of turncoat Griffin. The two rival adjutants were busily commanding and countermanding, even going so far as to post rival sentry details about the State Armoury. When a flood developed in south Georgia, it actually seemed for a time that the controversy as to which adjutant was to order out rescue details would prevent any relief being sent at all.

There was a lot of talk about what Uncle Sam might do to untangle the Georgia mess. The U.S. Constitution says in very plain language that the Federal Government must assure a "republican form of government" in every state. By no stretch of the imagination could the régime of 697-vote Hummon, put in power by the wool-hat putsch, be called a republic. Once before in American history a somewhat similar snarl was created, when in 1874 two men simultaneously claimed to have been elected Governor of Arkansas. In that situation, President Ulysses S. Grant stepped in and restored order.

According to law, Arnall could have appealed to President Truman to declare martial law in Georgia. Then the Secretary of War could actually have ordered Adjutant Griffin, as head of Georgia's national guard, to obey Arnall's orders—and clap Griffin into prison for treason if he refused to do so. This would have been very strong medicine, however, and Arnall had other ideas for effecting a cure.

A great deal of tension also arose over the question of who was to occupy the Georgia Governor's mansion. If Hummon came knocking on the door, backed up by an armed guard as he doubtless would be, would Arnall move his family out—or would he muster a guard of his own and defend the mansion against all comers?

This question was answered, however, when Arnall announced that he would rest his case with the courts of Georgia.

" I am moving out of the Governor's mansion," he said, " in the conviction that in good time it will be restored by the courts to its rightful occupant—my successor, M. E. Thompson."

No sooner had Arnall moved out than Hummon moved in with his wife and mother!

In the meantime, Arnall exercised his right to ask his Attorney-General, Eugene Cook, for an official ruling on the legal questions involved. Unless repealed, such decisions are binding. Refusing to be intimidated by threats of the surrounding Talmadge machine to lock him out of his office, too, Cook handed down a bold decision that Thompson was the rightful Governor. Hummon ignored the order, and his rubber-stamp legislature threatened to take away practically all the powers of Cook's office. And so Arnall was obliged to take the case to court.

Then I got a call to come into Duke's office. He looked weary but determined.

" Kennedy," he said, locking the door, " it looks to me like one phase of our Klan-busting is over. The word is that Hummon is planning to fire all of Cook's staff, me included. If Cook weren't an elected official, they'd try to toss him out too. But I'm not going to give them the satisfaction of firing me—I'm quitting."

I felt as if someone had taken a chair out from under me.

" Well," I said, " that's bad news for our side, and good news for the Klan. Too bad! "

Duke grinned.

" I'll always be bad medicine for the Klan, don't you worry," he said. " I just don't want to be associated with Talmadge's régime."

" What are you going to do? " I asked, sure that the grin hid more news.

" Go back to practising law. I'm thinking of running for Solicitor of Fulton County. If that Talmadge bunch stays in power they'll run hog-wild. The Capitol will reek with graft and corruption—and somebody ought to be in a position to ride herd on them."

" You'd be the man for the job," I agreed, feeling easier. " But what's to become of our case against the Columbians, and our suit to take away the Klan's charter? "

" Solicitor Andrews has all our evidence against the Columbians, and should be able to handle them all right. As for the suit against the Klan, Attorney-General Cook will have to carry on. Frankly, if Talmadge hangs on as Governor, I wouldn't be surprised if the courts let the Klan hang on to its charter."

" Well," I said, " it's been fun while it lasted. I'm not through with the Ku Klux yet. I'm going to stick with them on my own, and trip them up every chance I get."

" Good! Let me in on it whenever you think there's anything I can do. We've managed to cramp their style no end until now, and I'd hate to see them have everything their way under Talmadge."

We shook hands, and that afternoon Georgia was minus its Klan-busting Assistant Attorney-General.

The Kluxers, needless to say, were jubilant.

" We can all be thankful that Duke is out of the way," Dragon Green said at the meeting of Klavern No. 1 the following Monday night. " But we'd better keep our shirts on for the time being. So far as we know, that rat Kennedy is still on the job. As long as he's around to give the world advance notice of every move we plan to make, our hands are tied. Job No. One is—get Kennedy! "

Duke's return to private life brought immediate action from the Klan's attorney, Morgan Belser, who wrote Attorney-General Cook as follows:

> " In last night's *Journal* it is reported that you have expressed some apprehension that the General Assembly might divest you of your powers before you have an opportunity to try your suit against the Klan. In order that you may not be thus embarrassed, I am requesting the Clerk of Fulton Superior Court to add the Klan case to the jury trial calendar for Monday, February 3rd. I shall be glad to withdraw all special pleas and demurrers if that will enable us to proceed immediately with the trial of the case upon its merits.

" I find myself in a position to have to decline Mr. Belser's offer," Cook replied dryly. " It is public knowledge that only yesterday *Mr.* Herman Talmadge, by an alleged executive order, attempted to terminate the services of my entire staff, and that the former Assistant Attorney-General, Dan Duke, who has been handling this Klan case, resigned only a few days ago."

Judge Walter C. Hendrix noted that the calendar was full for the next thirty days, and ordered that the Klan case be scheduled at some time after that, with the state given preference as to the exact date.

Two months after the wool-hat putsch put Talmadge in power, Georgia's Supreme Court ruled Hummon out and Thompson in.

Upon receiving the news, Hummon telephoned his wife at the Governor's mansion and told her to " start packing." Then, carrying a large Bible conspicuously under his arm, he walked out of the Governor's office with the statement:

" This case will be taken to the court of last resort—the people of Georgia! "

CHAPTER THIRTEEN

BIGOTRY BEFORE THE BAR

BACKFIRE! That was the only word to describe what had happened to the Columbians' sixty days of grace.

They had asked for the postponement with a view to being brought to trial under a friendly Talmadge administration, but fate had intervened to take Old Gene from them, and now the courts had deprived them of their last hope, Hummon. The hostile atmosphere generated by the wool-hat putsch had not improved their chances, as the day of their appearance before the bar of justice drew near.

Still another event had taken place during those fateful sixty days—a book called *Southern Exposure*, by Stetson Kennedy, was published by Doubleday & Company of New York. At the time I delivered the manuscript I had no way of knowing that I would soon have to step out from under my Klan robe and into an open court-room.

Consequently the book contained a few choice tidbits on the Kluxers and barely hinted at the undercover explorations I have related here. Nevertheless, there was enough in *Southern Exposure* to evoke a howl of anguish in the Klaverns, and a renewed hue and cry of " Get Kennedy! " The only difficulty was, neither Klansmen nor Columbians knew Kennedy was Perkins, or vice versa. By the same token, my literary critics and readers did not know what I looked like either, since I had convinced Doubleday that it wouldn't be healthy to put my picture on the book jacket.

My publishers insisted, however, that I come to New York for a reception, and to do some lecturing against the Klan. I went, leaving Solicitor Andrews instructions on how to send for me when he was ready to go into court against the Columbians.

"Surely you're not going back down there?" my New York audiences cried. "They'll murder you!"

"I hope not," was all I could say.

"At least you'll have police protection, won't you?"

"That's the last thing on earth I want!" I had to reply. "Ten to one, the cops would turn out to be Klux, and take me for a ride."

"Would they dare bump off a white man—and an author at that? It's hard to believe they could get away with it."

"I don't think they'd come at me in Klan robes," I said. "But as they say in the Klaverns, there's more than one way to skin a cat. In my case, most likely I'd be arrested on a trumped-up charge of jay-walking or something. Then I'd be driven to jail through deserted back streets. At some spot where there are no witnesses, they'd simply shoot me, mess up their own shirts a bit, and deliver my remains to police headquarters with the explanation that I had resisted arrest."

"What *are* you going to do for protection?"

"Re-enter Atlanta quietly, stay with friends and keep off the streets, and try to protect myself," I replied.

In due time I received by registered mail a formal summons from Solicitor Andrews ordering me "to be and appear" in Fulton Superior Court, Atlanta, as a witness for the State of Georgia against the Columbians.

At the appointed hour I was there. The court-room was packed and overflowing into the corridors with Columbians, Kluxers, Klavaliers, wool-hatters and all sorts of good and bad Georgia folk. I spotted Ira Jett, Cyclops Vester Ownby, James Shipp of the American Gentile Army, and a host of other "buddies."

"Hi, Perkins!" they said, giving me the Klan shake. "Haven't seen you around lately."

If they only knew, I thought. In a few more minutes Perkins would be dead—and Kennedy would be very much in demand. I went into the ante-room where other witnesses for the State were sitting, with a deputy stationed at the door. Looking closely at the deputy, I wondered if I hadn't seen him before at some Klan function. . . .

At length the court clerk began to "call the roll" of witnesses who had been ordered to appear.

When he said "Stetson Kennedy" just about every head in the place started spinning.

I stood up and said, not very loudly: "Here...."

"It's *Perkins*!" Kluxers and Columbians roared in anger. "So he's the rat! Let me at him!"

There was a general rush in my direction. I looked around to see if the deputies were going to come to my rescue, but the ones I saw were glaring at me as fiercely as any of my arch-enemies. When the judge rapped loudly for order to be restored 'the deputies reluctantly went into action and escorted me back to the relative sanctuary of the state's witness-room.

"I want to warn the audience that if there are any further attempts to intimidate witnesses, I will order the guilty parties arrested!" the judge thundered. "The prosecution will now proceed to present its case...."

In the witness-room I was treated to a constant parade of my ex-comrades, who trooped by the door to glare, shake their fists, and mutter threats that they'd "take care of you later!"

"You'll never get out of Atlanta alive!" one direly predicted.

The deputy showed no inclination to discourage them.

Just then another deputy dashed in, and served me with a warrant as a witness for the Columbians!

Amazed, I ventured out into the corridor, where I found Duke standing in a doorway.

"What does it mean?" I asked him.

"Not a thing," he replied. "They served me with one too. They have no intention of calling us. But by making us witnesses for both sides they can keep us from sitting in the court-room and watching the proceedings."

So that was it—just spite! But that wasn't all the Columbians were doing to put me on the spot—as I discovered when I returned to the witness-room after having lunch in the court-house cafeteria.

"What comment have you to make?" a flock of reporters demanded.

" About what? " I countered.

" The banning of your book *Southern Exposure!* " they replied.

" Banned? " I said incredulously. " By whom? "

" By Solicitor Andrews! During recess some Columbians started handing out free copies, giving them to the deputies who have the jury in tow, passing them around in the audience, and planking one down in front of Andrews! "

" So what? " I asked. " It would do them good to read it."

" Maybe, but the Columbians ran around pointing to page 343, where it says ' The only way we're willing to give the niggers equality is by f——in' 'em white! ' "

" *I* didn't say that—I quoted a Kluxer who said it to me."

" It's not a question of who said it—*you're* the one who put it in print! Andrews took one look at it and said, ' Why, that's the most vulgar and obscene thing I ever saw! ' Then he sent the deputies out to every book store in Atlanta to ask for *Southern Exposure.* Told 'em to bring back two copies from each store, with receipts and the names of the clerks! "

" Then what? "

" Said he was going to have 'em all up before the Grand Jury on charges of selling obscene literature—and you too if you distributed any! "

" Nuts! " I said. " None of this makes any sense. When court adjourns this afternoon I'll personally inscribe and autograph a copy and present it to Andrews."

After thus speaking out for freedom of the Press, it occurred to me that if Andrews went through with his threat to arrest me, the Atlanta jail would be a very unhealthy spot. In the privacy of a cell the Klan-cops would really be free to do a job on me.

While I was sitting in the state witness-room mulling this prospect over, Andrews appeared at the door and beckoned to me. I followed him down the corridor to an alcove where we were alone.

" Kennedy," he said, whirling on me, " things have taken an ugly turn! They've got everybody so stirred up over that book of yours I can't even afford to put you on the stand as my witness! "

" Surely it can't be so bad as all that! " I said, really startled now. " What's so bad about using a naughty word? Every one of those guys uses it every day."

" I know, but you don't know the half of it! They've been reading the whole chapter you call ' Total Equality, and How to Get It.' Just listen to that rumbling in the court-room! Do you know what it means? "

" No."

" It means that the mob has forgotten all about trying the Columbians, and is ready to lynch you! You know Georgia as well as I do! Nigger-killing may be considered a misdemeanour, but nigger-loving is a capital crime! "

" But the court-room isn't judging the Columbians," I argued.

" It's not just the onlookers, I tell you! The deputies in charge of the jury are as worked up over this thing as anybody! That's why I sent 'em out looking for copies of your book, trying to cool 'em off. But they haven't cooled. Under the law they're not supposed to discuss anything with the jurymen, but for all I know they've been doing nothing else but! This is an important case, and we can't afford to muff it! With all the documentary evidence you've turned in we can still nail 'em—but the Columbians have fixed things so I can't use you! "

I knew Andrews was right, on all scores.

" Just put the Columbians out of business," I said. " That's all that matters."

" Right! " he said, shaking my hand—after looking around to see that no one was watching. " There's one more favour I'd like to ask of you, Kennedy, if you're game. The Columbians have subpœnaed you too—how about moving out of the state witness-room and into theirs? "

This was no small favour to ask, and we both knew it. In the Columbians' state of mind, they might very well jump me, deputy or no deputy, and regardless of the consequences.

" I'll give it a whirl," I agreed, not without misgivings.

" Good! Now let me at 'em! "

Andrews went back into the court-room, and I sauntered casually into the Columbian witness-room and sat down.

The room was packed with brownshirted Columbian stalwarts and their Kluxer and wool-hat sympathizers.

For a moment they were too flabbergasted to say anything.

" Of all the goddamed nerve! " Jett finally exploded, and the whole pack let out a howl and surrounded me. The deputy who was supposed to hold them in line just leaned against the wall and chewed on a toothpick.

"What's the big idea coming in here? " Jett demanded belligerently. " Aren't you through snooping? "

" I was subpœnaed as a witness for the Columbians, so here I am," I replied with a grin. While this was going on I had backed into a corner so that if they jumped me they wouldn't be able to pull me down from behind. The semi-circle tightened in front of me, and they began to call me all the things they had been itching to say since the trial got under way.

By that time I was as mad as they were, and was determined to get off my chest some of the things I had been wanting to say to the rats ever since the day I " joined."

They asked all the usual baiting questions, and soon enough got around to the $64 one.

" Would you let your daughter marry a nigger? "

" When any two people decide they want to get married, I don't think it's anybody's business what colour they are."

" Great Gawd! " exclaimed Jett, turning to the deputy. " Did you hear that? "

" People been lynched in Georgia for saying less! " the deputy agreed.

" Would you entertain a nigger in your home? " was the next question.

" I choose my friends on the basis of character, not complexion," I replied.

" I think anybody who associates with niggers is trash! " a burly new Columbian I had never met hissed.

" I think anybody who associates with Columbians is trash! " I countered.

At that, the big boy reached into his pocket and jerked out a large switch-blade knife. Out of the corner of my eye I could see that the deputy was not going to budge. The Columbian let out a roar and lunged at me, the knife aimed at my throat. Just as I was about to try to duck, he let out a scream of anguish, dropped the knife, and bent over and grabbed his ankle. Ira Jett had given him a powerful kick in the shins!

" Goddam you, Perkins or Kennedy or whatever your name is! " Jett yelled. " I hate your guts as much as anybody! But I don't want our boys to get in trouble by cutting your throat on the fifth floor of the court-house! "

Turning to the others, he ordered:

" Pipe down, all of you! We'll take care of this guy later! "

They subsided, and I sat down on the bench, to cogitate on the irony of having my life saved for the moment by a " Brother Klansman." At the same time, I debated the relative merits of submitting to the tender mercies of Klancops by getting myself arrested at the end of the day by presenting Solicitor Andrews with my book—or taking my chances on wading into a Columbian reception committee outside. After a while I went out into the corridor to a phone booth and put in a call to my union friend Charlie Pike, at whose home I was staying.

" What are the chances of sending over an escort at the end of the day? " I asked. " The Columbians are planning to grab me as I come out of the door."

" Sure thing," he said. " How many men will it take? "

" The Columbians are here in force," I replied, " but I think half a dozen good guys could wade through them."

" O.K., we'll be there at five. . . ."

I went back to the Columbian witness-room, feeling considerably improved.

Meanwhile, the wheels of justice in the case of the State of Georgia versus the Columbians ground on. Barred from the court-room by my dual-witness status, I had to rely on reports from others as to what was going on. It was about mid-afternoon when Betty Penland's brother, Clarence, returned from a session in the witness-chair.

" Do you know what Andrews had the nerve to ask me? " he said. " —' What time was it when you was beatin' on Hines? ' I told him, ' When you're beatin' on a nigger with a blackjack, you don't stop to see what time it is! ' "

As the afternoon wore on, a deputy suddenly popped into the Columbian witness-room and bellowed:

" Stetson Kennedy is wanted in the court-room! "

I was taken aback, and wondered if Andrews had changed his mind about putting me on the stand. The deputy ushered me down the hall. The moment I stepped into the court-room a woman's voice screamed:

" *That's him!* "

It was none other than my old friend, Nettie Meredith Stewart, of the Republican Women's Study Club. She was seated in the witness-chair, all decked out in a war bonnet, and evidently enjoying herself.

The deputy marched me up in front of her, where I stood silently with arms folded.

" He's the one! " she cried. " He came into my home and told me his name was Perkins, but his real name is Kennedy and he's the author of that filthy book *Southern Exposure*! He deceived me, that's what he did! "

Solicitor Andrews arose and turned to Loomis, Sr.

" I don't know what this is all about or what it has to do with this case," he said impatiently. " This man is not my witness—if he's yours, put him on the stand! "

Old Man Loomis spluttered in confusion. He had gone to great pains to try to discredit and smear me—and Andrews had neatly turned the tables on him.

" No—no," he mumbled, wiping his brow and dismissing both Mrs. Stewart and me with a wave of his hand. As I was led out of the court-room I could see that both judge and jury had enjoyed this little drama.

By this time the day was drawing to a close. When court was finally adjourned I was glad of it. My union escort arrived, bringing along a copy of *Southern Exposure*, as I had asked them to do. Taking out my pen, I inscribed it:

> To E. E. Andrews—
>
> I trust that upon closer examination you will find it not obscene, but socially significant.

With the book in hand, I walked into the court-room where Andrews was sitting at the prosecution desk. The

news photographers were all there, their cameras cocked to
record whatever might happen.

" Solicitor, allow me to present you with a complimentary
copy of my book," I said, holding it out to him.

Andrews, his thumbs cocked in his vest pockets, leaned
back and ignored the proffered gift. Finally I let it drop on
the table in front of him. Andrews refused to look at it, much
less touch it.

" All I've got to say," he finally declared, " is that the
next time you get ready to write a book, come to me and
I'll give you another word for it! "

And that ended that.

With my union escort, I went down the elevator and out
of the front door. The Columbians and Kluxers were drawn
up in force, waiting for me. Under the circumstances, the
fact that there wasn't a cop in sight was a neutral consideration. The Columbians had several cars pulled up at the
kerb, their motors already running, with evident intent of
hustling me off. But as we ploughed into the group, they
gave way, evidently deciding that tackling half a dozen men
would make a scene that would not help their chances in
court.

Once again they had to content themselves with curses
and threats that they would " Get you yet! "

That night Solicitor Andrews telephoned me at Pike's
house.

" Kennedy, you rascal, I had half a mind to go ahead and
throw you in jail on that book proposition! " he said.
" What's the idea of putting me on the spot like that? You
ought to pay me a commission for helping to sell the damned
thing! "

" Now, solicitor, don't get your bowels in an uproar," I
consoled him, resorting to the Georgia vernacular. " How's
the trial going? "

" Well enough," he said. " We weathered the storm today, thanks to your co-operation, and I hope I can wind it
all up tomorrow."

The next day, Loomis was called to the stand. Defiant to
the last, he still wore his brown shirt with the thunderbolt

insignia. He asked for permission to make a statement. Permission was granted, and he proceeded to talk without interruption for four hours and ten minutes. I was standing in Andrews' office behind the judge's bench, listening and looking through a crack in the door. It was not the raving, ranting Loomis of the street meetings. Instead, he gave a dispassionate account of his life and views on racism and nationalism.

" America must devote every energy to arming to destroy Red Russia, even if it means letting the rest of the world starve! " he concluded.

Court was then recessed for lunch, and Andrews came in for a drink of water from the cooler in his office.

" And some people tried to say that boy wasn't dangerous! " he said, shaking his head.

After lunch when court was reconvened Andrews proceeded to make short shrift of Loomis, nailing him with piece after piece of the documentary evidence and reports I had turned in to Duke during the preceding months.

Finally, Andrews demanded bluntly:

" Do you deny that on the night of August 27th at one of your street meetings, held at Exposition Mill Village, with an audience of hundreds of people, you said over a loudspeaker system: ' We don't want anybody to join who's not ready to get out and kill niggers and Jews. . .' ? "

Loomis thought for quite a while before answering. He had no way of knowing that I was Andrews' only witness to this statement—for all he knew, Andrews might have scores of witnesses waiting to swear that he had said it.

" I guess maybe I did," he said finally.

Andrews turned to the jury.

" Gentlemen, I put it to you that the defendant's statement constitutes clear and unmistakable incitement to riot! The prosecution rests. . . ."

The jury did not take long to reach its verdict—guilty!

" In order that justice and moderation be exercised as to you," the judge said in passing sentence on Loomis, " and at the same time protection be afforded the public and society, the court is not going to be as severe as the law would authorize it to be."

Loomis was given two years on the Georgia chain-gang, six months in jail, and two additional years on probation in the event that he ever again disturbed the peace. Burke and Jett were subsequently given lighter sentences.

Unrepentant, Loomis was led away.

" Jail can't hurt me! " he proclaimed cheerfully. " Hitler wrote a book in jail that did all right. I'll call mine *Thunder in the South!* "

Burke too had some notorious last words.

" They can put me behind forty feet of granite, and I'll still shout white supremacy! "

Klansmen, Columbians, and Woolhat Boys waiting to "get" Kennedy/Perkins when he emerges from the courthouse in Atlanta. Photograph by Marion Palfi, courtesy Center for Creative Photography, University of Arizona.

CHAPTER FOURTEEN

TRI-K ROUND-UP

THE Columbian trials marked the end—or so I thought—of my days as investigator inside the Klan. So I set out on a cross-country lecture tour to tell people of the things I had seen and heard inside the Klaverns, in the hope of broadening the counter-Klan campaign.

I spoke to hundreds of meetings sponsored by labour unions, churches and synagogues, Young Men's Christian Associations, the N.A.A.C.P., Anti-Defamation League of B'nai B'rith, American Jewish Congress, progressive veterans' groups, and also lectured at the University of Chicago, Ohio State, Atlanta University, Roosevelt College, City College of New York, Antioch, Wilberforce and the New School for Social Research.

Everywhere I met with a keen interest in the menace posed by the Klan, but also a general lack of information as to the extent of its postwar comeback. Given the facts, I found people eager to block the Klan's efforts to get another stranglehold on America.

Back in Atlanta, meanwhile, the Kluxers were still sweating under the heat which the Columbian trials had generated. The Klansmen knew the day was fast approaching when they too would have to appear in court to answer the charges which Duke and I had levelled at them.

For more than a year, the pleas of Klan attorney Morgan Belser that he was sick had won postponements of the trial to take away the KKK charter (even though he appeared in court almost daily on other cases). But at last the wheels of Georgia justice, having overturned the Talmadge wool-hat putsch and smashed the Columbians, were ready to come to grips with the Klan itself.

Still, the stalling tactics of the Kluxers had not been in

vain. Although they had been unable to bring the case to trial under a Talmadge administration friendly to the KKK, at least they had managed to stave it off until Governor Arnall was out of the way—and his successor, Thompson, showed no enthusiasm for an anti-Klan fight.

Equally important, the Klan's arch-enemy, two-fisted Dan Duke, had been obliged to leave the arena. In his place, representing the state, was the relatively slight figure of Eugene Cook. Though Cook had stood up against the wool-hat putsch when he was the only anti-Talmadge official left in the Capitol, the prospect of a Talmadge comeback was very real. In fact, Talmadge's campaign manager, Roy Harris, was boasting that Talmadgism was coming back to Georgia to stay. . . .

I was in the midst of my lecture campaign when I was startled one day by a news story date-lined Atlanta and headed: " Klan Documents Disappear."

The entire file of documents which Duke and I had amassed against the Klan had disappeared during the night from the Attorney-General's office! Reporting this event, Attorney-General Cook intimated that it might have a disastrous effect upon the prosecution of the court action to revoke the Klan's charter. The Grand Dragon, needless to say, waxed indignant.

" The Klan has enough members and friends inside the Capitol to get any information we might need, without stealing it! " he said with rare candour.

It was fortunate that I had turned over to Duke only photostatic copies of the evidence—the originals were still in my hands. I promptly wired Cook that I was sending him another complete set of photostats. At the same time, I offered to return to Atlanta to assist in any way I could with the preparation and prosecution of the suit.

Cook acknowledged receipt of the new batch of documents, and asked me to stand by. . . .

But the next thing I knew, I was reading in the papers that it was all over. In an informal settlement the Klan had pleaded guilty to the charge of violating its charter by making profits, in return for which Cook dropped all of the other charges Duke and I had so carefully documented!

It was all done very quietly. Nothing could be less damaging, in the " anything-to-make-a-buck " atmosphere of America, than to plead guilty to making a profit. The other charges, which properly pressed could have really hurt the Klan in the court of public opinion, vanished into thin air.

And so the educational value of the proceedings was almost entirely lost. Instead of days of exposure of the Klan's vicious operations which could have discredited it in every nook and cranny of America, there was only the single news story reporting the court order dissolving the charter. Even this story was devoted almost entirely to Klan attorney Belser's denials of the original charges.

" This dissolution of the charter works a final, and, I hope, conclusive interment to the Klan," he said—knowing full well it did nothing of the sort. Belser was simply resorting to a traditional Ku Klux trick—whenever the Klan is hurt it tries to hide its wounds by pretending that it has had a stroke of good fortune.

Cook's letter " informing " me of Georgia's negotiated settlement with the Klan did not make me feel any better.

" Dear Stetson," he wrote. " The Ku Klux Klan charter was revoked by an order of Fulton Superior Court a few days ago. In view of the fact that the Klan had violated its charter, I decided to eliminate all counts but that one proposition. While we could have proved many of the other counts, we did not feel it would be necessary. I want you to know that I deeply appreciate your offer to assist me in the trial of the case."

There was some satisfaction, of course, in the fact that the parent body of the Klan—the one which brought about the rebirth of the Klan in 1915 and under which Ku Kluxery had flourished ever since—was no more. . . .

On the other hand, I knew the heading which appeared on most of the news stories and editorials—" Klan Outlawed "—magnified the victory. By so doing the Press was actually doing the Klan a favour, by spreading the impression that the Klan had been sentenced to death, and the sentence carried out at dawn. Nothing is more favourable to the growth of the Klan than an attitude of public indifference. . . .

Actually, the Klan still had two charters left—the Federated Klans of Alabama Inc. and the Knights of the Ku Klux Klan of Florida Inc. Both of these charters give the Klan power to set up units throughout the forty-eight states and territorial possessions of the U.S.A.

" Can't something be done to revoke those charters too? " my audiences began to ask when I resumed lecturing.

" The legal problem is exactly the same as it was in Georgia, Kentucky and New York," I replied. " The Governors of Alabama and Florida could get rid of the Klan charters in their states in the same way if they wanted to."

" Then why don't they? " a questioner asked.

" You'll have to ask them," I said. " I've gotten together with a lot of organizations to make the demands. The Governor of Florida has never even acknowledged these demands. The Governor of Alabama said he saw ' no reason to revoke the Klan's charter at this time.' A little later, when a gang of 'Bama Kluxers invaded a Girl Scout camp and broke into the bedroom of the leaders, he appointed a special prosecutor to see if something could be done about the Klan's charter. But as the *Montgomery Advertiser* pointed out, ' The Governor might get more results if he would pick a prosecutor who was not such a notorious Kluxer himself.' "

" How do you feel about publicity on the Klan? " was another frequent question put to me during my travels about the country.

" I've heard editors who advocate a hush-hush policy in dealing with hate groups say it's best to let a sleeping dog sleep," I replied. " That's well and good—provided it's the dog that's doing the sleeping. The silent treatment is good only so long as it works, and Kluxers are especially immune to it. Anytime the Klan wants to be talked about, all it has to do is stage a masked parade and cross-burning."

" But do you think the news wire services should publicize such affairs? " a questioner persisted.

" There's no doubt but what the newspapers have given the Klan millions of dollars' worth of free publicity," I agreed. " For no reason at all, the news agencies habitually report the Klan's doings as though there were all sport and no terror. Most reporters are interested only in getting out a colourful story, so they scramble a lot of words like ' eerie, awesome and impressive ' with ' Dragons, Ghouls and Terrors ' and so serve as Press agents for the Klan. In this way the irresponsible Press has undoubtedly done more to build the Klan than all the Kleagles in the country. It's no wonder the Klan hands out ' KKK Press Kards ' to encourage sympathetic reporters to attend its functions."

" But haven't you done a lot of writing about the Klan? " one questioner teased.

" Yes," I smiled, " but I don't think the Klan ever rejoiced at seeing its name in print when I put it there. Publicity and exposure are two very different things. Those reporters and editors who have exposed and attacked the Klan have done a real job of cutting the ground from under it in their communities."

" What are some of the things that can be done to combat the Klan? " my audiences always asked sooner or later.

Stressing the necessity for organized action, I told how anti-Klan campaigns in union halls, the Press and pulpit had worked in many places. Pointing out the dual role of the Klan as a means of keeping both wages and political democracy at a low ebb, I suggested that it could best be fought by a citizenry armed with a union card in one hand and a ballot in the other.

To overcome the inertia of the authorities, I urged that mass pressure be brought to bear on the Department of Justice and its District Attorneys to vigorously prosecute every Klan violation of Federal law. I also called for pressure on Senators and Congressmen for passage of an anti-lynching law.

At the same time, I recommended campaigns for passage of laws to unmask the Klan. Working with the legal departments of various organizations interested in civil liberties, I had helped draft a model statute, based on the principle that the wearing of a mask is evidence enough that the wearer intends to commit some crime. This has been upheld by the courts, which laughed off the Klan's claim that such laws discriminate against it while permitting Hallowe'en parties and masquerade balls.

" Sometimes in order to hit a man you have to be close to him," I observed. " If you have difficulty getting action out of Uncle Sam, perhaps you can get your state legislature or city council to unmask the Klan. A couple of Southern states and a dozen towns have already adopted anti-mask laws. An ounce of this kind of prevention can be worth tons of cure. If such laws could be passed all over America, the Klan would be driven out into the open where it cannot live. If we can force it to unmask, its yellow streak will prove its own undoing."

Eventually my campaign to stir up trouble for the Klan brought me to Washington, D.C., where I found myself riding in a taxi down Pennsylvania Avenue towards Capitol Hill. On the seat beside me I had my capacious briefcase, stuffed with my Klan robe and documentary evidence against the KKK. I was on my way to pay a formal though unannounced visit—attired in Klan cap and gown—to the House Committee on Un-American Activities. . . .

This was no spur-of-the-moment decision but one that had been brewing for a long time. Ever since I first joined the Klan I had been doing my utmost to get the Un-American Committee to take some notice of the KKK's un-American activities. While I had expected very little action, I had succeeded in getting none at all. Knowing the history of the cordial relations between the committee and the Klan, I was not surprised. . . .

Back in 1934, when Congressman Martin Dies of Texas was head of the committee, he invited Imperial Wizard James A. Colescott to come to Washington for a " hearing." The Wizard went, and the committee asked no embarrassing questions, but simply let him use it as a sounding-board for Klan propaganda.

Soon afterward, Congressman Dies repaid Wizard Colescott's visit by going to the Georgia Capitol to speak. One of the items I had in the briefcase beside me was a copy of the Klan's paper, *The Fiery Cross*, reporting on that event. This is what it said:

> Big, blond, straight-shootin' Mr. Dies spoke in the Klan's Imperial City of Atlanta on invitation of Elks

Lodge No. 73. More than a hundred patriotic, fraternal and civic organizations joined with the Elks in sponsoring the occasion, including the Knights of the Ku Klux Klan.

Conspicuous among the honour guests with the speaker on the platform was Imperial Wizard James A. Colescott. A dozen other national leaders of the Klan also sat on the stage. One of the latter, scanning the vast audience which heard the speaker, declared that fully half of the persons present were Klansmen and Klanswomen.

" How faithfully he followed the doctrine which the Klan had been laying down for the past twenty years," commented Imperial Wizard Colescott in an interview after the celebration. " His programme, which unquestionably is the programme of all real Americans today, so closely parallels the programme of the Klan that there is no distinguishable difference between them."

A few days later, the Klansman wired the Congressman:

> EVERY TRUE AMERICAN, AND THAT INCLUDES EVERY KLANSMAN, IS BEHIND YOU AND YOUR COMMITTEE IN ITS EFFORT TO TURN THE COUNTRY BACK TO THE HONEST, FREEDOM-LOVING, GOD-FEARING AMERICAN TO WHOM IT BELONGS.

After World War II had ended, the Un-American Committee came under the acting chairmanship of Congressman John Rankin of Mississippi. The revival of the Klan, its public outrages and inner chicaneries which I helped to expose led to a widespread popular demand that the Un-American Committee launch a real probe of the KKK.

" There's no sense sending anyone down to Georgia to investigate the Klan," Chairman Rankin argued. " If you want to know about the Klan the thing to do is call the Grand Dragon up here and have him appear before the committee."

The committee was split on the question, and when a vote was taken it was decided to drop it.

" The committee has decided that it lacks sufficient data

on which to base a probe," the committee's chief counsel Ernest Adamson announced.

" After all," Rankin observed, " the KKK is an old American institution."

" The threats and intimidations of the Klan are an old American custom, like illegal whisky-making," added Congressman John S. Wood, another committee member.

Later the committee came to be chaired by Republican J. Parnell Thomas.

"I promise the most active year of the committee's existence, let the chips fall where they may, whether on the Columbians, the Ku Klux Klan or the Communists! " he declared.

Thomas appointed a three-man " Sub-Committee on Fascism," consisting of Congressmen Wood, John McDowell (Republican, Pennsylvania) and Richard B. Vail (Republican, Illinois). The latter, incidentally, is a steel manufacturer who had been " cited " by the National Labour Relations Board for refusing to comply with an order to cease his anti-union activities.

The Sub-Committee on Fascism held one fifteen-minute session, at which the pro-fascist rabble-rouser Gerald L. K. Smith was invited to testify as an " expert against communism." After that the Sub-Committee adjourned to announce " there is no fascist threat in America."

This prompted me to address myself to the committee once more. In a letter I offered to come to Washington at my own expense and turn over to the committee trunkloads of documentary evidence of the Klan's un-American activities. Specifically I offered proof of the Klan's subversion of the 14th and 15th Amendments of the Constitution (which guarantee the civil and voting rights of Negroes), its violation of Federal election laws, and its treasonable conspiracy to interfere with the operation of other national laws.

Months passed, but the committee never even acknowledged my offer of a Klan probe on a silver platter.

It was this stone wall that made me decide to call on the Un-American Committee in person to force it to either act on the Klan or admit publicly that it had no intention of doing so. . . .

As the taxi in which I was riding sped through the grey

concrete canyons of Federal office buildings and neared
Capitol Hill, I pulled my Klan robe from my briefcase and
began to slip it on.

Suddenly the cab swerved, and almost climbed the
kerbing. Looking up at the rear-view mirror, I saw that the
driver had caught sight of my Klan robe. From the look of
terror in his eyes, he must have thought he was being taken
for a fatal ride.

" Don't get excited," I said, " I'm just going to have a
little fun with some Congressmen. You can put me out at
the side door of the House office building."

I had " cased " the building earlier in the day, and found
that while armed Capitol police were stationed at all the
regular entrances to question visitors, there was a side door
which was unguarded. It led into the basement, and there
was a stairway I could take to the second floor where the
committee had its offices.

The driver continued to watch me closely in the mirror,
and when we pulled up beside the House building he heaved
a sigh of relief.

" Here you are," I said, handing him the fare. Waiting
a moment for the sidewalk to clear, I clamped the hood
down over my face and dashed for the side door.

I made it without attracting any attention, and was glad to
find the stairway deserted. Briefcase in hand, I began to
climb. As I approached the first floor I looked carefully
down the hall to see if anyone was in sight. To the left at
the front door I could see a Capitol guard sitting at his
desk, but his back was turned to me. Hurriedly crossing the
hall, I climbed to the second floor. There were some people
in the hall, but they soon disappeared into offices. Tightening my grip on the briefcase, I strolled casually down the
hall until I came to a sign over a door which said:

Reception Room
Committee to Investigate
Un-American Activities

The door was standing wide open. Two girls inside were
busily typing, and there was a man sitting behind a desk.
Standing in the doorway, I knocked.

The girls screamed and fled from the room, but the man, who had already caught sight of me out of the corner of his eye, just sat there and arranged papers, pretending not to see me. I decided he must be trying to make up his mind what to do or say.

I walked in and stood silently in front of him.

" Hello," he finally said, with a good deal of uncertainty in his voice.

" Hello," I replied.

" What can I do for you? " he asked dubiously.

" Months ago I wrote this committee offering to give it evidence of the un-American activities of the Ku Klux Klan," I said. " Since I can't seem to get a written reply, I've come for an oral one."

" Oh yes," he said, somewhat relieved to know I was not a real Klansman. " I'll let you speak to our chief investigator, Mr. Robert Stripling. Have a seat, and I'll tell him you're here. Let's see, you're Mr. —? "

" Kennedy," I said, taking the chair he offered. " I'm sure he received my letter—I sent it by registered mail."

" Well now, Mr. Kennedy, if you'll just wait right here I'll be back in a moment," he said, and disappeared into the adjoining office, looking back nervously over his shoulder before closing the door.

I sat there, with my mask and hood still on, and waited. . . .

Minutes went by, and nothing happened. Picking up my briefcase, I opened it, adjusted the eye-slits on my mask, and began to arrange the documents inside.

After a while a number of people began to gather in the hall and peer in the doorway—but no one ventured inside.

Suddenly there was an explosion and flash. It was all I could do to maintain my composure. Then I realized a flash bulb had gone off in the doorway. The Capitol Press had evidently arrived—but was not in any hurry for close-ups until they found out whether I was dangerous.

I continued to sit there, sorting my papers and wondering what sort of reception Stripling might be arranging. Then I saw the uniforms of Capitol police, standing in the hallway with the reporters. But they too kept their distance.

At least fifteen minutes must have passed before two of

the police, one of them a sergeant, finally squared their shoulders and marched stiffly into the room.

"You'll have to come with us!" the sergeant said. I could see they were both ready to pounce if I made a false move.

"Very well," I said, "but I'd like to reassemble my papers first."

By that time the documents were spread all over my lap. The Capitol cops just stood there, looking slightly silly, while I took my time putting them all back into my briefcase. When everything was ready I stood up.

"That does it," I said.

We walked out of the room, with me in the centre and an officer at each arm. The crowd in the doorway parted to let us through, and four other Capitol police fell in behind us as we started down the hall.

"You can't do this to me—I know Mr. A-y-a-k!" I protested to the sergeant.

"Who the hell is he?" the sergeant replied, no doubt thinking Mr. Ayak must be some new power in Washington.

"He wants to *Save America*," I said.

"I don't get you," the sergeant replied abruptly.

I had been watching his face, and decided he really didn't know what it was all about.

"I was just trying out some Ku Klux passwords on you," I explained. "—Thought you might happen to be a Brother Klansman."

"Oh," he said, laughing at last. "Nothing like that— though I wouldn't be surprised if some of the city police could throw the passwords right back at you!"

"Where do we go from here?" I asked.

"Down to the guard-room. Lieutenant Marion Wilson wants to ask you some questions. Congressman Rankin gave us orders to take you away. He was there in the next room with Stripling. You'd better be glad Rankin decided not to talk to you—he packs a pistol as long as your arm, and might have lost his temper!"

A bit shaken by this information, I arrived at the guard-room, which turned out to be in the basement not far from the side door where I had entered the building.

Lieutenant Wilson was talking on the phone, but he motioned to the sergeant, who promptly frisked me to see if I were carrying any concealed weapons.

"You never know," the sergeant said to me, slightly apologetic. "Just last week we picked up a Tennessee mountaineer wandering through the halls. He was packing two pistols, and said he was gunning for the President!"

I understood then why the reporters and even the cops had been handling me with such care. Deciding the time had come for me to unmask, I pulled off my hood and wiped my brow with my handkerchief. The cops seemed relieved to be able to see who they were talking to.

Lieutenant Wilson, a clean-cut young man in his thirties, put down the telephone and turned to me.

"Got any identification?" he asked without preliminaries.

I handed him my driver's licence and social security card. He made a couple of notes, and then looked up.

"Now what's the big idea?" he asked.

I told him, and he listened carefully. Towards the end he began to smile a little. Without asking any further questions, he picked up the phone again and dialled an extension number.

"His mental assay seems to be okay," he drawled, politely informing whoever it was on the other end of the line—probably Rankin—that I appeared to be sane.

There was a long silence on the lieutenant's part, until he finally said, "Right, sir!" and hung up.

"You can go," he said, turning back to me, "but I'd advise you not to wear that thing out on the streets. The city police might not be so understanding!"

Thanking him for his consideration, I pulled off my robe, and stuffed it into my briefcase, and started through the door.

"And don't come back here in it, either!" he called after me.

Outside, I found the Capitol Press waiting eagerly to find out what manner of Klansman had come calling on the Un-American Committee, and why. I told them, and the next morning the story was spread across the country. The committee's chief investigator Stripling tried to wriggle off the hot spot by saying he would " not talk to anyone in Klan garb."

Consequently, I resolved to pay the committee a second visit before leaving the capital. This time I left my Klan robe in my hotel room, but took along my briefcase full of documents. When I knocked on the door of the reception room the two secretaries, recognizing the briefcase, half screamed but held their ground. The man at the desk seemed surprised that I had come back, but after a considerable wait I was finally shown in to see Stripling.

" Are you aware that this committee has already investigated the Ku Klux Klan, back in 1934 when Congressman Dies was chairman? " he blustered indignantly.

" Are you aware that after that so-called investigation the Klan Wizard told reporters that the programme of this committee so closely parallels that of the Klan there is no distinguishable difference between them? " I countered.

" That's a lot of crap! " Stripling snapped.

" Then how do you explain the fact that this year the committee voted not to conduct any investigation of the Klan? "

" That was the Wood Committee, and this is the Thomas Committee," Stripling declared. " We are definitely interested in information about the Klan."

" Well, I offered Thomas a trunkful of it months ago, and he's never even acknowledged the offer."

" Your communication has been referred to our Sub-Committee on Fascism," Stripling said with finality. " You will no doubt hear from its chairman, Congressman McDowell, when he returns to the Capitol."

With that, I took my leave of the Un-American Committee. . . .

The yeast I had planted began to ferment, and there was a flurry of organizational and editorial demands across the country that the Un-American Committee look into the Klan. Finally, the question was asked on the floor of the Congress as to what, if anything, the Sub-Committee on Fascism was doing.

" We have investigators working in the Deep South, in the Far West, in Texas, Chicago, Detroit and Philadelphia,"

Congressman McDowell responded. " We expect to open public hearings in about two weeks involving some pretty important people."

Ten days later, I picked up the newspapers to read that McDowell had changed his mind, and the Sub-Committee on Fascism was going out of business!

" Our investigators have tracked down all leads from every source," he said blandly, " and have found there is no evidence of any organized, active fascism in America."

Later, Chairman Thomas was clapped into a Federal prison for having forced a number of his Congressional employees to " kick back " to him certain percentages of their salaries every month. This was unfortunate in a way, for I had hoped I might be able to eventually persuade some Federal agency to ask him under oath whether he was the same Thomas who was inducted into the Klan in an abandoned house on Fair Street in Patterson, New Jersey, during 1925. A man named Talbot says he saw a certain Thomas pay the Klectoken fee, another fellow named Ralph says he was initiated on the same night, and two other witnesses named Roy and Arch could tell plenty if called upon to do so under oath.

The House Un-American Committee, though somewhat eclipsed by Senator McCarthy's Permanent Investigating Committee, is still witch-hunting its way into everything from college campuses to church pulpits. But it has never yet stuck its head into a Klan Klavern.

Sometime after my unmasking of the pro-Klan Un-American Committee in the nation's capital, it became necessary for me to revisit the capital of the Invisible Empire, Atlanta. In preparation for this foray back into Klan territory, there was not much I could do except grow a beard and buy some dark glasses.

By this time Hummon Talmadge had, by demagoguery as adept as his father's, and with the backing of the textile and Coca-Cola empires, reclaimed the Governor's seat in Georgia. One of the first acts of his administration was to re-issue the Klan a corporate charter as a tax-exempt charitable order, with jurisdiction in all forty-eight states! Judge

T. Hicks Fort, in approving the charter under the name of " Original Southern Klans, Inc.," said he " could find no evidence of illegal intent."

Upon arriving in Atlanta I learned that Sam Roper—who had taken over as Imperial Wizard after Sam Green passed on " from the Invisible Empire to the Empire Invisible," as the Klan says—had opened up new offices. The new Klan headquarters, I was told, was in the West End neighbourhood, near Wingo's Café, where the Klavaliers had held their final Klonvokation. For some reason I felt a strong urge to inspect the new headquarters. . . .

Taking a cab to West End, I climbed out a few blocks from the address of the new Klan headquarters. Approaching from the opposite side of the street, I found it to be located in a rather dingy office building. Crossing the street at the corner, I walked back and examined the entrance.

A number of shingles were hanging there, including that of a portrait photographer, a real estate concern, and one which said simply " S. W. Roper, A.G.K."! The initials I of course recognized as standing for " Association of Georgia Klans." His office was on the second floor, together with a number of others. After a moment's hesitation, my curiosity got the better of me, and I began to climb the stairs.

As I neared the second floor I suddenly heard the Wizard's familiar voice. I paused a moment, listening, until it became apparent that he was dictating a letter. Sticking my head cautiously over the banister, I saw that the door to his office, at the head of the stairs, was closed.

Continuing my ascent, I entered the hallway, and almost fell over a large overflowing waste-basket.

Could it be the Wizard's? Would he be so careless?

I had been out of the Klaverns for some time, and he was probably feeling pretty secure, I thought. Lifting my dark glasses, I glanced at the contents of the basket. My eye promptly focused on the red letterhead emblem of the Wizard's office! Remembering how well my salvaging of the Columbians' waste paper had panned out, I suddenly wanted very much to lay hands on the Wizard's waste-basket.

But how?

I was hardly dressed to pose as a janitor. If the Wizard were to pop out of his office at the wrong moment, my goose would be burnt to a crisp. I had no desire to tangle with the 200-pound ex-cop.

There was also the problem of transportation. I wanted the contents, not the basket itself. But I had nothing to put the stuff in, and there was a lot of it.

I walked on down the hall, looking at the various offices. At the end of the hall I came to a door marked " Toilet." I went in. It was a small, single-unit affair. But there was a lock on the door. I tried the lock and it worked. Maybe I could get as far as this room with the waste-basket, stuff the contents into my overcoat, and make a get-away!

But there was still the question of what, if anything, I could say to the Wizard if he or his secretary were to step out and catch me in the act of carting off his waste-basket to the men's room. On the long chance that he might not recognize me, I wondered what explanation I could give him. Finally I had it . . . I tossed the roll of toilet paper out of the window. . . .

Unfortunately the Wizard's office was at one end of the hall by the stairway, while the toilet was at the other. After first peering out to see that the hall was still clear, I went out to look for a rear exit or fire escape. There was none.

Wandering back to the waste-basket, I could hear Roper still dictating—

" Now, Brother Kligrapp, you know perfectly well I cannot run the Imperial Palace unless each and every Klavern promptly sends in its dues every month . . ." he was saying.

If he was sending out collection letters, he might be at it for some time, I thought, remembering the 159 Klaverns in Georgia alone. But would the contents of the waste-basket prove to be worth the risk? Reaching out quickly, I pulled a handful of papers from the top of the basket and stuffed them into my overcoat.

Safely locked in the toilet once more, I pulled out the sample and had a look at it.

The very first item turned out to be a piece of a bank statement that had been torn in half, from the West End branch of the National Bank. It was the top half, and was for the account of the " Death Benefit Association " of the KKK. If I could just lay hands on the other half of that statement, I would have something concrete to lay before the U.S. Treasury Department in demanding that it pounce on the Klan's assets to satisfy that unpaid tax lien!

Examining the other papers, I found bits of letters addressed to the treasurers of various Klaverns, referring to their financial status. That, too, I thought, should certainly interest the T-men. If they knew who handled the purse-strings of the local groups, and had these letters to prove it, they should be able to pin down the records and accounts of a lot of Klaverns!

I knew then that I had to go through with the salvage operation. Going back to the basket, I listened once more. Roper was still at it. Taking a double breath, I picked up the basket and holding it in front of me walked casually but quickly towards the toilet.

When I was still some twenty feet away, a man popped out of the real estate office. I could see by his air that he worked there, and was not a customer. Seeing me with the basket, he stopped and stared.

" Ain't no corncobs nor paper in the toilet," I snickered in my best Georgia boy accent.

" That's funny," he said, with a puzzled look. " There was plenty of paper in there this morning. Somebody must have swiped it to wipe their noses with."

But he disappeared down the stairs, and I disappeared into the toilet and hurriedly locked the door behind me.

Without taking time to inspect anything, I began stuffing the paper into my pockets. My overcoat pockets were soon filled. Next, I stuffed the pockets of my suit coat under-neath. This only half emptied the basket. I filled my trouser pockets. Still more to go! Taking the larger flat sheets, I loosened my belt and shoved them inside my undershorts. Just as I was scraping the last few papers from the bottom of the basket, I heard footsteps coming down the hall.

I had heard that ponderous tread many times before in Klan initiations—the Wizard was coming!

Had he noticed that his waste-basket was missing? Was I trapped?

The tread came to a halt in front of the door, and the knob turned. Then he shook the door to make sure it was locked. The next few seconds would tell, and I held my breath—thinking how appropriate it was to be trapped in a toilet.

But then I heard the Wizard's steps retreating down the hall. If he had not already missed his basket, would he not miss it on the way back to his office? If so, he might either return, or simply lie in wait to see who came out. . . .

I waited a few more minutes. Nothing happened.

Should I try to put the basket back in its place? If I didn't, the Wizard would in a matter of minutes find it in the toilet and plunge into hot pursuit. On the other hand, if he were already lying in wait and caught me with it, my chances of getting away would be very slim indeed.

I looked down at myself. The bulging papers made me look pregnant in all directions—like " Mr. Five-by-Five," as the song says.

I decided to leave the basket and make a dash for it.

Turning the lock silently, I cracked the door and peered down the hallway. It was deserted, and the door to the Wizard's office was closed.

I opened the door and started for the stairway. I decided that if the Wizard came out I would let his face tell me whether to continue walking or start running.

Just as I reached the head of the stairs, the Wizard's door did open suddenly. But instead of the Wizard, out came a good-looking blonde, at least six feet tall. I had thrust both my hands into my overcoat pockets and was holding the coat out like a tent to hide the bulges. The big blonde stared at me so curiously she failed to notice the waste-basket was missing. I could hear her footsteps continuing down the hall toward the toilet.

The moment the stair hid me from her sight, I began to sprint, expecting to hear her scream at any second when she stumbled on the empty basket. On the street, I looked hurriedly about for a taxicab. There was none in sight!

Ducking around the nearest corner, I continued to

search for a cab. Still no luck! After turning three corners, looking back over my shoulder all the while, I finally climbed aboard a trolley. While I knew this might not prove entirely safe, it was better than walking my way out of the neighbourhood.

With each block that went by I relaxed a bit more. When we finally passed a cab stand, I got out and boarded one.

" The Jefferson," I said to the driver.

But I had no sooner settled back than it occurred to me that the Wizard just might put in a riot call to Chief Ass-Tearer Carter, who might in turn get out a Fiery Summons through the taxi radio station for all cab-drivers to be on the lookout for me.

I studied the driver's face, and was glad I couldn't remember having ever seen him at a Klan meeting. But I knew the odds were ninety-nine to one that he belonged to the tribe. If it came to a showdown, I knew my best chance would be to leap from the cab the first time it slowed down or stopped for a traffic light—I didn't want to be delivered at full speed into Carter's ham-like hands. Each time the radio clicked on my heart echoed, but after about a twenty-minute ride I arrived safely at the hotel.

In my room I bolted the door, emptied my pockets on the floor, and got down on my hands and knees to examine my haul.

First, I went after anything that looked like figures or financial statements. I not only found the other half of the piece I had first plucked from the basket, but three more besides!

They showed some very interesting things, giving the fictitious names in which the Klan accounts were kept, the account numbers, the bank branches, the amount on hand and other such data. There was even one big sheet on which Roper had toted up some of his balances—and noted that certain sums had been taken out of Klan accounts and put into other accounts!

Next, I tackled the letters. There were a good many copies of originals which the Wizard had for some reason or another decided to write over. Then there were—torn up but still readily pieced together—dozens of letters from

Klan officials throughout the country. And finally, there were several scores of envelopes, bearing return names and addresses of Klansmen who had mailed in their $1 assessments for the Klan's Death Benefit Association. Some of these had little notes of transmittal, while others, according to an old Southern custom, had " $1 " written on the flap of the envelope.

Armed with such documents, there was no reason why the T-men could not launch a major round-up of the Klan's financial resources!

Should I take it to Collector of Internal Revenue Allen in Atlanta, or directly to the Treasury Department officials in Washington?

I decided this was too big an opportunity to strike a mortal blow at the Klan to take any chances. I called the airport and reserved space to Washington that afternoon— under the name of Lester Harrington.

I spent the rest of the day before plane time piecing together the bits of paper with Scotch tape and paste. When I had finished, I had a real stack of dynamite.

At the airport I decided it might be a good idea to put in a call to Collector Allen. I didn't want to alienate him any more than necessary, and at the same time I wanted to be able to tell his Washington superiors that I had not gone over his head without letting him in on things.

I waited until they made the first call for plane loading, and then put in the call.

" Mr. Allen," I said, and gave my name. " You may recall that I have been in touch with you a number of times in recent years about the possibility of collecting on the tax lien outstanding against the Ku Klux Klan? "

" Oh yes, Mr. Kennedy—what's on your mind now? "

" The same thing," I said. " I've just come into possession of some very interesting documents that have been salvaged from Wizard Roper's waste-basket—"

As I talked, I could hear two men whispering at the other end of the line. One of them was Allen—and the other was Roper!

" What a coincidence," I said. " Mr. Roper is there with you now—"

"Well, er, ah, yes, he is," Allen replied. "We were just going over the question of the Klan's taxes. You will bring these documents you say you have to me?"

"It so happens I have to leave for the North immediately," I said. "But I must stop off in Washington—and I thought I would turn the documents over to the Revenue Bureau there, and let them forward copies back to you."

"Ah, yes, hmmm. . . . Well, I will look forward to receiving them. Thank you very much for calling."

The next morning I was closeted with Internal Revenue Commissioner George J. Schoeneman, and spread everything I had on the table before him.

"I think we've got the goods on them at last," I said. "They can't very well pretend to be inoperative or broke on the basis of these bank statements and letters."

Schoeneman called in a number of his assistants, who pored over the documents.

The director of criminal prosecutions seemed especially impressed.

"These are of very great interest," he said. "You are giving them to us?"

"I would like to retain the originals for my personal files," I said, remembering how Klan documents had disappeared from official files in the past. "But you're welcome to make copies."

"Splendid! We'll make two sets of copies—one for our legal department here and the other for Collector Allen in Atlanta."

Then began another one of those waiting periods in which I felt as if I had lit a bomb with a long fuse. . . .

When several months had passed, I could contain my impatience no longer, and so sat down and wrote Collector Allen.

"How about it?" I asked in effect.

"The data which you submitted to the Bureau of Internal Revenue in Washington were duly forwarded to me," he wrote in reply. "Since it has to do with this year's financial activities of the Klan, you may be sure that next year when the taxes for this year are computed, these data will be taken into consideration."

This was simply not true. I wrote again to Allen, pointing out that the bank balances shown had been accumulated through the years, and furthermore could and should be confiscated in partial satisfaction of the $685,305.08 lien already outstanding against the Klan.

But the collector did not reply. Neither did he collect, that year nor in any of the years which have followed.

(An interesting sequel to the efforts to make the KKK cough up what it owes the U.S.A. came sometime later, when former Revenue Commissioner Nunan was haled before a House Committee investigating tax scandals. Nunan was asked to explain how it was that four giant corporations he had represented as legal counsel since stepping down from his post as commissioner had not been required to pay a single dime of two million dollars they had been assessed in taxes. Another Nunan client who owed the Government $812,000 was allowed to settle for $4,500—and then he was sent a $35,000 refund!)

It is a sad fact that the one man who can with one word to the Klan put it out of business for all time has refused to speak. That man is Uncle Sam, and the word is:

" Remit! "

I had bowed out of the Klan feeling certain I had accumulated more than enough evidence for the authorities to crush it. But the repeated refusal of public officials on every level to act on the evidence gave the Klan a new lease on life.

Secure in the knowledge that I could no longer penetrate their Klaverns—and that the authorities would probably not prosecute even if someone took my place—the Klansmen who had been scared away by the years of exposure returned to the fold. New membership drives were launched at cut rates, and the Klavalier Klub resumed operations as the " Black Raiders " and " White Circle," unleashing a new reign of terror. . . .

I couldn't help feeling disappointed and disillusioned by this turning of the tide. At the same time, I knew that the struggle against the Klan had not been in vain. By passing inside information on the Klan to democratic forces, I had provided the ammunition which enabled them to hold the

Klan's postwar growth to a small fraction of what it otherwise might have been. Instead of roping in nearly nine million members in all forty-eight states as it had after the first world war, the Klan had been held down to a few hundred thousand in twenty-seven states.

But, thanks to the refusal of the authorities to act more vigorously, the struggle against the Klan would have to go on. . . .

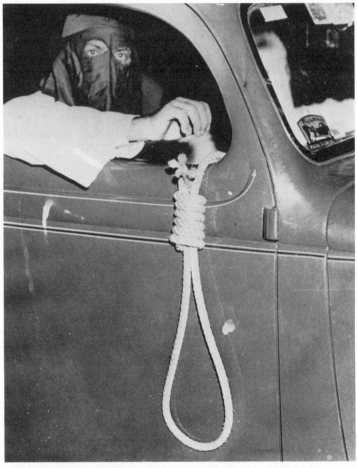

The Klan staged a parade through the black section of Miami on the eve of the primary election in 1939 warning voters to stay away from the polls. Photograph courtesy UPI/Bettman Newsphotos.

CHAPTER FIFTEEN

MEETING IN MACON

" Hello—New York? Atlanta calling . . ."

" Yes, go ahead," I said. " Hi, Bob. What's up? "

Some months had passed, and I had resumed my lecturing in the New York area. Meanwhile, I had succeeded in finding someone to take my place inside the Klan, and I knew a call from Atlanta could only mean that the Klan was planning something devilish. Of course " Bob " was not the real name of my pipeline into the Klaverns. He called me " Bill " over the telephone for the same " security " reason—to avoid the prying ears of Georgia switchboard operators who might recognize the " notorious " name of Stetson Kennedy and relay our conversation to the Dragon.

" I've just come from church," Bob said, " and the deacons have announced a big shindig to be held in Macon next Monday night. The call is going out to the brethren all over the country. They're going to have a parade with all the trimmings, and then a big ceremony in the city auditorium."

When Bob said " all the trimmings," I knew he meant the Klan was going to march with masks and burn fiery crosses.

" Has the city given them permission to parade and use the auditorium? " I asked.

" Both," he answered. " You remember how that Macon church was founded, with Police Chief Bowers as head man. Practically all the city officials have got religion, if you know what I mean! The whole idea back of this show they're planning is to put a damper on the union organizing campaign out at the textile mill."

" Well, maybe something can be done to put a damper on the brethren instead," I said. " Are you going to be able to cover the affair? "

" I don't think so," Bob replied. " My wife's sick in bed."

" I just might be able to cover it myself, in that case. Maybe one of the newspapers will send me down."

" In your church garb? "

" Sure."

" I dunno," Bob said dubiously. " The brethren are still hot on your trail. The ' Bishop ' has sent some picture of you all over the place, and if they got a good look at you it would be too bad. . . ."

" I've taken worse chances than that," I said. " And I think this is worth doing! Thanks for calling, and if anything else turns up, let me know."

I lost no time sending the tip-off on the meeting to some real church leaders I knew in Macon, Georgia. Acting on it, and with the co-operation of one of the local newspapers, they generated so much steam that the city fathers had to cancel the Klan's permit to parade. But the Klan had a written contract for the rental of the auditorium, and the city council refused to cancel it, saying they were afraid the city might be sued for damages.

When I spoke to the editors of the *New York Post* about covering the meeting in my robe " from the inside," they enthusiastically agreed to fly me down. I sent my robe out to be laundered—but it came right back with the message that I could wash my own dirty linen! I had to go out myself and explain to the manager of the laundry, who was a Catholic, and his workers, who were Negro, what I was up to.

I also took my automatic out of mothballs, and gave it a good going over. Since my " pistol toter's permit " was good only in the State of Georgia, I packed the automatic and shoulder holster into my briefcase. About ten o'clock Monday morning I boarded a plane for Macon. On the passenger list my name appeared as " Will Jenkins."

Around noon the *New York Post* hit the stands with a big story, with photograph of their special correspondent Kennedy who was flying down to Macon with robe and mask to cover the Klan Klonvocation that night.

My plane was due to arrive in Macon at four-fifteen in the afternoon.

It was about three-thirty when my wife in New York got an urgent call from Atlanta.

" Is it true that Bill is flying down to Macon to cover the Klonvocation tonight? " Bob asked, so excited he forgot to use any sort of code.

" That's right," my wife replied. " He ought to be landing in about forty-five minutes."

" You'd better do something quick! " Bob said. " Some loyal Kluxer up there in New York read in the paper about Kennedy's coming, and phoned Dragon Green down here at the Imperial Palace! He's already ordered a squad of Klavaliers to meet the plane! And they're Macon boys, so Kennedy won't recognize them! "

" What can I do? " my wife asked weakly.

" I'll be dadblamed if I know," Bob answered. " It's a cinch the Macon cops won't be much help. What was the idea tipping off the Klan anyway? "

" We didn't know the *Post* was going to print an advance story," she said. " How about the labour unions—anybody we know in Macon? "

" Say, that's an idea," Bob said. " Starnes is stationed there now! You ought to be able to reach him by telephone. . . ."

" Thanks—and goodbye! I don't want to lose a minute! "

" Hold on," Bob said, " my wife is up and about now, and I thought I'd jump into my car and go to Macon after all. I can't get there before Bill lands, but maybe I can do some good. . . ."

" O.K., good luck! "

On the plane, I was of course blissfully ignorant of all this.

But the moment the plane touched the ground at Macon airport, I spotted a group of five men whose looks I didn't like. As I walked into the station, I could feel their squint-eyes boring into me. The only other passenger to alight at Macon was a woman, and she was met and whisked away by her family. I looked around for a cab. There was none in sight. The airport is several miles out of town.

" What can I do about transportation into Macon? " I asked the man behind the desk.

"Doesn't seem to be any right now," he said unconcernedly.

The five men, meanwhile, were standing at the other end of the station, talking in low tones among themselves and watching me. I decided I had better get ready for trouble, just in case. Ducking into the men's room, I locked myself in a toilet compartment and got into my shoulder holster. The snug feel of the automatic under my armpit was reassuring, but I still didn't like the odds.

I walked outside the station and stood in the roadway, and the five men followed. There was only one car on hand. One of the men got into the driver's seat. I kept my distance, and they stood about uncertainly.

"Want a lift into town?" one of them called out with a show of friendliness.

"No, thanks—I'm expecting some friends to pick me up," I said, wondering how the devil I was going to turn up any friends in that isolated spot.

"Maybe they couldn't make it," the man said. "We're going right in—be glad to take you."

"Much obliged," I answered, "but I'm sure they'll show up any minute now."

"You could leave word at the desk that you'd already gone in," the man insisted. "That way there wouldn't be no mix-up if they do come, and if they don't come you won't be stranded. Won't be no taxi until plane time tonight, neither."

While he talked, several of the other men approached. No one else was in sight. I slipped my hand beneath my coat to the automatic as though I were fumbling for cigarettes in my shirt pocket. I had often wondered what I could do in such a spot if the brethren were to throw a gun on me and order me into a car. I had long ago decided that my chances, if any, were somewhat better out in the open, on the street—that I would make them get me the hard way. Now that the time had come to put this principle into practice, it still seemed a good idea. There was no longer any doubt in my mind that I was up against a Klan reception committee.

"Well, whadaya say?" the man asked impatiently.

Two of the approaching men had their hands in their coat pockets—for all I knew on pistols of their own. But when they saw me reach inside my coat, they stopped in their tracks. It was a question as to who would make the first move.

Even if the odds had been better, I wanted to avoid gunplay if at all possible. On their part, they seemed determined to take me with them. If there were shooting, I could visualize the Kluxers in court testifying in one voice that I had tried to rob them at gun point.

Just then a cloud of dust came roaring into the airport!

Another contingent of Klavaliers, I thought. Now I'm done for!

Out of the dust rolled a station wagon, and three men tumbled out and surrounded me.

" Whadaya say, you ole son of a gun! " a familiar voice boomed out. It was Starnes, slapping me on the back and glaring at the Klavaliers. " Your wife just called about seven minutes ago and said you were coming in. We got here as fast as we could. Climb in! "

The Klavaliers climbed into their car too, and followed close behind.

" Looks like the yellow dogs are trailing us," Starnes said. " I recognize two of them—dirty scabs, been giving us hell out at the textile mill. But I don't think they have guts enough to tackle us."

" Slow down," said a union brother on the back seat. " I'd like nothing better than to tangle with them."

Starnes slowed, but so did the Klavaliers. Evidently they didn't like the more equal odds.

" Probably they're just trying to find out where I'm going to be staying, and will try to pick me up later," I said.

" Then we'll have to shake them," Starnes said. " Just watch me! I'm practically the dirt-track champion of Georgia from shaking all kinds of union-busting thugs! "

We careened off into a clay road, with the Klavaliers in hot pursuit. The choking, blinding dustcloud our car kicked up would alone have thrown most pursuers off the track, but the Klavaliers, accustomed to it, came on. Our speedometer climbed around ninety.

" I don't know," I ventured. " Maybe I would be safer with the Klavaliers."

" They are kind of stubborn," Starnes admitted. " But I know how to fix them! "

We screeched out of the dirt trail on to an unpaved but gravelled road, wide and straight. Starnes glanced from his speedometer to the distance between us and the Klavaliers. We were doing about fifty when he suddenly twisted the steering wheel, throwing the car into a counter-clockwise skid in the middle of the road. As the nose of the car came back into line with the road—but in the opposite direction to which we had been going—Starnes suddenly stamped on the accelerator, bringing the car out of its skid, and speeded head on towards the oncoming Klavaliers! Just when it seemed that a collision was unavoidable, the Klavalier at the wheel lost his nerve and took to the woods. Their car crashed into the underbrush, while we zoomed on our way.

" That's mighty rough treatment," I gasped, wiping my brow.

" I knew the yellow bastards would turn chicken," Starnes said. " They're only tough when they know they're not going to get hurt."

" I was going to check into some hotel, but I'm not so sure those guys won't find me," I said.

" Don't worry—we'll put you up at Brother Paul Harding's here," Starnes offered.

" Sounds good to me," I said. " Now tell me about this phone call you said you got from my wife. I didn't even know you were in Macon."

" Seems like the paper you're writing for busted out in print ahead of schedule and somebody up in New York phoned Klan headquarters in Atlanta that you were on the way down," Starnes said. " Then the fellow you call Bob got wind of it, and phoned your wife in New York, and she phoned me," Starnes went on. " I didn't talk to her long—there wasn't much time left."

" I was never so glad to see anybody," I said.

" Oh, and Bob said to tell you he's going to try to cover the meeting too."

" Good. How does this Klan clambake seem to be shaping up? "

" The town's lousy with Ku Klux," Starnes said. " Licence plates from all over the South, and some from outside the South too."

" If any of our union brothers want to help out, I wish they'd take down the licence numbers of any Klan cars at the auditorium tonight," I said.

" How can we be sure they're Klan cars? " asked Harding.

" Some of the Ku Klux put on their robes before they get out of their cars, and some will wait until they get inside the auditorium," I said. " Those who wait will be carrying their robes in little satchels or wrapped up in paper."

I went home with Harding and hung out my robe in preparation for the meeting. At the appointed hour, Starnes came by and drove me to the auditorium. We found a deserted alley where I put on my robe and let down my mask. I walked alone to the auditorium entrance. Outside there were a group of Mercer College students, a stack of leaflets in their hands, talking to a police captain.

I picked up one of the leaflets. It was a vigorous attack on Ku Kluxery and bigotry.

" Why can't we hand them out? " one of the students was asking the police captain. " I thought we had freedom of speech and Press in America."

" It's not a question of that," the captain said with a smirk. " You're creating a fire hazard, which is contrary to City Ordinance 8597. . . ."

I walked on up the steps. Here Klansmen in robes were busily handing out a full line of KKK hate propaganda and membership application blanks among the spectators standing around. The police made no effort to stop them.

At the doors, robed and masked Klavaliers stood guard. Atop the auditorium, perched on the roof, I could see other Klavalier guards, their robes flapping in the wind. What a spectacle, I thought—the public barred from an auditorium built by tax money and dedicated to the public welfare! This is the way it must look when storm troopers stage a putsch and take over public buildings and the halls of government. I wondered if I might be getting a preview of an American-style putsch.

I marched on in, feeling safe behind my mask from the prying eyes of the Klavaliers. There were several thousand Klansmen on hand, including women and children. Even the kids were decked out in full Klan regalia, with hoods and masks. The Kluxers, like the Nazis, lose no time regimenting and indoctrinating their children.

I kept wandering around in the alcoves, hoping to come across my friend Bob before he put on a robe, so I could thank him for probably saving my life. It was not until some time later that I learned that Bob was outside at the time— probably saving my life again!

He bumped into Starnes standing on the sidewalk, who was trying to spot union-busters as they entered.

" Where's Kennedy? " Bob asked breathlessly.

" Just went in," Starnes replied.

" Oh, my Gawd! " said Bob. " We've got to get him out! "

" What's the trouble? "

" The Dragon has set a trap for him! In ten minutes the Klavaliers are going to lock all the doors—and the Dragon is going to order everyone inside to unmask! As soon as a Klavalier spots Kennedy he's to whistle—and all the Klavaliers will grab him and take him for a ride! "

" But how in hell are you going to find him? It's worse than looking for a needle in a haystack! "

" I know, but I've got to try," Bob said, and dashed into the auditorium. By this time the ceremonies were under way, and everyone was masked. Bob reluctantly lowered his visor, thinking his search was hopeless.

The first I knew of all this was when I heard Bob's familiar voice from somewhere behind me whispering, " Hey, Bill! " It took me a minute to locate him. He was wandering aimlessly among the Terrors and Ghouls on the sidelines repeating " Hey, Bill! " every few feet.

" Whadaya say, Bob? " I asked.

" Is that you, Bill? " he whispered. " I've found so many wrong ' Bills '! You've got to get out of here quick! "

" What's wrong? "

" Any minute now the Dragon is going to order the doors locked, and make everybody unmask! "

" Jehoshaphat! Let's get a move on! "

" You better head for the door alone, and if a Klavalier tries to stop you, make like you've got to vomit or something! "

" Okay . . . here I go! "

I started for a door, as fast as I could without attracting too much attention. Not one, but two Klavaliers were guarding it.

. I began to sway drunkenly. They peered intently into the eye-slits of my mask, trying to see more of my face.

" Too much rot-gut liquor," I belched, stumbling between them. They looked at each other, while I swayed uncertainly, as though I were about to pass out and roll down the stairs.

" Pass, Klansman," one of them finally said.

I stumbled on out into the night, really feeling groggy.

Back in the alley, I got out of my robe and hid it in Starnes' car. By now I had decided I had better keep some distance away from the auditorium. I circled it from across the street, taking down out-of-state licence numbers as I went. I always made these numbers available to both local and Federal authorities, as well as to various organizations concerned with the defence of civil rights. Sometimes the numbers proved very useful.

The Mercer College students were still standing about dejectedly.

" There ought to be some way to let the world know that most of the people of Macon are against the Klan," I heard one of them say.

The remark gave me an idea, and I went up and introduced myself.

" I have my Klan robe over here," I said, " and while I sort of hate to have to fight fire with fire, it might be a good idea to stuff it and string it up in effigy."

" That's an idea! " one of them said. " We could put a placard on it saying something like ' No Kluxers Wanted Here.' "

" I'm for it," another said. " I've got a rope at my house, not far from here."

" I can go turn out the placard and bring some rags for stuffing," another volunteered.

Off they went, and in about twenty minutes we were all reassembled in the alley.

" They don't teach us how to tie lynch-knots at Mercer," the lad with the rope laughed. " I guess I'll have to improvise something."

Meanwhile, I carefully removed the embroidered " Mystic Insignia of a Klansman " from the front of the robe, knowing this to be the most expensive part of it. It would come in handy for future use.

" What about stringing it up to a lamp-post? " a student asked.

I looked at the Klavaliers posted atop the auditorium.

" We might be able to swing it and make a getaway before those guys could get down to the street," I said. " But that's not our only worry. I know the habits of the Klavaliers, and its a cinch they've got some plain-clothed guys in that crowd standing out in front."

" What do you think we ought to do? " the student asked.

I looked around the square. Directly across from the auditorium the Young Men's Christian Association had a three-story building.

" Help me roll this thing up in a bundle so it'll look like I'm travelling, and I'll go see if I can get a room at the Y.M.C.A.," I said. " I'll try to hang it out a window," I explained. " It shouldn't embarrass the Y, since it's for a good cause."

We wrapped the rope, stuffing and placard into the robe, and I marched into the Y with it. They had one room left, and I handed them a dollar for it. On the way up I said to the Negro man who ran the elevator:

" Isn't that the damndest monkeyshines going on across the street? "

" Some white folks does some funny things," he said with a surprised grin.

My room, unfortunately, didn't look out over the square in front of the auditorium.

" Where's the toilet? " I asked the porter who had just brought me up in the elevator.

He led me down the hall. The lavatory window was just what I needed!

As soon as he had gone I hurried to my room and brought the bundle into the lavatory. There was no lock on the door, so I had to take my chances on someone—possibly a Klansman—coming in.

Quickly I lowered the effigy out the window, and tied the end of the rope to a towel rod. A murmur like far-off thunder rose from the crowds on the street. I sped through the hall to a fire escape at the rear, down into an alley and on to the street.

Already the Klavaliers posted atop the auditorium had spotted the effigy, and were on their way down, shouting curses. News photographers had discovered it too, and were banging away with flash-bulbs. Traffic was jamming as drivers stopped for a look, and the crowd craned their heads back and pointed to the swinging " Klansman." I lost myself in the crowd, and watched the Klavaliers as they debated what to do. One of them clambered up on a ledge, and by stretching was barely able to touch the hem of the robe with his fingers.

But just as he braced himself to lunge at it, the effigy began to rise slowly through the air! I looked up, and saw a large black hand hauling away at the rope—my friend of the elevator! Then the rope was fastened, and the effigy hung high, well out of reach.

The Klavaliers had seen the black hand too. With an oath, one of them ran into the Y.M.C.A. and up the stairs, four steps at a time.

I began to wonder what might happen to the Negro, and to wish I had never thought of the effigy idea.

But after about five minutes the Klavalier was back, crestfallen.

" I couldn't find hide nor hair of the black rascal! " he said. " The door to the toilet is locked, and the manager swears he doesn't know anything about it."

" I hate to let the black bastard get away! " another Klavalier said.

" I can't believe he cooked up the idea," the first Klavalier said. " Some nigger-loving sonovabitch put him up to it! That looks like a real Klan robe all right—I bet this is some more of that rat Kennedy's doings! "

" We've got to get the damned thing down. If the Dragon sees it he'll let out a roar that can be heard from here to Atlanta, and skin us alive! "

" If you climb up on my shoulders I think you can reach it."

Amid the jeers of the audience, the Klavalier climbed atop his companion and gave a heave. The two Klavaliers fell in a heap in the shrubbery, with the Klan effigy— decapitated by the pull—falling in a heap on top of them. The crowd roared with laughter. Red-faced, the Klavaliers tossed the effigy into the back seat of an auto, and sped off into the night.

I never saw my white Klan robe again (though I was soon to acquire the embroidered green satin robe of a Kleagle) except as it appeared in the photos on the front pages of newspapers all over the country the next morning. Instead of merely reporting on the big Klan demonstration, the news stories led off with the story of the Klansman hanged in effigy and the anti-Klan protest of the church-people and college students of Macon.

We had stolen the show, and the Klux were as mad as wet hornets.

The last time the author saw his Klan robe was when he hung it in effigy from a window in the Macon, Georgia, YMCA across the street from the auditorium where the Klan was holding a klonvokation. He barely got away via the fire escape.

CHAPTER SIXTEEN

TERROR IN MIAMI

BY this time I was beginning to experience more than a little battle fatigue from my struggles against the Klan. Although I was tempted to settle in some quiet New England country-side, far from the marauding Kluxers, I chose instead to go back down South and settle in the heart of the Klan's Invisible Empire. My father had died, leaving me a small tract of land at Switzerland, Florida, about eighteen miles south of Jacksonville. The population of the hamlet of Switzerland is approximately eighty-seven, and my piece of land, which embraces a small lake, lies on the outskirts, with no neighbours within shouting distance. My wife and I came in like pioneers and began to clear the land and make a home. We decided to call the place Beluthahatchee—a Seminole Indian name meaning Happy Hunting Ground, or Never-Never Land.

One evening as I was smoking my pipe and hoping I would never, never tangle with the Klan again (I had established a new identity in the neighbourhood as " Bill Kennedy "), my radio, which had been presenting Pee Wee Jenkins and his Border Riders in a rendition of that popular ballad " Wham, bam—thank you M'am; and I hope you're satisfied! " suddenly broke off.

" We interrupt our programme to bring you a special news bulletin from Miami! " the announcer of the nearby Jacksonville radio station said. " A dynamite blast of block-buster proportions has just demolished a sixteen-unit apart-ment building in the Carver Village Housing Project for Negroes. The prospective occupants had not yet moved in, so there were no casualties. Police said the blast, which shattered windows and jolted persons from their beds within a radius of fifty blocks, was the most powerful ever detonated in the Miami area. It was caused by two 100-pound bundles of dynamite. A third bomb, consisting of eighty sticks of dynamite tied together, failed to explode. Police Chief Walter Headley said he does not think the Ku Klux Klan is involved in any way, and adds that he has reason to believe that Reds are responsible. One Negro has been arrested."

" Here I go again! " I called to my wife.

She knew I wasn't kidding, and without a word began to pack a valise and my automatic. . . .

On the way south by bus I had much to think about. There were a bunch of tough babies running the Miami Klan, and I knew I would have a tough time pinning anything on them. While I was too thoroughly exposed to stick my neck into a Klavern, I planned to hang around Klan-infested bars and, by posing as a Georgia Kluxer on vacation, try to get some leads on the bombing. Besides, if the brethren were to do any masked demonstrating, I thought it would be safe enough to join in.

As the bus rolled southward along the palm-draped Indian River it was difficult to think of such things as bombings and Ku Kluxery, but when we finally reached the Miami city limits I recognized with a jolt the vacant lot where, some years earlier, a large billboard had blossomed with the legend:

WELCOME TO MIAMI!
John B. Gordon Klavern No. 5
P.O. Box 181
Buena Vista Station

Getting that sign torn down was one of the first blows I had helped to strike against the Klan. By digging into court records I managed to track down the owner of the lot—and then located some Catholics and Jews among his customers. Representations were made, and in short order the sign came tumbling down, never to rise again.

Those were the prewar days when many members of the Gordon Klavern, not satisfied with the Klan's programme of terrorism, helped set up the grey-shirt outfit which called itself the " White Front." As White Fronters they swaggered about in black boots and Sam Browne belts, boasting,

" When Hitler has killed all the Jews in Europe, he's going to help us drive all the Jews on Miami Beach into the sea! " These bully-boys were finally put out of business when squads organized by the Jewish War Veterans called their bluff. Upon getting word that the White Fronters were terrorizing some innocent Jew, the vets descended on the scene and in the mêlées that followed invariably came out on top. It also helped when I uncovered the fact that the White Fronters' propaganda was being printed by Hitler's *Welt Dienst* agency in Erfurt, Germany.

Scurrying back to the security of their Klan masks and dens, they resumed their night-riding, establishing through the years one of the bloodiest records of violence against Negroes, Jews and Catholics of any Klanton in the Invisible Empire. One of their favourite stunts was to stage an " Americanism " programme each year in the local Masonic Temple. These affairs—which consisted of nothing more than a few robed Klan windbags making inane speeches— were always packed to capacity, even though the price of admission was $10. The secret of the Klan's success was not hard to find—business men and politicians were intimidated into buying the tickets.

" We're from the Klan! " a strong-arm Kommittee calling on Jewish merchants would say. " Maybe you've noticed we've been letting the Jews off light lately—how many tickets do you want? "

Miami's politicos were given much the same treatment by a battery of professional telephone solicitors to whom the Klan paid commissions.

" Nobody can hold office without Klan support! " the politicos were told. " —How about ten tickets for your friends? "

These were the sort of " karacters " I was up against. . . .

After the bus pulled into the station I checked my bag and walked down to Biscayne Bay to stretch my legs. Miami appeared to be her usual self, busily preparing to give the tourists a run for their money during the approaching winter season.

Before doing anything else I telephoned some friends, a

young couple who are always in the forefront of moves to
upbuild democracy.

" Hi, Stet—I was hoping maybe you'd come down and
pitch into the bombing investigation," Harry said. " Why
don't you come out and stay with us? We have a guest
room now, and would be glad to have you."

" Be right out," I replied. " You can brush me up on the
background to this business, and if and when I turn up
anything you'll know what organizations can push it the
hardest."

So I checked out of the bus station and into Harry's home
in the suburbs.

" Well, what's the lowdown? " I asked when we settled
down to dinner.

" Looks like the Klan is up to its old tricks," Harry
replied. " But I never heard of them using so much dynamite before. During the war I saw what blockbusters
did in Europe, but I never saw a more finely pulverized
pile of rubble than that apartment building in Carver
Village! "

" I'm sure it's something of a record for the Klan, all
right," I agreed. " My files are choked with such cases all
the way across and up and down the country, from Cali-
fornia to New Jersey and Birmingham to Chicago, but this
is the first time they've used more than a handful of dynamite
sticks on one job."

" The stuff's as easy to get around here as a drink of
water," Harry said. " Most of the dynamite plants are
located just outside the city limits, and you don't need a
permit of any kind, no matter whether you want to buy a
stick or a carload! "

" Isn't there something that can be done to tighten up on
that situation? "

" It's worth trying. I'll pass the idea along to one of the
labour unions, and let them press the authorities."

" What's the story about Carver Village—has there been
any agitation over it? "

" Plenty! It started a couple of months ago, after we
succeeded in getting 216 units of the big Knight Manor
housing project, which was originally built for whites only,

set aside as Carver Village for Negroes. The Village section fronts on a Negro neighbourhood, but some of the whites in Knight Manor began raising hell, and then a lot of other people joined in."

" Who? The Klan? "

" Well, not openly. . . . Most of the agitation has been coming from an outfit that calls itself the Property Owners' Association."

" That's routine Klan procedure in handling housing ' problems,' " I assured him. " It's the same story all over the country. What do you know about this outfit? "

" Not a whole lot," Harry admitted, " except that it's brand new. Got started a couple of weeks ago, with demands that the police move in and throw the Negroes out of Carver."

" I thought the Carver section was still empty? "

" Not entirely. Some of the buildings are already occupied, and the rest are ready for occupancy. About the only thing to be thankful for is that the Klan planted its bombs under an unoccupied building. If there had been people living in it, there would have been nearly a hundred killed. That's what everybody's worried about—especially the Negroes who're living there. These first explosions may have been intended to scare them out, and if they don't get out I wouldn't put it past the Klan to plant bombs right under them! "

" And are they moving out? "

" Not a single family! They've asked the police to post night watchmen, but all they've gotten so far is a promise that an occasional police car will drive by during the night."

" And what do the city fathers have to say about all this? "

" Nothing constructive," Harry replied ruefully. " The newspapers aren't mentioning it since the bombing, but the truth is that the city commission, after being needled for a week by this new Property Owners' Association, agreed last week to condemn Carver Village as a ' menace to the public safety '—and turn it into an office building! "

" But if Carver has already been condemned for Negro occupancy, why would anyone want to blow it to bits? "

"You'll have to ask the Klan that," Harry said grimly. "The occupants, helped by white and Negro friends, got an injunction to force the city officials to come into court and show cause why the property should be condemned. The hearing is set for December 17th, but I guess the Kluxers didn't want to wait that long—or else they wanted to give the court something more to think about."

"Has the bombing changed the legal proceedings in any way?"

"Well, no, except that city commissioner Leslie Quigg is going along with the Property Owners' Association in demanding that the police come in and move the Negroes out without benefit of any court order."

"Quigg?" I exclaimed. "He used to be police chief here before the war, and let the Klan run wild with police escorts for their parades and everything! A couple of his cops picked up a Negro hotel porter who was accused of winking at a white woman and drove him outside the city limits on the Tamiami Trail and castrated him!"

"I wouldn't know about all that," Harry said. "That was before my time in Miami."

"Well, I think I've heard all I can stomach for one night," I said, polishing off my coffee. "I'll probably be having a busy day tomorrow, and had better get some sleep."

Early the next morning I went to Carver Village to look around. Harry had not exaggerated the extent of the damage—even the refrigerators with which the apartments had been furnished were blown to bits. I struck up a conversation with a Negro man who emerged from one of the occupied buildings.

"Looks like you're on a pretty hot spot," I observed.

He looked at me closely, trying to see whether I was being sympathetic or voicing a threat.

"We'd make it hot for whoever done it, if the police would just let us set up guards!" he said defiantly.

"Good!" I said. "Everybody has a right to protect themselves against invasion and attack."

"Don't worry," he said. "We're watching from our windows as best we can!"

" Nobody thinking of moving out, are they? "

" Nobody! We been forced to live in them black shacks down in the foggy bottoms too long to give up decent homes without a fight, now that we got 'em! "

Nodding agreement, I left him looking at the ruins. Making my way to the nearest bar in the white neighbourhood, I ordered a beer, and, after drinking a bit of it, turned to the man sitting next to me.

" Some fireworks you folks have been having around here! " I ventured.

" Yeah," he grinned. " There won't be no niggers moving into that building no time soon! "

" Looks to me like the Ku Klux are on the job . . ." I said tentatively.

" I dunno," he said suspiciously. " But whoever it was sure done a good job! "

" You wouldn't happen to know a Mr. A-y-a-k here in Miami, would you? I'm down here on vacation from Georgia, and I'd kind of like to get in touch with him."

" Can't say as I do," the man said, clamming up.

He clammed up so fast, in fact, that I decided he undoubtedly was a Klansman and knew what I was talking about, but was under orders from the hierarchy not to talk to any strangers about the bombing, no matter what passwords they might have. So I had another beer and talked of other things. Then, just as I was leaving, he called after me.

" If you're interested in this Carver Village thing, why don't you come to the meeting the Property Owners' Association is having tonight? It's just around the corner, and starts at eight."

" Much obliged," I said. " I might do that. See you later."

I spent the rest of the day making the rounds of all the old hangouts in Hialeah and other suburbs where I knew the Kluxers took their beers. But I couldn't find a damned soul who would confess to knowing Mr. A-y-a-k. I'm sure I talked to many a Klansman, but their lips were sealed.

That night at dinner Harry and I compared notes.

" I took your question about tightening up on dynamite to Local 809," he reported. " They're a wide-awake bunch, with both white and Negro members, under solid progressive leadership. They sent a committee to the fire chief, who it seems has charge of such things. He promised to see what he could do about tightening the local laws. The way things stand now, anybody can go up to any fire station and get a permit to buy dynamite, just by saying they need it to get rid of a stump or make a swimming pool or something. But as far as the big dynamite depots outside the city go, he can't do a thing about them. Said he ' hopes and prays ' the state legislature will do something about that when it meets a year from now! "

" That should give the Klan plenty of time to level all of Carver," I said wryly—little thinking that the lightning would strike twice in the same spot.

After dinner I went to the meeting of the Property Owners' Association. Except for the change in faces, it was an exact replica of all the meetings of similar associations which I had attended in Atlanta and elsewhere. The leader renewed the demand that the police evict all Negroes from Carver.

" We didn't want what has happened to happen, and we don't want it to happen any more! " he shouted. " I'm afraid there's going to be bloodshed both ways if this thing keeps up! "

In a thinly veiled threat, he declared that all the hardware stores in the vicinity were doing a rush business, selling arms and ammunition to white residents.

In the days that followed, Mayor Chelsie Senerchia began to get anonymous telephone threats to " Get the niggers out of Carver Village or we'll blast them out! "

Still no police guards were posted.

Meanwhile, I dug into old newspaper files to document my recollection of earlier Klan terror campaigns aimed at depriving Miami Negroes of new housing. Sure enough I found the accounts of how shortly before World War II the Klan had nipped in the bud a projected housing project for Negroes in the Pinewood section. Then, the Klan had been content to use fire instead of dynamite, burning the first

Negro houses that were built, and touching off fiery crosses on the project's boundaries while a Kluxer with a loud-speaker proclaimed:

" Yes, sir, ladies and gentlemen—this is the Ku Klux Klan! Whenever the law fails you just call on us! We're going to see to it you don't have to sleep with niggers like they do over on Miami Beach! "

(Actually, Miami Beach is one of the two remaining cities in the U.S.A.—Palm Beach being the other—where Negroes are not permitted to establish homes or even remain on the streets after nightfall.)

At that time, too, I noted, there were several " property owners' associations " fronting for the Klan in agitating against housing for Negroes.

One would think that such a record would be more than enough to prompt the authorities to question the Klan about the current bombing. But even after I turned over to Harry the news clippings I had uncovered, and a civil liberties organization waved them under the nose of the police chief, he refused to question any Kluxers. To generate some more steam, we organized a community-wide telephone campaign to ask the chief why he did not rake the Kluxers over the coals. I was one of the first to put the question to him.

" Why, the KKK is an American, legal, law-abiding organization! " he spluttered.

This prompted me to go to the court-house and dig into the records of corporate charters. Sure enough, I dug out a charter issued to Ku Klux Klan of Florida Inc. on September 7th, 1944, as a tax-exempt " charitable " order!

In addition, I discovered that Governor Fuller Warren's own administration had on July 31st, 1949, authorized the Original Southern Klans Inc., a Georgia corporation, to set up Klaverns all over Florida!

Switching my investigations from the court-rooms back to the bar-rooms, I learned that the Gordon Klavern had split, the majority affiliating with the Southern Klans, of which Bill Hendrix of Tallahassee was Grand Dragon, while the remainder were now calling themselves " Den No. 2 " and were paying tribute to my old buddy, Wizard Sam Roper of Atlanta.

Passed on to various civil liberties groups, this information helped them to put the screws on the Governor, who sent in his "special investigator," one Jefferson J. Elliott, who somehow looked vaguely familiar to me. . . .

One morning about two weeks after I arrived in Miami, the phone rang while I was still having coffee at Harry's house. He had left earlier for the Jewish community centre where he works.

"Guess what?" he said, his voice shaking just a bit.

"O.K., what?" I asked.

"I just had a call from the Coral Gables Jewish Centre—they found a bundle of dynamite on their front step this morning!"

"Ye gods!" was all I could say.

"Somebody had thrown it during the night, but it hit a palm tree, so the fuse got knocked out," Harry continued.

"No clues?"

"No clues. There was a watchman on duty at the centre all night, and a police patrol car was supposed to drive past every twenty minutes—but nobody saw a thing."

"H'm. . . ."

"Now I know exactly how they must feel out at Carver! It's not going to be easy teaching kids to play games, knowing somebody might toss some dynamite your way any minute!"

"What's being done?"

"Everybody's demanding action, but the authorities aren't even promising much, much less doing anything," Harry said.

Another week went by, and the terrorists struck again. This time their target was the Hebrew School and Congregation, but once more their home-made bomb failed to explode. Still no one was even questioned—except a couple of Negro stump-pullers who were thrown into jail for having a few sticks of dynamite in their car.

Evidently taking police inaction as a cue to bomb as much as they pleased, the terrorists waited two weeks and then went back to Carver. Two of the three bundles of dynamite they planted failed to go off, but $22,000 damage was done to an eight-unit building.

A large group of Negroes—many of them residents of Carver—gathered at the scene. One man emerged from his shaken home carrying a shotgun—and the police promptly pounced on him.

" What are you doing with that gun? " they demanded.

" Protecting my family and people," the man replied steadily.

" Get in! " a cop ordered, taking away the gun and shoving the man into the back seat of a radio patrol car.

But the Negroes were in a militant mood. About five hundred of them pressed around the police car so it could not move. Silently, they opened the door of the car and motioned for the arrested man to come out. Out he came, and walked off through the crowd, while the frightened police radioed frantically for help. Virtually every squad car in Greater Miami answered the " riot " call with sirens screaming; but there were no further attempts to arrest Negroes that night.

But neither did the police post any guards at Carver. Two nights later, at four o'clock on a Sunday morning, the terrorists blasted Carver for the third time. Then, at half-hour intervals, there were two successive blasts in Jewish neighbourhoods, destroying thousands of dollars' worth of stained-glass windows in a synagogue. A few days later, the terrorists broadened their attack on minorities still further by hurling bombs at Catholic churches.

" The whole world knows that only the Ku Klux Klan goes after Negroes, Jews and Catholics, all three," I said to Harry. " Maybe now somebody will move against the KKK! " But not one law enforcement agency did.

By this time over a quarter million dollars' worth of property had been destroyed, and it was only a miracle that human life had been spared. The Council of Churches, Ministerial Alliance and Rabbinical Association joined forces to sponsor a mass meeting to demand police protection, and the Anti-Defamation League of B'nai B'rith set up a Co-ordinating Committee Against Bombing.

But when a community committee called on Assistant

Police Chief Youell with a demand that he post guards at the most likely targets of the terrorists he refused.

" We just can't make night watchmen out of our officers," said he.

At this point, Jewish war veterans went to see Sheriff J. B. Henderson.

" If the law enforcement agencies won't protect us, we'll protect ourselves! " they said. " We ask that you swear us in as special deputies so we can establish guards over our own institutions."

The sheriff agreed, and the vets promptly rigged flood-lights atop Jewish institutions and set up round-the-clock patrols. But when a group of Negro vets from Carver applied for the same privilege, the sheriff had a change of heart and cancelled all the deputizations.

State Attorney-General Richard Ervin suggested that the sheriff ask Governor Warren to send in the state militia—not to protect the buildings of minority groups but " as a precaution against anti-Negro rioting."

As for the F.B.I., it stubbornly refused to do anything to stem the terror, saying it could not see where any " Feder-ally guaranteed civil rights " had been violated.

By this time the winter tourist season was just around the corner, and the business interests which cater to this multi-million-dollar industry were beginning to fear the terrorism would cost them plenty by keeping visitors away.

" Why not mobilize the tourist interests to demand that state and Federal authorities do something to stop the bombings? " I suggested to certain people who were in a position to start the ball rolling. " Sometimes officials will jump when business men crack the whip, when they won't do a thing for minority or civil liberties groups. They're much more sensitive to purse-strings than to heart-strings."

It was not until December 7th—two and a half months after the first bomb exploded—that the U.S. Attorney-General, spurred on the one hand by mass meetings all over the country and on the other by the Florida tourist industry, finally ordered the F.B.I. to " investigate to see whether it could investigate."

" There was a mailbox damaged in one of the explosions,"
the chief of the F.B.I.'s Miami bureau told reporters.
" Maybe that gives us an entrée into the case."

The terror did not run its full course until Christmas Eve.
That night there was a final, fatal explosion.

The terrorists planted a bomb under the bedroom of Mr.
and Mrs. Harry T. Moore, Negro residents of Mims, a small
town north of Miami. Moore was killed instantly. His wife
died after a week of suffering.

" I want to die," she told friends and relatives who
gathered at her bedside. " Harry and I did all we could to
win justice for all people; others must carry on."

Even though Mrs. Moore said she had a " good idea " who
planted the bomb, neither the local police nor Governor
Warren's special investigator Elliott nor the F.B.I. bothered
to take any statement from her before she died!

Moore was a two-fisted saintly fighter for democracy, who
throughout his life was in the forefront of the struggle of his
people for a greater measure of justice. At the time of his
murder he was not only state secretary of the N.A.A.C.P.
but also leader of the Progressive Voters League of Florida.
This latter organization had done a magnificent job in
getting Florida Negroes registered to vote. And in 1950
when I campaigned for the U.S. Senate from Florida as
an independent " colour-blind " candidate on a platform
calling for a " live and let live " foreign policy and " total
equality " at home, Moore's organization unanimously
endorsed my candidacy.

" With a programme like that, aren't you afraid we'll be
called Reds? " one of Moore's followers asked at the state-
wide convention in Ocala at which I spoke. (Neither the
Republican nor Democratic nominees deigned to acknowledge the Negroes' invitation to appear.)

" We've been called black so long, I don't see why we
should start worrying now about being called some other
colour," Moore replied.

This, I feel sure, is the real reason why Harry Moore and
his wife were so brutally murdered. That he had set out with

such success to arm Negroes with ballots was bad enough in the eyes of white supremacists, but that he should then provide such fearless leadership in the use of the ballot was too much.

The murder of the Moores brought to a head the national and international demand that something be done to halt the Florida terror.

" The State of Florida is making every effort to find the guilty parties," Inspector Elliott assured the Press. " We've found some tracks near the scene. . . ."

" Tracks? " snorted a speaker at a south-wide protest meeting of the N.A.A.C.P. which I attended soon afterwards in Jacksonville. " There are tracks all over Florida! If a white man and woman had been dynamited to death, you can be sure the police would have had a hundred Negroes in jail the very next day—*any* hundred! "

During the course of the meeting I reported my discovery that the State of Florida had given the KKK sanction in the form of corporate charters . . . and offered to provide the necessary evidence to strip the Klan of this cloak of legality. The offer was referred to the Florida N.A.A.C.P. attorneys for action.

As the meeting progressed, we received telephoned and written messages that the building was going to be bombed. As each of these warnings came in, they were reported to the conference by the chairman. But no one left the meeting, and attendance actually increased.

" These people who go around throwing bombs just don't understand us," Mrs. Edith Simpkins, an N.A.A.C.P. leader from South Carolina said. " They think that bombs drive us apart, when in reality they bring us together! "

On the final day, someone did sneak into the basement and turn on the gas in the heating system—without lighting it. The entire building was soon filled with fumes, and there was considerable danger of an explosion. Fortunately, the gas was shut off and the building aired without mishap.

During this same period, the Civil Rights Congress sent a large delegation of white and Negro leaders to Tallahassee to demand action of Governor Warren. Warren not only posted a large reward for information leading to conviction of the terrorists, but invited the delegation to have luncheon at the Governor's mansion. It was the first time whites and Negroes had partaken of food together there since Reconstruction days.

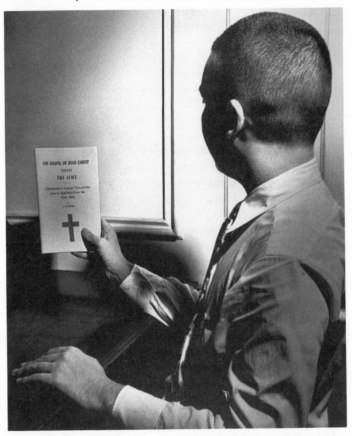

J. B. Stoner, who later served time for the deaths of some young girls in the dynamiting of a black church in Alabama. He is shown here with a copy of his book *The Gospel of Jesus Christ vs. the Jews*. When posing for this picture, he told the author that he would not show his face because "I don't want people who are not my friends to be able to recognize me." Photograph by Marion Palfi, courtesy Center for Creative Photography, University of Arizona.

CHAPTER SEVENTEEN

NIGHT RIDE IN SUNNY FLORIDA

I HAD no sooner returned home after investigating the terror in Miami when the news of another atrocity in south Florida sent me packing again. In fact, my wife scarcely had time to launder my Klan robe.

The account given by the radio announcer was cryptic in its brevity.

"Last night two Negro prisoners were shot by Sheriff Willis McCall of Lake County when they attempted to escape while being transported to a new trial ordered by the U.S. Supreme Court. One of the Negroes, Samuel Shepherd, was killed instantly, while the other, Walter Lee Irvin, is lying near death in a Eustis hospital."

There is of course nothing extraordinary about Southern law officers killing Negroes who are said to have resisted arrest or attempted to escape—it happens every day. But these were no ordinary prisoners, and McCall no ordinary sheriff. The two victims were part of the ill-fated " Groveland Four," whose case attracted world-wide attention after they were accused of raping a white woman in Groveland, Florida. Now, McCall's Police Special revolver had in effect reversed the Supreme Court of the United States, and I resolved to get to the bottom of the matter if I could.

So I boarded a plane for Orlando, where I could get a bus for Eustis. When my plane landed, I bought copies of the local papers, and boarded the first bus for Eustis. As we rolled through orange groves dotted with lakes and palms it was difficult to believe that such an outwardly tranquil countryside could spawn such bitter race hatreds and Ku Klux violence. But of course I knew without reminding myself that it is not climate or soil that gives rise to these things, but rather the greed of a handful of men who stand to profit by keeping plain people at each other's throats.

I settled down to study and make notes on the news reports of the shooting. McCall's story was simple enough— too simple, in fact. His car got a flat tyre, his prisoners attacked him in an attempt to escape, and he was obliged to shoot them. The chief difficulty on the face of this was that the two prisoners were handcuffed together, were unarmed, and still McCall had emptied his gun into them. A photograph published with the news stories showed the two Negroes lying in a ditch. It was taken, the caption said, by the woman editor of the Eustis paper, who " happened to be visiting " with her flash camera in the vicinity of the shooting.

There was also a wire service rehash of the background story of the " Groveland Four." I was living in south Florida when the case first broke, and was familiar with all its details, so it was easy for me to distinguish between fact and fiction and to fill in between the lines.

" The case of the Groveland Four arose in 1949 when a group of Negroes kidnapped and raped a young white house-wife," the story began.

Actually, it arose when the woman in question failed to come home one night. She and her husband were out riding and had a flat tyre. Some Negroes stopped and offered to drive her to a gasoline station to get assistance. She was next seen the following morning in the company of a service station operator. The story was that she arrived after daylight, saying she had been kidnapped by the Negroes, but could not identify any of them. It was not until the next day that she cried " Rape! "

" Feelings in the small citrus-growing community were roused to a high pitch by the crime," I read on. " Three young Negroes, Samuel Shepherd, Walter Lee Irvin and Charles Greenlee, were arrested and charged with the crime. A fourth suspect, Ernest Thomas, was shot and killed while resisting arrest."

The truth is that the Klan stepped into the picture with parades and cross-burnings, and so terrorized the Negro community that the inhabitants fled from the town. To placate the Klan-led lynch mob, McCall did what a lot of other Southern sheriffs have been doing in recent years—he legalized the mob by swearing it in as a posse.

A mass manhunt was launched, and scores of Negroes were caught in the dragnet and carted off to jail. Although the husband of the " wronged " woman took a leading part in all this, it was not until after the Negroes were in jail that he pointed to the three " guilty " ones. The posse found Thomas at the home of a relative, and riddled him with a volley of rifle, shotgun and pistol fire.

" Wasn't it possible to capture him alive? " a reporter asked.

" He tried to get away," a member of the posse laconically replied.

Turning to a deputy who had been assigned to lead the posse, the reporter asked, " Where were you at the time? "

" I was looking the other way," the deputy said.

Its bloodlust quenched for the time being, the deputized lynch mob disbanded.

During the months that passed before the youths were brought to trial, McCall jubilantly announced that he had obtained signed confessions from all three of them. With this, his political stock soared to new heights. When the trial finally began, the local Press, aided and abetted by the Klan, fanned the fires of hatred until a new lynch mob formed and pressed on the court-house doors.

" Let us have the black bastards! " the mob howled. " No use wasting taxpayers' money on a trial! "

Instead of dispersing the mob, Sheriff McCall addressed it from the court-house steps.

" Just let us handle this thing, and you can rest assured they'll be legally executed! " he solemnly promised. By saying this, he made his own political future dependent upon the outcome of the trial.

Significantly, the prosecution never introduced the signed confessions of which McCall had boasted. This strongly supported the prisoners' complaints that they had been beaten and tortured while in jail.

With the lynch mob still milling outside, the lily-white jury brought in its verdict.

"Guilty!" the jury said of all three. Mercy was recommended only for Greenlee, who was sixteen years old at the time.

"I sentence you to death in the electric chair!" the judge said to Shepherd and Irvin. To Greenlee he said, "Life imprisonment!"

McCall had made good his promise, and his constituents were satisfied. Triumphantly he delivered his prisoners to the State Penitentiary at Raiford, and Shepherd and Irvin were clapped into "Death Row" to await execution.

Turning back from my thoughts to the news story, I read on:

"Following their convictions, the National Association for the Advancement of Coloured People appealed on behalf of Shepherd and Irvin. Florida's Supreme Court upheld the sentences, but the U.S. Supreme Court early this month ordered a re-trial on the grounds that the first trial was conducted in an inflamed atmosphere by a jury from which Negroes had been systematically excluded. It was while the prisoners were being transported to this new trial that the shooting took place."

What the news story neglected to say was that in addition to the court action undertaken by the N.A.A.C.P. the Civil Rights Congress had through mass meetings succeeded in focusing national and international attention upon the case of the Groveland Four. Also not mentioned was the effect of the high court's decision on McCall's political standing. The electric chair and the mob had been cheated of their prey, at least temporarily. In Lake County the openly expressed sentiment was: "Those niggers have lived too long already."

The instant I stepped off the bus in Eustis I knew I was in a lynch town. There was the very same tension I had felt at Monroe, Georgia, after the Klan staged a quadruple lynching there. . . .

Very few Negroes were to be seen on the streets, and the whites all seemed to be walking stiff-legged, like dogs about to leap. I took a room at the Fountain Inn Hotel, where I was told everybody from F.B.I. agents to news reporters had checked in.

"I'm afraid you'll have to carry your own bags up the stairs," a corn-fed young lady behind the desk apologized. "Our coloured bell-hops and elevator boys decided not to come to work today."

"I can manage," I said. "There's just one bag and a typewriter."

"Are you a reporter too?" she asked. "I guess it's a terrible thing to say, but I almost wish we could have a nigger-killing more often—we've never had so many nice young men in town."

After depositing my baggage, I got in touch with Thurgood Marshall, chief counsel of the N.A.A.C.P., who quickly brought me up to date on developments. Irvin, after a number of blood transfusions, was now out of danger and had regained sufficient strength to talk. His doctors were going to let him be questioned for the first time that afternoon. As Irvin's attorney, Marshall was to be the first to see him—but he was to be accompanied by a court reporter, and—none other than the Governor's special investigator, Jefferson Elliott.

The story Irvin told that afternoon rocked the entire world. He said that even before leaving the State penitentiary in Sheriff McCall's automobile he and Shepherd had been "teased" with threats that they would "not live long enough to be re-tried." Instead of taking the highway to Tavares, McCall had turned off on a deserted backroad route and was followed at some distance by Deputy James Yates in another car. After driving along this road some distance, Irvin said, the sheriff radioed his deputy:

"Is everything clear?"

Shortly afterwards, Irvin continued, Sheriff McCall said he thought he had a flat tyre. He stopped the car, got out, and bent over a front wheel. Then he got back in and drove on. In a short time the front tyre was flat. Sheriff McCall again got out, came around the car, opened the door, and ordered his prisoners to get out. Then, Irvin said, before they could stand erect, the sheriff began to empty his gun into them, continuing to fire after they started to fall and even after they were lying on the ground.

Though in great pain and only semi-conscious, Irvin said he heard the sheriff radio his deputy:

" Come ahead—I've fixed them both good! "

The next thing he knew, Irvin said, the deputy was standing over him and saying, " This one ain't dead—hand me your gun! "

When the deputy first pulled the trigger it failed to fire, and the two men went around in front of the car to fix the gun in the glare of the headlights. Then the deputy returned and shot him through the neck as he lay there, Irvin said.

" After that, I decided I'd better play dead," he added.

" Are you absolutely certain that neither you nor Shepherd made any attack on the sheriff or attempted to escape? " Attorney Marshall asked Irvin.

" We didn't make a move—didn't have no reason to," Irvin replied. " After all, we were on our way to a new trial and were hoping everything was going to turn out all right in the end."

While this was going on in Irvin's hospital room, I was busy with my own investigation—at the reception desk out front.

" I'm a newspaper reporter, and I wonder if you would be good enough to tell me what time it was when Irvin was admitted to the hospital? " I said to the nurse.

" You're the only one who's asked," she replied, " but I guess it's all right. Wait just one moment, please."

She pulled out a card file and ran through it.

" It was 1.17 a.m.," she said.

" Does the card say anything else? "

" Yes—it says ' Pulse imperceptible.' "

In other words, the officers of the law had taken over two and a half hours to get Irvin to the hospital six miles away, and upon delivery he appeared to be dead! Nor had any of the investigators, Federal or state, bothered to make this basic inquiry!

The next morning, a coroner's jury was empanelled by Judge Truman Futch to determine the cause and fix the blame, if any, for Shepherd's death. First, the jury went to Irvin's bedside. He told them the same story he had related the day before. The white jurymen sat there and blinked at him as he talked. Then, without asking any questions, they silently filed from the room.

Next, the jury visited the site of the shooting, and poked about in the sand. It developed that some school-kids had beaten the police and F.B.I. to the job, and had found some unfired pistol cartridges. They took them along to school, and the teacher in turn handed the cartridges over to the F.B.I.

That afternoon, the jury set up shop in the lobby of the Fountain Inn. I have watched many a Southern coroner's jury at work on similar cases involving Negroes killed by whites, and greater mockeries of justice never existed. This one turned out to be the most crass of all. With an appreciative audience of townsfolk listening in, a parade of witnesses trotted across the witness-stand to corroborate everything Sheriff McCall said. Not once did Judge Futch—who chewed nonchalantly on a matchstick throughout the proceedings—or any of the jurymen ask any question which would suggest that they believed one word of Irvin's account of what had happened.

Actually, the most notable things about the inquest were the questions *not* asked and the witnesses *not* called.

For instance, a monitor from the police radio station at Tavares, through which all police radio calls pass, was put on the stand. Yes, he remembered very clearly hearing Sheriff McCall radio for an ambulance to take Irvin to the hospital. But did anyone ask him whether he had heard the sheriff radio his deputy earlier about the road being clear? Or " fixing them good "? No. Perhaps it was just as well, for this monitor had not gone on duty until midnight. The monitor on duty at the time of the shooting, about 10.30 p.m., was not even called to the stand.

Throughout the proceedings, Sheriff McCall sat on the sidelines looking very much a public servant who had seen his painful duty and done it. With him sat his wife, looking just like a wife who felt sure her husband would be vindicated. Between them they had a small brown valise.

A number of farmers who lived in the vicinity of the shooting were put on the stand.

" Did you hear anything? " the judge asked.

" Yes, sir—a whole bunch of shots, around about ten-thirty," they all replied.

No one asked if there had been an interval between the shots, as Irvin's testimony indicated there had been before the deputy arrived and delivered the *coup de grâce*.

Other witnesses, the first to arrive at the scene, testified that both Negroes had appeared to be dead, and that they were not handcuffed together.

This didn't jibe with what the woman who photographed the bodies had told me earlier. She was present, so I called her aside.

" Were they handcuffed together or weren't they? " I asked. The woman had hopes of selling me a set of the photos, so she wanted to be nice to me.

" They certainly were when I arrived, and I was one of the very first," she whispered. " But everybody else is saying different, and I guess I shouldn't talk so much. They told me not to talk."

I went back to the hearing. At the foot of the table around which the jurors sat, State Prosecutor J. W. Hunter was in the witness-chair, describing the scene of the shooting as he had found it.

Earlier, McCall had claimed credit for discovering that Irvin was still alive and for sending for an ambulance. But in my pocket I had a news clipping published just a few hours after the shooting, in which Hunter was quoted as saying it was he who discovered Irvin was not dead and that he had ordered the wounded man to be taken to a hospital. But Hunter said nothing of this on the stand—and no one asked.

It was now getting near supper-time, and the supply of witnesses was exhausted. When it became apparent that Judge Futch was about ready to wind up the proceedings, Sheriff McCall, as though by afterthought, came forward with the small brown valise.

" Your Honour," he said, " I've got something here that may be of some interest to you and the jury—I didn't notice it until this afternoon."

Slowly, dramatically, he put the valise on a table, opened it, and drew out a man's coat.

" I found this here powder burn on the coat I was wearing that night . . ." he said, holding up the left sleeve.

Inspector Elliott, as though acting on cue, stepped forward.

" Let me have a look at that," he said, whipping a magnifying glass from his pocket and scanning the burn closely. " Hmm . . . very interesting—very interesting! "

" Inspector, can you tell us what significance that powder burn might have, if any? " Judge Futch asked.

" Yes, sir, I think I can qualify as something of a ballistics expert," Elliott responded.

" Take the chair! "

" In my opinion this is by far the most conclusive piece of evidence yet offered," Elliott said deliberately, still examining the coat sleeve. " It proves beyond any doubt that when this shot was fired a terrific struggle was taking place. If you will look closely you will see that the burn begins beneath the elbow, and gets larger toward the shoulder. That means the sheriff must have thrown his elbow up to protect his face, twisting the sleeve, and more or less firing back over his own shoulder. He came very close to shooting himself! "

Duly impressed, the jurymen passed the coat around among themselves, and threw up their own elbows to see how it might have happened. Obviously, everyone was more than satisfied, and anxious to render the verdict.

" Does anyone have any further evidence to offer or testimony to make? " Judge Futch asked, looking around the room. " How about you gentlemen of the Press? Any questions? "

My colleagues seemed as satisfied with the day's work as everyone else in the room; they had no questions.

I looked at my note pad.

There were plenty of questions in need of answers.

First of all, who was the radio monitor who was on duty at the time of the shooting? What had he heard, and what had he entered in his log book? Did the log book show any signs of having been altered?

What about the pistol slugs? The F.B.I. had finally gotten around to sifting all the dirt in the area of the shooting—

had they found anything to indicate that the Negroes had been shot while falling or lying on the ground? What was the meaning of the unfired cartridges the school-kids had found on the ground? Did they show any marks of a firing pin to bear out Irvin's story that the sheriff's gun had missed fire? If not, wouldn't this indicate that the sheriff's gun was empty when the deputy first pulled the trigger, and that in their haste to reload it and dispatch Irvin before witnesses arrived the two officers had spilled cartridges on the ground?

What about fingerprints on the sheriff's gun? Were the deputy's prints there too? I knew the F.B.I. had the gun in their custody—but no one offered testimony about fingerprints, and no one asked.

Above all, what about an autopsy? This was supposed to be a coroner's inquest to fix the cause of death, and here it was about to conclude without hearing any autopsy, either written or oral! An autopsy might very well show that the victims had been shot while lying on the ground.

These were but a few of the questions which cried out for answers. But Shepherd was dead, and there seemed to be no one to ask for him. Was I a proper person to ask these questions, and was this the proper time and place? If I pointed to these gaping holes in the " Case for McCall," might not someone rush to plug them? If the radio log book had been doctored, for example, I didn't want to give anyone a chance to improve the erasures.

These were questions, obviously, for a grand jury to spring —preferably a Federal one. After, all, Prosecutor Hunter had indicated that a state grand jury would be speedily summoned. And since the case involved both an officer of the law and ward of the Supreme Court, I took it for granted there would also be a Federal jury probe. I couldn't believe that Uncle Sam would accept a whitewash of the shooting —and lose face before the whole world.

So I decided to hold my fire. There was one question, though, that I felt might as well be asked then and there.

" What about an autopsy? " I asked mildly, looking up from my notes.

" Autopsy—autopsy? " Judge Futch muttered, as though

he had never heard the word before. " Let's see—" He
went over and had a whispered conference with Prosecutor
Hunter. Then, resuming his chair, the judge announced
with finality, " The doctor who made the medical examination wasn't able to get here."

And so the farce drew to a close. In time for supper, the
jury returned a verdict of " justifiable homicide," ruling that
McCall had fired in " self-defence and line of duty."

Spectators and jurymen alike rushed to shake the sheriff's
hand. For the first time since the hearing began, McCall let
himself smile, and then broke into a broad beam.

Of course, the sheriff and his deputy may be as innocent
as new-born lambs; but if that is the case, they themselves
should be the first to insist upon grand jury probes to establish
the facts.

Sheriff Willis McCall of Orange County, Florida, who shot two of the "Groveland Four"
who were handcuffed together during transportation to a new trial ordered by the U.S.
Supreme Court. Photograph courtesy *Orlando
Sentinel.*

CHAPTER EIGHTEEN

INVESTIGATING THE INVESTIGATORS

THE morning after this whitewashing (by an all-white jury after listening to an all-white parade of witnesses before an all-white audience), Eustis looked like a town that had had its face lifted. The streets thronged with white folks in a holiday spirit. Negroes, however, were still conspicuous by their absence.

I spotted Inspector Elliott going into his room at the Fountain Inn. He had been out to buy all the morning papers telling of the exoneration of McCall, and was obviously in an expansive mood.

Acting on a hunch I had long been wanting to pursue, I followed him into his room. Remembering me only as a newsman, without knowing my name, he invited me to sit down.

" I'm glad this business is all over so I can do a little fishing," he said. " Hard to beat these lakes around here for large-mouth bass, and the weather's perfect."

Boasting of his prowess with rod and gun, Elliott showed me the cards he holds as an expert marksman. I decided the moment had come to play the ace up my sleeve.

Reaching for my wallet, I pulled out my Klan Kard and handed it to him. There is nothing on a Klan Kard to show what it is—unless you know its symbolism.

" Well, well! " Elliott grinned delightedly. " I see you know Mr. A-y-a-k. . . ."

I had scored a bull's-eye!

" Sure do," I answered, " and Mr. A-k-a-i too."

" What newspaper did you say you're with? " Elliott asked, with increased interest—and caution.

" The *Southern Outlook* over in Birmingham," I answered, " but I work out of Atlanta."

" I see you're a member of the Headquarters Klan," he said with respect. " I'm a member of the East Point Klavern."

" Small Invisible Empire we live in! " I cracked. " I used to know a bunch of the boys out at East Point."

We both began to rattle off the names of some of our Atlanta brethren, and were soon mutually satisfied with each other's identity as a Klansman. Elliott opened up immediately.

" On the basis of that Kard you just showed me "—by which I knew he meant I was to keep what he was about to say strictly secret " in the sacred unfailing bond of Klannishness "—" I don't mind telling you that when those niggers were first delivered to the state pen they'd had the hell beaten out of them," he declared in a burst of confidence.

" The penitentiary officials were so afraid somebody might try to pin the beatings on them they took pictures of the scars and sworn statements from the prisoners," he continued. " The devil of it was, they sent copies to the F.B.I. before they did to us at the state capitol. We had a hellova time keeping the stuff out of circulation! "

I remembered that a Federal grand jury had actually tried to pin down the prisoners' stories that they had been beaten while in jail in Lake County—but no such documents as these were ever placed before it. If what Elliott said was true—and for once I was inclined to believe a Brother Klansman—it meant that local, state and Federal law officers were all linked in a conspiracy to suppress evidence!

" After that, the Governor sent me over to get a coherent story from them nigger rapists," Elliot went on. " I did, and there's no doubt about it—they had been beaten before breakfast, after breakfast and at all hours of the day and night! "

He recited these facts, not with any sign of regret, but rather with a grim " Aren't we devils? " smile.

Suddenly there was a knock on the door. I gripped the arms of my chair, wondering what might happen if some fellow journalist were to walk in and call me by name. Sure enough, in walked Stephen Trumbull of the *Miami Herald*.

" Hiya, Stet? " he said cheerfully. I looked at Elliott, and was glad to see my nickname meant nothing to him.

" Well, what do you make of the coroner's verdict, off the record? " Trumbull asked, turning to Elliott.

" Oh, it'll assure McCall's election for at least two more terms! " Elliott grinned.

I had heard enough, and wanted out. For all I knew, Trumbull might start at any minute to regale Elliott with tales of my anti-Klan exploits. After first turning the conversation back to fishing, I glanced at my watch.

" I'm going to have to dash off a story," I said. " See y'all later."

I did dash up the stairs, three at a time, to my room on the next floor. There was a good chance Elliott might be asking, " Who's that guy? " and Trumbull might be telling him, " Kennedy, the Klan-buster." I felt like I had a bear by the tail.

This thing was big—and I decided the best thing for me to do was to get out of town with it while the getting was still good. At last I felt sure I had something the F.B.I. could not fail to act upon. The beating of prisoners, and still more the suppression of evidence concerning violation of Federal law, is strictly the business of the F.B.I. But I had to remember that, according to Elliott, Florida F.B.I. agents had been partners to the conspiracy! The best hope for getting action, I decided, was to grab a plane for Washington and tell the story at F.B.I. headquarters.

I would have to move fast, for if Elliott discovered who I was he would probably start covering up his tracks—and perhaps even set up some sort of " interception " party for me. I wanted the G-men to swoop down on him, the sheriff, the state prison and the prison bureau simultaneously in an effort to get the hidden photos and reports.

I would have to take the bus back to Orlando, and catch a plane there. Then I realized I didn't have enough money with me for a plane ticket to Washington. I looked in my wallet—there wasn't even enough for a plane ride as far as my home in Jacksonville. Catching sight of my camera, I decided I should be able to hock it for enough to get to

Jacksonville, where I could pick up some more money and go on from there.

It occurred to me that if I checked out of the hotel, bag and baggage, and Elliott became suspicious, he would be apt to move even faster in covering up. Leaving my bag in the closet and my clothing scattered about the room, I slipped my toothbrush into my inside coat pocket, hung the camera strap over my shoulder, and started through the door. Just as I was about to close it behind me, my eyes fastened on a pint of whisky standing on the table. It was straight Bourbon, and I thought it might stand me in good stead before my mission was over. But I couldn't find the cap. I looked on all the tables, in the bathroom, and on the floor. At the same time, I half expected to see Elliott come bounding in. Finally I slipped the bottle, uncapped, into my pocket beside the toothbrush.

Hurrying past Elliott's floor and down to the lobby, I paused for just a moment.

" What time does your cafeteria begin to serve lunch? " I asked the corn-fed one behind the desk.

" Eleven forty-five," she answered sweetly.

" Good! " I said, making a bee-line for the bus station.

" When does the next bus leave for Orlando? " I asked the clerk.

" Twelve fifteen—if it's on time," the man said.

This meant a two-hour wait, and I wanted to do my waiting as inconspicuously as possible. Even as I stood there, I saw Sheriff McCall drive past in a limousine police car, tipping his five-gallon Stetson cowboy hat to his admirers along the kerb.

I didn't want to buy a ticket just then, but waited until no one was watching and then ducked into the men's toilet. Locking myself into a compartment, I settled down for a long wait, But as I bent over, the forgotten open bottle of whisky poured out, soaking my coat, shirt and underclothes. Instantly, I smelled like someone who had been wallowing on a bar-room floor in a thirty-day drunk. Since I had brought no other clothing with me, there was nothing I could do but sit there and reek. All I could hope for was that most of the fumes would evaporate before I reached F.B.I.

headquarters. By the time the bus arrived, even though I hadn't felt like taking a drink, I was pretty well intoxicated just from inhaling.

Once on board the bus I felt safer, but knew I was not yet completely out of danger. If I were discovered, it was entirely possible that the bus might be overtaken, and that I would be taken into custody and then " worked on " along some deserted road.

I arrived in Orlando without mishap, however, and went straight to a telephone booth.

" There's a plane leaving for Jax in seventeen minutes," the airport informed me. " I don't think you can make it."

" When's the next one? " I asked.

" Not until ten tonight."

" Hold everything—I'm going to try to make it! "

I sprinted outside, and began shouting for a taxi. There was only one in sight, and a man was already sitting in the back seat.

" Where can I get a cab in a hurry? " I asked the driver. " I just got word my wife's having a baby in Jacksonville, and I've got to catch a plane in seventeen minutes! "

" Don't seem to be no other cabs around right now," the driver said unconcernedly.

Just then the man in the back seat spoke up. He was clutching a half-empty bottle of whisky, and I think he must have gotten a whiff of my spilled Bourbon and decided I was a kindred spirit.

" Whazzat? " he blubbered. " Wife having a baby? . . . Come on, get in. . . . I got nothin' else to do. . . . Take you anywhere you wanna go. . . ."

I jumped in, not being inclined to look my gift horse in the mouth, and off we went to the airport.

" Here, have a li'l drink," my benefactor said, waving his bottle at me. " If you're havin' a baby you'll need a li'l drink."

" Not right now, thanks," I said, trying to figure out how I was going to buy a plane ticket even if we got to the airport in time.

" Say," I said to the driver, " this whole thing has caught me by surprise, and I need ten bucks more to cover the price of the ticket. I've got a hundred and fifty dollar camera here—how about letting me have the ten dollars, I'll give you an I.O.U. for fifteen dollars, and you can hold the camera for security? Just give me your licence number and I'll redeem the camera in a couple of weeks."

" I dunno . . ." the driver said dubiously. " I don't know that I got ten bucks I can spare."

I was beginning to think I would never get off the ground, when my new-found friend spoke up again.

" Here," he said, pulling out his wallet and extracting a ten-dollar bill. " I'll let you have it, and take good care of your camera too."

This caught me by surprise. As badly as I wanted to get on that plane, I didn't want to take a chance on losing my camera. The cab-driver would stay put, but there was no way I could be sure of ever locating this man again.

" Thanks very much, but I don't want to impose on you any more," I said.

By this time we were pulling into the airport. The seventeen minutes were up, and I could see the solitary two-engined plane at the ramp, her props already turning. I paid the cab fare, thanked my friend, and ran for the ticket counter.

" You'll have to hurry, sir! " the clerk said. " We've been holding the plane for you! "

" Look," I said breathlessly. " My wife's having a baby and I'm caught with ten dollars less than the price of the ticket! Can't one of you fellows let me have it, and hold my camera for security? "

The two clerks looked at each other. Then they looked at my camera and sniffed at me. I still reeked of Bourbon. Just when I was about to abandon hope I felt someone at my elbow.

" Here—take the ten dollars and keep your camera! "

It was my drunken friend again, who had finally sobered to the fact that I was afraid to leave my camera with him. He slapped a ten-dollar bill down on the counter, and the clerk began writing out the ticket. My friend handed me his card, wished me a good trip, and then I ran for the plane.

The hostess, taking the ticket and a whiff at the same

moment, changed her smile to a frown. All the other passengers sniffed too as I made my way up the aisle to my seat. But I was on my way at last, and didn't mind their grimaces.

When I had relaxed a bit I summoned the hostess and asked her about connections at Jacksonville for Washington. She promptly put an end to my relaxation by advising me there was a plane leaving twenty minutes after ours would arrive. If I missed that I would have to wait six hours. Such a long wait meant I could not talk to the F.B.I. until the following day. I still felt it was my duty to report before that, so the F.B.I. could move during the night before the conspirators could be warned and the evidence destroyed.

" Is there no stop between here and Jacksonville? " I asked.

" Only for five minutes at Daytona Beach to take on mail."

When we reached Daytona I was standing at the door of the plane.

" There won't be time to leave the plane," the hostess said.

" The toilet . . ." I whispered urgently. " Be right back! "

I put in a rush call for my wife, collect. There was a delay. " This is urgent! " I told the operator. " Official business . . ."

Meanwhile, the loudspeaker began to announce the departure of my plane, while I sweated inside the phone booth. There was a rap on the door.

" We're taking off, sir! " the hostess said emphatically.

Then I heard my wife's voice.

" Pack me a bag and bring some money to the Jacksonville airport! " I blurted, and hung up. When the hostess climbed back into the plane I was right at her heels.

As we pulled up in front of the hangars at Jacksonville, I could see my wife waving from the crowd. The first thing I did—after embracing her—was to go into the men's room and get out of my Bourbon-soaked clothes (it was some time before my wife would believe I wasn't drunk).

Then I put in a call to Washington. Hinting vaguely at what I had, I told them I would get in around midnight.

It was after 1 a.m. before I was finally cloistered at F.B.I. headquarters with Leonard Kaufman, assistant chief of the civil rights section. He listened intently as I told him the whole story, taking careful notes as I talked. I told him everything, that is, except what Elliott had said about F.B.I. agents in Florida being linked in the conspiracy. There would be time enough to pursue that matter later, I thought, after the F.B.I. had acted against the other culprits. But I did venture to suggest that Kaufman send in non-Southern agents to look for the evidence—before dawn if possible.

" Non-Southern agents? " Kaufman exclaimed. " You're not trying to imply that any of our Southern men are biased in any way, are you? "

" Well, let's say I have some indication that a few of them might be, but I don't want to be more specific until I've had a chance to track down the leads I have."

This didn't satisfy Kaufman, but he thanked me for my information and assured me that appropriate steps would be taken.

I checked into an hotel, and fell asleep hoping I would awake the next day to read that the F.B.I. had blown the Florida terrorism wide open.

But there was nothing of the sort in the papers. The story from Eustis was that Irvin had been sent back to the penitentiary to await re-trial. Prosecutor Hunter had changed his mind about calling a state grand jury to probe the shooting. He was satisfied, he said, with the coroner's findings. Nor was there anything to indicate that a Federal jury would be empanelled.

Bitterly disappointed, I caught a train for New York City. There was nothing more I could say to the F.B.I. If it did not choose to act on the information I had given, my only recourse was to take the facts directly to the American people.

" So here you are! " my literary agent exclaimed when I walked into her office. " Your wife has been trying to reach you by long distance all morning! You're to call Operator 1 at Switzerland."

" Give me the phone! " I said. " The Klan must have paid her a visit! "

Soon I heard her reassuring voice over the wire.

" What in hell are you doing up there? " she bellowed. " F.B.I. agents are swarming all over our place! When I went down the road to our mailbox this morning there were two of them perched on top. Said they couldn't find the house. Been sitting there since dawn, waiting for somebody to show up! Imagine paying the salaries of such lousy detectives! "

" What did they want? "

" Damned if I know—said you had cast aspersions on their integrity or some such rot, and they intended to get to the bottom of it. Wanted to know where you were."

" Didn't the agents want to know anything about the McCall case? "

" Never even mentioned it."

" Is there anything in the papers or on the radio down there to show that they've acted on the information I gave them? "

" Not a word."

" Well, I guess you can handle the F.B.I. all right."

" Sure can—I got rid of 'em by trying to sell 'em some chickens."

" What about the Ku Klux and Brother Elliott—haven't seen any signs of their being on our trail? "

" Not so far, but don't worry about that. Your buddy Woody Guthrie blew in right after you left, and he's out in the woods now getting in a little practice with the army rifle. Sits back on his haunches, leans the rifle over a log, puts the butt in his crotch, and sights it like it was a cannon. Knocking off one-gallon jugs at three hundred yards every time! Damnedest thing you ever saw! "

" Well, hold the fort, and I'll get back just as soon as I can," I promised. " I think I'd better stick up in this part of the country where I can break the story wide open if the F.B.I. doesn't act. I won't give them more than about ten days."

While I was waiting, I sent a wire to a friend in Orlando asking him to phone the Fountain Inn in Eustis and tell them I had been called away unexpectedly, and to hold my baggage until further notice.

I also sat down and wrote a letter to U.S. District Attorney

Herbert Phillips in Tampa, Florida, who has jurisdiction over the southern part of the state. I outlined to him the same information I had given the F.B.I., and offered to testify before a Federal grand jury. By the time I received his reply, the ten days and my patience had expired. His letter was the last straw. In it he said he had no intention whatever of calling a Federal jury to look into what he derisively said " the F.B.I. refers to as ' the McCall case.' "

Just as I had felt it my duty to report my findings to the authorities as fast as possible, I now felt it to be equally my duty to give the facts to the people, so they could build a fire under the officials to move them to action.

And so, at one of the mass meetings which were being held in New York to protest the Florida terror, I told the whole story.

As a result, strong new demands were made upon the U.S. Attorney-General to order a Federal grand jury probe. At the same time, Florida's Governor Warren was called upon to fire " Kluxer-Inspector " Elliott. Warren, himself a Klansman, refused to do anything. Elliott issued a statement saying " I am not a Klansman," but he did not deny that he had been a member of the East Point Klavern, nor did he deny any of the other statements he had made to me.

About that time I received an invitation from the N.A.A.C.P. in Miami to tell my story to a meeting of Negro, Jewish, Protestant, Catholic and labour leaders there.

" You're not going back down there without at least waiting for this thing to cool off? " my New York friends protested. " If that bird Elliott doesn't get you, the Klan will! "

In Miami, we met in the courtyard of the Lord Calvert, a Negro hotel. The local Press was represented, but only Jack Bell, columnist for the *Miami Herald*, dared report my remarks. Even his account got only as far as the midnight edition before being killed by the paper's editors.

But bonfires had been kindled at both ends of the country, and the heat was on the Administration to act. . . .

It was not until October of 1952—one year after the bombs began to burst, and one month before the national election—

that the U.S. Department of Justice finally sent in two special prosecutors to call a Federal grand jury to probe the Florida terror.

Thirty-nine witnesses were subpœnaed, including twelve Kluxers who were ordered to bring in the Miami Klan's records. Before testifying, each witness was required to swear not to reveal what questions he was asked or what answers he gave.

I went before the jury on October 24th. Somehow it overlooked pledging me to secrecy, so I am at liberty to reveal what went on inside. To begin with, I told the jurymen the whole story of my investigation of the shooting of Shepherd and Irvin, and the questions which had gone unanswered at the coroner's inquest. I also told them how I discovered Inspector Elliott's Klan connection and heard the story of the suppressed evidence.

U.S. Prosecutor Emory Akerman was especially interested in what I had to say about Elliott.

" We've found a good many indications that that guy has been going around glossing over things! " he confided.

Then I told the jury everything I had been able to learn about the Miami Klans, and directed them to a list of Miami auto licence numbers I had jotted down while attending a Klan parade at Live Oak, Florida. The Miami contingent, I informed them, had been the largest in the parade. They had driven through the streets shouting: " You folks are lucky; we're from Miami where we have both niggers and kikes to contend with! "

The jury was also interested in my findings on the operations of " property owners' associations " acting as fronts for the KKK.

" Mr. Kennedy, you have been inside the Klan and are familiar with its operations," the jury foreman leaned forward and said to me. " There is an important question which perhaps you can help us to clear up. The Klansmen we have had on the stand all insist that the Klan does not maintain any sort of apparatus whatever for flogging, bombing and so on. What is the truth about that? Someone has mentioned a Klokann committee—is that the flog squad? "

" No, sir," I replied. " The Klokann is a five-man committee responsible for investigating the qualifications of new applicants for membership. The flog squad is called the Klavalier Klub, or Military Department of the Klan."

" Who gives the Klavalier Klub its orders? " the foreman asked. " That's what we're trying to put our fingers on."

" Its leader is called the Chief of Staff, but refers to himself as the ' Chief Ass-Tearer,' " I explained. Pulling my Klavalier Kard from my wallet, I explained its symbolism to them. " For several years now, all Klavalier Klubs have been under strict orders not to undertake any action without the prior approval of the Exalted Cyclops of the Klavern and the Grand Dragon of the state."

" That's what we wanted to know! " the foreman said with satisfaction. " Thank you very much for your testimony."

The grand jury finally handed down indictments against twelve Klanspeople, including one Klanswoman. Five of them are now behind bars.

But Irvin is also behind bars—back in Death Row awaiting execution in the electric chair. While the State of Florida had no time to investigate the shooting, it was not satisfied with the punishment already inflicted on the Groveland Four, and lost no time renewing its demand for Irvin's life. Wheeled back into court in a half-paralysed condition, Irvin was again tried by a lily-white jury. This time, however, the State first called a few prospective Negro jurors—and then dismissed them " for cause."

The defence called Herman Bennett, a professional criminologist, to the stand. He said he had examined plaster casts of footprints made at the scene of the alleged rape, and while they fitted Irvin's shoes he could prove the shoes were empty when the footprints were made with them! Under cross-examination, Deputy Yates admitted he had made the plaster casts *after* Irvin was arrested. But when the judge called for the casts, the law officers said that unfortunately they had been lost on the way to the trial!

And what of the other principals in the tragedy? They are very much at large.

Elliott is still on the job as the Governor's special investigator, " investigating " the handiwork of his Brother Klansmen.

. . . McCall, as Elliott predicted, has been re-elected sheriff —and made a director of the Florida Sheriffs' Association. The sheriffs also invited Grand Dragon Bill Hendrix to address them, and applauded when the Klan Chieftain said: " Harry Moore wasn't just a nigger, he was a trouble-maker in our state! "

" Who can say that justice in America is colour-blind? " my wife asked, as we added a thick folder marked " McCall Case " to the chamber of horrors that is my filing room.

" Not I," I replied, marking the file not closed, but pending. . . .

At the same time, the authorities were marking all these events a " closed book."

The year was 1952, and America was in the throes of election campaigning. With a view to keeping at least half an eye on the Klan and its political machinations, I subscribed through a friend to the KKK's official newspaper, *The Klansman*, published at nearby Jacksonville. Since I had bowed out of active membership in the Klan the Invisible Empire had been rent by a severe schism. The ascendancy of Atlanta cop Sam Roper to the Wizard's throne after the death of Sam Green did not sit well with some state Klan leaders, who had ambitions of their own.

And so Florida's Grand Dragon Bill Hendrix, the Dragon of the Carolinas Thomas Hamilton, and Alabama Dragon Lycurgus Spinks got together with other dissident Klan leaders and in a Klonvokation held at Jacksonville broke with Roper and established a rival Klan of their own, which they proceeded to call the " Southern and Northern Knights of the KKK." It was claimed, extravagantly as usual, that 150 Klepeers (delegates) representing 650,000 Klansmen in 302 Klaverns in twelve states were present. Jacksonville was named as the new Imperial City, and a mysterious Wizard who signed his edicts merely " Nathan II " (thus claiming to be the legitimate successor to the Wizard of the original post-Civil War Klan, Nathan

Forrest) was elected. By tracing the licence number of the limousine which thereafter headed Klan parades, I discovered that " Nathan II " is none other than Jacksonville attorney Edgar Waybright, Sr. In addition to his duties as Klan Wizard, Waybright also served as Duval County chairman of the Democratic Party. . . .

As Democratic chairman, Klan Wizard Waybright promulgated a fourteen-point " party platform " which was unanimously adopted by the executive committee on January 4th. Upon examination, I found this Democratic Platform to be pretty much a replica of the Klan's official " Kreed " and the Klan line which *The Klansman* was plugging with every issue. The platform asserted that the party " strongly favours social and educational segregation of the races," and opposes " all isms, Fair Employment legislation, the Genocide, Human Rights and all other proposals of the United Nations as overriding the U.S. Constitution."

Neither the state nor national committees of the Democratic Party did anything to disavow this platform, and others patterned after it were widely adopted by other county committees throughout the South.

At the same time, Governor Herman Talmadge of Georgia and Governor James Byrnes of South Carolina (former U.S. Secretary of State) were publicly threatening to abolish the public school systems in their states if the courts ever ordered an end to race segregation. Talmadge predicted further that if such a court mandate is ever handed down, " blood will flow in rivers."

No doubt inspired by these pronouncements, Florida Dragon Hendrix went into action. At a meeting held in Orlando during July, allegedly attended by delegates from ninety-seven organizations in thirty-one states, he formed what might be called the S.S. of the KKK—an " American Confederate Army for White Christians." In an announcement brazenly sent through the U.S. mails and widely published in the Press, Hendrix declared:

" If necessary this organization will bear arms to uphold our Constitutional rights! If the Supreme Court ever outlaws racial segregation, all members will take this as a violation of our Constitutional rights! "

In addition, he said his Klan army was compiling lists of members of the National Association for the Advancement of Coloured People and the Anti-Defamation League of the Jewish B'nai B'rith fraternity, and " if law and order ever break down we will hold them responsible "!

Since the Southern woods are full of Kennedys, I decided after some deliberation to establish contact with the new Klan army. With a bit of string-pulling, password-passing and money-paying, Hendrix issued me on July 18th a Commission as Colonel—complete with the Klan's gold seal. Though the circumstances required that I promptly " disappear," these credentials were to stand me in good stead. . . .

The next thing I knew, Hendrix had paid a $600 qualifying fee as a candidate for Governor of Florida! In this guise he was granted permission to hold " political " rallies in public parks and auditoriums all across the state. While Hendrix laid down the Klan line, Klan Kleagles flitted through the crowds handing out Klan membership application blanks.

Then, when Eisenhower became the Presidential nominee of the Republican Party, things began to happen thick and fast. Wizard Waybright set out to use the Klansmen in Democratic Party machines to deliver those machines over to the Republican Party!

Reasons for this were not hard to find. To begin with, the big industrialists who put up big money for the Klan are naturally inclined towards the Republican Party, dominated as it is by big-business interests. More particularly, Eisenhower forsook the public interest by renouncing Federal claims to tidelands oil deposits—and this meant that the private oil cartels would be able to acquire these riches from the states.

But these were reasons which the Klan hierarchy could not very well present to the Klan rank and file. It was Eisenhower's stand on civil rights, and his record as an enforcer of racial segregation in the U.S. armed forces, that opened up the possibility of swinging the traditionally Democratic South into the Republican camp.

" My policy for handling coloured troops will be absolute

equalitative treatment, but there will be segregation where facilities are afforded," Eisenhower had said in 1942—and the Klan proceeded to make much of this fact.

On July 16th of that same year, a directive bearing Eisenhower's signature went out to Red Cross clubs in London, ordering that, " Care should be taken so that men of two races are not needlessly intermingled in the same dormitory or at the same tables in dining halls."

In 1945, when there were more Negro recruits for the Army than could be absorbed into the existing all-Negro units, he ordered the formation of additional Negro units rather than permit Negro recruits to be integrated with white units.

And in 1948, testifying before the Senate Armed Forces Committee, Eisenhower said that the armed forces are not concerned with " social reform," and added that " a certain amount of segregation is necessary in the Army."

Finally, when in campaigning for the Presidency Eisenhower announced his opposition to civil rights legislation by Congress, the Klan took off the wraps and went all out for Ike.

Using my new Klan credentials, I took a long chance and got in touch with the Klan's new Kludd (who had succeeded Dr. Young), the Reverend A. C. Shuler of Jacksonville. This was the same man whose plans to establish a branch of the Columbians I had managed to forestall during my earlier investigations. I found Shuler to be a garrulous character, and what he told me was an earful.

" Of course the KKK likes Ike! " he declared.   " All things considered, the Republican Party has what it takes to save America! We believe with ex-President Hoover in a strong air force to knock Russia off her feet, and we don't mind going along with Eisenhower in rearming Western Europe, provided those countries do all they can to arm themselves. But General MacArthur is right about recapturing the Far East first, because it is there that the future —the wealth—lies! "

" In what way is the Klan supporting Ike? " I asked.

" Mostly our Klanspeople are just keeping quiet, going to church—and talking for Ike," he replied with a sly wink.

" As for me, I'm packing my bags to hit the sawdust trail! That's how we did it back in 1928—sent out Klan preachers all over the country with revival tents, and by mixing a little politics with religion we managed to deliver five Southern states to Hoover, and saved the country from the Catholicism of Al Smith. This time we can make an even broader appeal, and I predict we will deliver at least five Southern states to Ike! "

As the Presidential campaign progressed, a great many Southern newspapers, reflecting the sentiments of their big advertisers, joined in the effort to swing the South to Eisenhower. Wizard Waybright printed 100,000 copies of a leaflet containing a photograph of Democratic Vice-Presidential nominee John Sparkman conferring with three Negroes, and captioned it, " Good Democrats and real Southerners have no alternative but to vote for Eisenhower and Nixon to maintain our individual freedoms and way of life! "

To cap the campaign, which included a whirlwind of cross-burning and terrorism designed to keep Negroes away from the polls, Wizard Waybright's Democratic committee staged a big election-eve rally in the Klan's Imperial City, Jacksonville. Governor Byrnes was the featured speaker, while Wizard Waybright lurked in the background. . . .

On election day, more Negroes than ever before in American history defied the Klan terror and marched to the polls —but nevertheless at least five million were kept from voting. The hate propaganda did its work, and Kludd Shuler's prediction that five Southern states would go for Eisenhower came true (as for Dragon Hendrix, he polled 11,200 votes as Klan candidate for Governor of Florida).

Since then, the Klan has had good reason to rejoice.

In his State of the Nation message to Congress, Eisenhower has piously proclaimed his belief in the equal rights of citizens—but made no mention of the crying need for Federal laws against job discrimination, lynching and the poll-tax price tag on voting.

The new Republican-dominated Congress likewise lost no time making it clear that it too has no sympathy for civil rights laws. Since time immemorial, civil rights Bills have

been bottled up in the Senate by the unlimited right of
Senators to speak for ever (filibuster). On January 7th,
1953, the *New York Times* reported:

" The Senate today smashed by roll call vote of 70 to 21
an effort by a bloc of declared liberals to change its debate
limitation rule so filibusters might be curbed. The plain
prospect thus raised was that no civil rights Bill was at all
likely to be enacted by this Congress. The vote by which the
effort to curb filibusters was smashed was initiated by
Senator Robert Taft, Republican floor leader, with the
support of the Democratic hierarchy and of almost every
powerful and veteran Senator of both parties."

" It can no longer be said that the South is the chief
stumbling-block in the path of civil liberties," observed
Clarence Mitchell, Washington director of the National
Association for the Advancement of Coloured People.

Another signal victory for the Ku Klux ideology is represented by the McCarran Immigration Act, which represents
a perpetuation of the Johnson Immigration Act of 1924 (that
which Kludd Young said the Klan spent a million dollars to
push through Congress). Sponsored by Republican Senator
Pat McCarran—who is also the author of the U.S.A.'s
concentration camp law—and Republican Congressman
Francis Walter, the new law bars coloured races almost
entirely, while favouring immigration by north Europeans.
Instead of working for repeal of this racist law, Eisenhower
has asked for special quotas to let in migrants from eastern
Europe, most of whom are diehard German Nazis.

There was still more rejoicing in the Klan Klaverns when,
on April 5th, 1953, Republican Secretary of State John
Foster Dulles shocked the world by bluntly announcing that
the Eisenhower Administration has no intention of ratifying
either the United Nations Covenant on Human Rights or
the U.N. Convention on the Political Rights of Women.
Dulles' statement immediately brought to my mind the
many diatribes I had read in *The Klansman*, in much the same
language.

Pointing out that the Human Rights Covenant contains
thirty articles as compared to the ten articles of the American
Bill of Rights, the news commentator Dorothy Thompson

complained that many new laws would be needed to enforce the Covenant's provisions in the U.S.A., " if, indeed, they could be implemented by any except a socialist state."

Similarly, the Eisenhower Administration has refused to ratify the Convention against Genocide. Drafted by the U.N. in 1948 to punish " acts committed with intent to destroy, in whole or in part, a national, ethnical, racial or religious group as such," this Covenant had by 1951 been ratified by enough nations to make it the law of the world, but the U.S.A. refuses to back up its signature of the original document.

" The failure of the U.S. Senate to sign the Genocide Convention has caused the whole world to question American motivation, to doubt her purpose to build world brother-hood, co-operation, and justice," the Methodist Federation for Social Action observes. " These stands contradict the democratic stands of our American forefathers."

They are, however, in strict accord with Klankraft, and I wonder what ex-Kludd Young would say as to the prospect of America being Kluxed if he were still alive today?

In 1981, Horace Glass (*left*), publisher of the *Mandarin* (Florida) *Advertiser*, ran a story on Kennedy's Klan-busting. Klan members wrapped a ten-foot cross with copies of that edition and tried to burn down the paper's office. The cross (being examined by Kennedy) fizzled because the papers had been wrapped too tightly to burn. Photograph by Jody Glass.

CHAPTER NINETEEN

FIRE!

" We double-dog dare Kennedy to ever again show himself around a Klan function, masked or otherwise! "

This challenge, signed by the Wizard himself, appeared in the KKK's official paper *The Klansman*, published at Jacksonville, just eighteen miles from my home at Beluthahatchee. In addition, the Wizard hinted that the Klokann had at last tracked me down and knew where I was living, and the Klan would soon settle accounts with me. There was just enough detail in the story to convince me that for once the Klan was not bluffing.

Some of my friends strongly urged me to pull up stakes and move to a healthier clime. But Florida is my birthplace, and I am attached to it. I did not want to give the Klan the satisfaction of forcing me to abandon Beluthahatchee.

Counter-Klan preparations, however, were obviously in order. My first concern was with the safety of my Klan files, which by this time filled four filing cabinets. I dare say I had more material on the Klan than the Klan had on itself. Above all, I did not want this damning evidence to fall into the hands of the Klan and be destroyed. Nor did I have any intention of turning the original documents over to the House Un-American Committee or any other Government body where Klan-minded elements might bury or destroy it for ever.

After due consideration, I decided that the most appropriate repository, where the material would be entirely safe and at the same time readily accessible to contemporary and future students of Ku Kluxery, was the New York Public Library's famous Schomberg Collection dealing with Negro history. So I made the necessary arrangements, and when I had notice that the last insured parcel had been received in New York and its contents recorded on microfilm, one of my major worries came to an end.

Shortly after this, my wife and I went off for a brief lecture tour. It was late one night when we returned to Beluthahatchee. When I stepped up to unlock the front door, I found it standing ajar, evidently smashed open with an axe. I reached in and flicked the light switch. Nothing happened. I struck a match, and the scene of desolation which met our eyes was enough to turn the stomach. Not a stick of furniture or piece of clothing remained. The floor was littered with rubbish. We felt our way to the kitchen, and struck another match. Even the plumbing had been disconnected and carted off. Cup-hooks on the wall, worth two cents each, had been unscrewed and pocketed.

That night was a dark one for us. Kicking out a clear space among the litter, we slept on our coats on the floor. In the morning when we stepped outside we discovered that the young orange and grapefruit trees which we had set out had been dug up and taken away. I walked down to the lake, and saw the contents of my filing cabinets floating in the water. Angered at not finding my Klan files, the Kluxers had resolved to steal or destroy everything in sight. Walking out to the road, I received a final blow when I saw that the fence which surrounded our property had been pulled from the posts and carried off. It was a bleak picture, and we had very little money with which to begin repairs.

" What do you say? " I asked, turning to my wife. " I can't ask you to stay . . ."

"You don't have to," she replied, picking up a broom which the Kluxers had apparently dropped in the dark.

Without another word, she attacked the rubbish on the floor, while I went down to the lake and fished out what I could of my papers and spread them on the bank to dry in the sun. Later, I reported everything to the sheriff, but never even received a reply.

Slowly, we refurnished our home and replanted the citrus grove. At the same time, we built up quite an arsenal until at length it boasted, in addition to my ·32 automatic and the Springfield army rifle, a ·38 revolver, ·12-gauge pump gun,

·16-gauge automatic shotgun, a double-barrelled shotgun and a ·22 rifle. I also acquired a ferocious German shepherd watchdog, who had a reputation for chewing up intruders. We seldom left home at night for more than a few hours at a time, and when we did we always left lights burning and a radio blaring.

But one night I left my wife at home while I went to Jacksonville to address a strike meeting of shipyard workers. Just as she was about to retire she heard the whistle of a chuck-will's-widow.   The nights at Beluthahatchee are filled with the plaintive calls of these birds—but this particular whistle did not sound very bird-like. Reaching under the bed pillows, she took my automatic in one hand and her revolver in the other. Then she switched off the light and stepped out of the side door. In the darkness of the pine woods surrounding the house she saw the glow of a cigarette being tossed to the ground. . . .

At the same moment, four autos full of cursing, shouting Klansmen turned in at our gate and drove slowly up the driveway. Without waiting any longer, she emptied one pistol in the direction of the cigarette, and the other over the tops of the cars. There was a loud crashing as the Klansman in the woods plunged off through the palmettos. The cars, turning through the orange grove, also beat a hasty retreat, and sped off down the highway towards Jacksonville.

To ensure a still hotter reception in the event the Klan were to pay us a further visit, we began to hold practice mobilizations from time to time. In these drills we practised slipping out the rear and side doors without lights, and taking up battle stations behind various trees and logs. Whenever we had guests staying with us they were also issued weapons and assigned to stations. I rigged a floodlight which would light up the approach to the house, while leaving us in the dark. Then we would all begin firing, reloading and flitting from station to station to give an impression of numbers. The result sounded like a rather hot war, and served notice on the surrounding countryside that we were well prepared for unwelcome guests. A number of my Negro neighbours, and a few of the whites who belonged to the shipyard workers' union and lived within sound of these volleys, promised to "come a-runnin'" to our aid if we ever got into a pitched battle with the Klan.

My folksong-singing buddy Woody Guthrie came to visit us again about this time. Though he chose to sleep outdoors in a hammock rigged with zippered mosquito netting, he always leaned the army rifle against the tree. One morning, to rouse him from a late sleep, I took the automatic shotgun and fired five blasts into the sky over his head. Without waiting to unzipper the netting, Woody plunged through it, grabbing his rifle as he went, and raced barefoot through a smouldering campfire to his station.

"Well, I'll be a suck-egg mule!" he swore when he finally awoke to the fact that it was a false alarm. "I thought the Ku Klux had snuck up and caught us by the short hair for sure!"

A few nights later, the Kluxers did just that.

It was about three o'clock in the morning when I was awakened by the acrid smell of smoke. Peering out of our bedroom window to the south, I saw that the pine grove was a mass of flame. Driven by a brisk southerly wind, the fire was racing through the lush underbrush and pine needles directly for the house.

Rousing my wife (and the sleeping watchdog), I prodded Guthrie from his hammock. He and I began cutting small pine saplings which could be used to beat out the flames, while my wife got in the car and raced down the road for help. Soon she was back with a half-dozen white and Negro friends in various stages of attire. They were led by Tom Appleby, the white chairman of the union's strike committee, and Fred Jones, the Negro co-chairman.

Tying wet cloths over our faces and dipping the saplings in the lake, we fanned out and approached the oncoming fire in a frontal attack. The heat was so intense and the smoke so dense that for a time I did not think we could work close enough to the flames to strike back at them. Hot cinders kept falling on our hair and clothes, and we had to retreat long enough to beat them out and catch our breath.

"Let's go at it where it's thin, cross over, and attack it from behind!" I called out.

Just then Appleby let out an anguished yell. My first thought was that his clothing had caught fire or he had been ambushed by a Kluxer.

" Call off this damnfool watchdog of yours! " Appleby cursed. " He just bit a chunk out of my rear end! "

" I suspect the s.o.b. has Nazi blood! " I called back. " He probably licked the hands of the Kluxers while they applied the torch to the woods! "

We finally fought our way through the flames and launched a flank attack. The ankle-deep ash burned through our shoes, but the air was cooler and not so smoky. For a long time it seemed that the fire would win and reach the house. Frequently when we thought we had extinguished a stretch of it, it would burst into flame again the moment we turned our backs. My wife kept bringing buckets of water in which we soaked our sapling brushes.

Finally we got the fire under control, when it was less than a hundred yards from the house. Taking it easier, we methodically liquidated the far reaches and isolated pockets of flame that kept springing up. At last there was no more fire to be seen except a score of stumps, which blazed away like torches, brightly but harmlessly.

We stopped and wiped our brows. The house had been saved, but the beautiful pine grove was no longer green but black. The young trees had been destroyed, and the older ones would be stunted for years.

" I'm going to take a walk over to the south fence to see how this thing was started," I said.

" We'll come along," the men chorused.

We walked together through the smouldering ash, which crunched under foot and puffed up to spill over into our shoes. When we reached the fence we saw that the fire line began inside of it. Every inch had burned inside my property, but nothing outside of it.

" They waited until the wind was just right," Guthrie said bitterly, spitting into the ashes.

" They're a mean bunch of bastards! " Jones echoed.

" Let's go back to the house," I said.

We walked down the highway this time, and as I passed

through the gate I saw in the half dark a small white card sticking in a crack.

" Somebody strike a match," I said. The night sky was turning grey, but it was not yet light enough to see very well.

" Here you are," Jones said, cupping the flame in his hand. I held the card in the glare, and read aloud:

Since Eighteen Hundred Sixty-Six
THE KU KLUX KLAN
Has been riding and will
continue to do so as long as
the WHITE MAN liveth.

" So the cowards left their calling card! " Appleby said.

" Strike another match," I said, " I think there's something on the other side."

Jones lit up again, and I read, crudely lettered in pencil:

S. K.—You are finished;
We have just begun!—KKK

" Well, they came close, but they missed," Jones said.

" Yeah, but next time they may come on you with dynamite," Appleby said slowly. " You're on a mighty hot spot. Maybe you ought to move off it."

" Didn't the Klan toss a stick of dynamite~at your strike meeting last week? " I asked.

" Sure did! " Appleby scowled. " Blew the front steps of our hall plumb away! "

" But you're still out on strike, aren't you? " I pursued.

" Sure are, and we aims to stay out until we gets our demands or all hell freezes over! " Jones replied.

" You can say that again, buddy! " Appleby declared, slapping his union brother on the back.

" Well, I feel the same way about hanging on to my home here at Beluthahatchee," I said.

" You know you can count on us," Appleby assured me. " I keep my varmint gun loaded, and would like nothing better than to nail me a Ku Klux pelt to the side of my barn."

" Come on up to the house and have some beer! " my wife called out.

We went, and stood around the smouldering campfire.

The sun was just coming up through the cypress trees that stand in Lake Beluthahatchee. But the air was cool, and I kicked up the fire a bit. My wife passed around the beer bottles, and poured one for herself.

" To hell with the Klan! " Appleby toasted, and we all drank to it.

" You know," I said, " it's not these old-fashioned bed-sheeted Kluxers who worry me so much nowadays. . . ."

" How's that? " Appleby asked.

" I'm talking about these new-fangled, plain-clothed Kluxers who've brought our country to the brink of depression and war. Take all these new laws, for instance—the Taft-Hartley Act to bust up our unions, the Smith Act to tell us what to think, and the McCarran Act to toss us into concentration camps if we think otherwise. It's no wonder the Klan keeps boasting that Ku Kluxery has come to be the law of the land! "

" If you ask me," Appleby said slowly, " the biggest Kluxer of all is Joe McCarthy. He may not be a member of the Klan, but he'd sure make a good one! "

" McCarthy makes the Grand Dragon look like an earthworm by comparison," I agreed. " He's pulling every trick in the Ku Klux bag, and then some. The guy was cut out to be a bar-room bouncer, but he's got all the makings of another Hitler, including big money backing. Unless we get together and cut him down to size mighty quick, he just might turn out to be a greater curse on the world than Hitler ever thought of being! "

" I can't believe America will ever fall for a foul fighter," Appleby said. " Just the other day one of his gumshoers was hanging around our union headquarters, asking fool questions. . . ."

" What kind of questions? "

Appleby laughed, and knocked out his pipe on the heel of his shoe.

" Wanted to know what kind of folks come to visit you out here at Beluthahatchee."

" What did you tell him? "

" ' Some of the best in the world! ' "

" Thanks, pal," Guthrie said, taking a mock bow.

"The man wanted to know all about you," Appleby continued. "I asked him, 'Do you have any evidence of Guthrie ever committing any un-American act?'

"'Well, there's this,' he said. And then he reached in his bag and pulled out a picture of you—the one where you got a sign painted on your guitar saying 'This machine kills fascists!' Me and Fred here both laughed so loud the man fell all over himself getting away from there!"

"How 'bout getting out that machine and making us a little music?" Jones said to Guthrie.

Woody went in the house and came back and stood in front of the fire. He threw his head back, and a cigarette hung from his lip as he tuned his guitar.

"I been standin' here thinkin' and drinkin', and drinkin' and thinkin'," he said, "and I wish I could outwhite Mr. Whitman, and outburn Mr. Burns, and outsand Mr. Sandburg, and outpush Mr. Pushkin, and come up with the answer to this KKK hate fire that goes creepin' along the yellow highway line goin' and comin' out there. And I just kinda believe that if us folks will work together same way we done here tonight we can stomp out that hell-fire way on back past the gateposts and fencelines down all the highways and byways of America to the place where the stuff gets its first goddamned start of the earthlife.

"So here's a little song that I'll just fish up, fry up, and serve up as I go along. . . ."

As the sun rose higher over the lake and the burning stumps sputtered and went out, Woody thumped his guitar and sang:

> Name that I was borned with, name that I've got still,
> Rings out by the sound of Beluthahatchee Bill;
> You Kluxers tried to scare me, with your words of swill,
> But you'll never scare me none, not Beluthahatchee Bill.
> Beluthahatchee Bill, old Beluthahatchee Bill,
> Freedom-lovin', freedom-huntin', easy-ridin' Bill;
> You can swing me and hang me, and beat me to your
>   fill,
> But you'll never slack my speed none, not Belutha-
>   hatchee Bill.

I'm from down through South America, like mossy
   mossy moss,
I'm from up across old Canada, where Paul Bunyan got
   so lost;
I'm from Pittsburg Beer and Gary Steel, and you know
   I tell you true,
When I tell you I'm a Christian, a Buddhist and a Jew.
You tortured me with blow-torches, and dumped me
   from your car,
You tried to burn my home up, and set my woods on
   fire;
You can dynamite my house, and dig my grave upon
   the hill,
But you'll never keep me in it, not Beluthahatchee Bill.
Beluthahatchee Lands means Never-Never Lands,
Never-never bloodied by your bloody hands,
Never-never caught in your kid-like traps,
Never-never drained like turpentine saps,
Never-never scared by all your screams and squeals,
Never-never done in by all your dirty deals.
You can try your best to kill us, but you know you never
   will,
Ever scratch a finger of Beluthahatchee Bill!

The new wave of racist solidarity is exemplified by this march
in 1987 in Pulaski, Tennessee, involving Klansmen, Nazis,
skinheads, and paramercenaries.

KLUXED AGAIN?

MY REWARD for the decade I spent as a counterterrorist agent in the unclean racist underworld came one night after I had spoken to the Dallas branch of the NAACP. Among those gathered around was a little girl about five years old, who gave me a big hug around the knees and looked up and said, "I know what you do—you spy on mean white folks, and then come tell us what they're fixin' to do."

While the Klan I have written about here is that which emerged in the wake of World War II, my account is hardly a period piece, as the Klan does not change its spots all that much. The motto most frequently seen on Klan calling cards is "Here Yesterday—Today—Forever!" and with rival Wizards and Empires proliferating all over, we are obviously not rid of it yet.

It is my hope that the 1990 edition of this book—originally published around the world over three decades ago but not in this country—will provide a few pointers for my fellow Americans as they cope with the Klan of today and tomorrow. To set my report in its historical context I thought it might be well to add a thumbnail sketch of the Klan as it was before and after my midcentury brush with it.

Publishers had long bedeviled me to write a history of the KKK, but, knowing how much deviltry it had committed, the task seemed too formidable. A number of excellent ones are now available, including Wyn Craig Wade's *The Fiery Cross* (New York: Simon & Schuster, 1987) and David M. Chalmer's *Hooded Americanism* (New York: Franklin Watts, 1981). I have also written an account of Klan terror during Reconstruction, *After Appomattox*, scheduled for publication by University Presses of Florida in 1990. In it I submit that the history of racism in the South was symbolized by successive changes of uniform: from Confederate gray to Ku Klux white to police blue and eventually back to white again (often superimposed upon the blue).

Twice before in our nation's history the Ku Klux Klan has boasted, with reason, that it had America "Kluxed." The first

273

occasion came with the overthrow of Reconstruction, when the original Klan in effect dictated the terms of the "Deal of '76" setting aside the total surrender of the Confederacy at Appomattox, making dead letters of the constitutional amendments asserting black rights, and abandoning the freedmen to the not-so-tender mercies of their former masters. The Kloran of the KKK, rather than the Constitution of the USA, became the governing instrument in the former Confederate states insofar as any black rights were concerned. It was not the total autonomy sought by secession, but it was enough for white supremacy's purposes.

Real power at that time was in the hands of former Confederate generals who served as Grand Dragons over the state Realms of the Klan's Invisible Empire. Blacks were dealt with by an elaboration of the black codes to extend them into an all-pervasive system of Jim Crow apartheid, which insinuated itself throughout the nation, including its armed forces. The United States of America became an integrally racist state, no less than the Union of South Africa, and in this sense it is fair to say that America as well as the South was Kluxed.

The changeover from Klan white to police blue took place as soon as the reign of terror had done its work and the new laws and regulations took effect, jointly enforced by lawmen and lynch mobs.

The second Kluxing of America took place during the mid-1920s when the Klan—"reincarnated" in 1915 in the wake of the Leo Frank lynching—elected a number of Klansmen to Congress and a half dozen as governors, controlled a number of state legislatures, saw to the passing of a racist immigration law virtually barring all black, brown, and yellow people, marched twenty abreast from dawn until dusk down Pennsylvania Avenue in the nation's capital, and inducted President Warren G. Harding in a ceremony conducted in the Green Room of the White House.

I taped the inside story of that last event a quarter of a century later in a deathbed confession by the Reverend Alton Young. Young had spent his entire life as a Klan official and was Imperial Klokard (national chaplain) when he served on the five-man team that made a Klansman out of Harding.

The reason he was revealing all, Young said, was that the only Klansman who had visited him in the hospital wanted to borrow ten dollars!

Young was so nervous he forgot and left his Bible in the car, he related, so Harding had to send for the White House Bible. The only deference paid him as president was to allow him to rest his elbow on the edge of the desk while he knelt to take the long oath to obey without question the every edict of the Imperial Wizard of the Invisible Empire. As a token of appreciation, Harding presented each member of the team with a War Department auto license tag, so they could run red lights with impunity any time they felt like it.

Things have changed somewhat since then.

Throughout its bloody history the Klan has shown itself a master at exploiting issues based on bigotry. Lately it has produced Klan "border patrols" to turn back Hispanics at the Rio Grande; patrol boats manned by robed Klansmen along the Gulf waterfront, featuring effigies of Vietnamese fishermen hung from the yardarms; ritual lynchings just to show that the Klan still knows how; inflammatory propaganda campaigns on such issues as school busing and "reverse discrimination"; paramilitary boot camps conducted jointly with Nazis and Skinheads; a computerized hit list of antiracists; and a national conspiracy with "The Order" of the "Aryan Nations" to provoke race riots and establish white rule.

Alarmist? Perhaps, but better too much alarm than too little. When this book was written, I said that of all of America's homegrown fascist groups, the Klan was the most likely to succeed. While a racist/terrorist takeover seems unlikely, their hate-mongering, dress rehearsals, and practice assassinations can do a lot of damage. A 1988 inventory compiled by the Anti-Defamation League lists at least 67 active racist organizations and 50 hate sheets being published on a regular basis.

As Jim Crow in the USA served as the prototype for apartheid in the U of SA, the KKK has served as role model for the death squads that keep many oppressive regimes in power around the world. It was not for nothing that Reconstruction blacks referred to the Ku Klux as "night-assassins." We know that they killed NAACP leaders Medgar Evers in Mississippi and Harry T. Moore in Florida, and no man can say with certainty that they were not behind the assassination of Martin Luther King.

Recently I spoke to students at Stetson University, and while they are aware that they face some problems out there, not even the black students feel that the Klan is one of them. Here's hoping they are right.

While the bedsheet brigade is bad enough, the greatest threat to human rights in America today are certain plain-clothed Klux in Washington, D.C., and certain black-robed men on court benches.

There is more than one way of being Kluxed, and we need to think about ourselves and the kind of people we elect to public office. Like my good buddy Woody Guthrie used to sing:

> As through this world I've rambled,
> I've met lots of funny men;
> Some will rob you with a six-gun,
> Some with a fountain-pen.

Stetson Kennedy
Beluthahatchee,
Florida
Spring 1990

HOW TO KAN THE KLAN: A HANDBOOK
FOR COUNTERTERRORIST ACTION

THE QUESTION "What can we do about the Klan and other organized hate groups?" is frequently heard from readers and audiences.

Drew Pearson, predecessor to Washington columnist Jack Anderson, once generously labeled me "the nation's number-one Klan-buster." To justify the title further, I drew up a ten-point program called "How to Kan the Klan," which civil rights and labor groups distributed widely. Governors Ellis Arnall of Georgia, Reuben Askew of Florida, and Jim Folsom of Alabama acted on some of them, as did others. But when I survey the battlefield today and see how things are going, I must confess to feeling that the time I spent Klan-busting might have been better spent girl-watching or bass-fishing.

Of course, things might be worse had we not done what we did. One suspects, however, that the veteran who gave an arm and a leg fighting "the war to end wars" had much the same misgivings as successive generations rushed off to fight other wars that came along. But since I believe in the sun even while it is raining (as the saying goes), I am including here an update of weapons at our disposal in this ongoing struggle against Ku Kluxery and other forms of racist terrorism. (The reader might want to see also *What to Do When the Klan Comes to Town*, published by the National Anti-Klan Network, now the Center for Democratic Renewal, Atlanta.)

Charter revocation. When I drafted the first *quo warranto* pleading for revocation of the KKK's corporate charter as a tax-exempt, nonprofit, eleemosynary (charitable/fraternal) organization in 1947, and Governor Arnall acted on it, Klan propagandists said they could operate just as well or better as an unincorporated association. The truth is, however, then and now, that such a charter provides a considerable degree of immunity not only from taxation but also from liability and prosecution of individual Klansmen for the Klan's "corporate" acts. Moreover, these charters, issued by a particular state but "authorizing" nationwide activity, represent a stamp of moral and legalistic sanction by society and government for a clandestine criminal conspiracy to deprive certain categories of Americans—by intimidation, terrorism and violence—of rights guaranteed them by federal and state constitutions and law.

The plain fact is that the Klan is no more entitled to a nonprofit, tax-free charter as a fraternal group than the Mafia or the Miami Boys crack cocaine cartel. The successful Georgia revocation proceeding was based upon these contentions, plus the fact that the KKK had lied about its purposes in its application for incorporation and had engaged in activities not stipulated in the charter.

Alabama and several other states followed Georgia's lead, but before the ink was dry on revocation orders, secretaries of state elsewhere—and even in those same states—were handing out new charters automatically upon receipt of the required fee (usually $10.00). At this writing, it appears that states are vying with one another in issuing Klan charters to whoever wants one.

The esteemed purists of the American Civil Liberties Union may contend, with the Klan, that the KKK is just as entitled to charters as the NAACP, Knights of Columbus, or B'nai B'rith and that no secretary of state is entitled to make a priori judgments as to corporate intent. There is nothing a priori, however, about the Klan's actual intent, purposes, and record or the many legislative and judicial findings on the subject.

I will come to grips with the ACLU/KKK contention later on, but a final word here on the considerable educational value of revocation proceedings. Hanging the Klan's blood-stained linen on the line for all the world to see not only exposes its true terrorist nature but makes it abundantly clear that, far from being the pillar of society it claims to be, the Klan is rejected by the body politic as beyond the pale, criminal, and cancerous.

Antimask laws. Anytime a person walks into a bank with a mask on, we do well to regard it as prima facie evidence of criminal intent. We would do equally well, I think, to look upon the mask of the Klan in this same light. The Klansman may not be after our bankroll, but he is after something infinitely more precious and irreplaceable—our constitutional rights to life, liberty, and the pursuit of happiness. The Klan-minded will argue that antimask laws would spoil the fun of Halloween and Mardi Gras, but we know a hell-bent Klansman when we see one. The bank guard does not wait to draw until the masked bank-robber presents a note saying "This is a stick-up!" Neither does the masked rights-robber have to carry a sign for us to know that he is bent upon making a second-class citizen or dead citizen out of someone. I am proud to say that my native State of Florida has an antimask law. Every state and municipality ought to have one.

A registry of Klux? In 1923 the State of New York adopted a law requiring corporations and associations (other than fraternities, benevolent societies, and labor unions) that have an oath as a condition of membership to file a copy of that oath and the names of all officers and members. Anyone joining with knowledge that the group had not complied with this law could be prosecuted. A Klansman was, and the Court of Appeals upheld his conviction in these words: "The danger of certain organizations has been judicially demonstrated. . . . It seems reasonable to separate the known from the unknown . . . the sheep from the goats."

Upon appeal to the U.S. Supreme Court (*Bryant v. Zimmerman*, 278 U.S. 63) in 1928, the Court held that many secret organizations do not violate the peace or interfere with the rights of others but that on the other hand the state may take notice that certain societies are evil and dangerous and may legislate against them, provided the classification in such regulations is reasonable. In the case of the Klan, the Court felt that the abundant congressional and judicial findings of its criminal intent and deeds were more than sufficient.

That this principle is subject to abuse was demonstrated, however, when forces opposed to apartheid in America began to mobilize a quarter-century later and Florida and some other states enacted laws requiring the NAACP to hand over its membership lists. Happily, the courts ruled that this was not a reasonable distinction.

Can Klansmen be lawmen? A question related to that of whether the KKK is entitled to cloak itself in the corporate mantle is whether a member is qualified to serve as a law enforcement officer. As we have seen, law officers tend to gravitate into the KKK and the Klan into law enforcement. A case in point arose in Jacksonville, Florida, in 1983, when it was called to the attention of the sheriff that Officer Robert McMullen was serving as kleagle (organizer) for the Klan in Duval County. After first being put into the Records Department, he was eventually dismissed and the case went to court.

I submitted what amounted to an *amicus curiae* brief to the U.S. District Court, pointing out that the Klan oath requires one to "come to the aid of a Brother Klansman in any extremity, treason, rape, and malicious murder alone excepted." Translated into practice, this oath has resulted in Klan-staged jailbreaks, providing false alibis, destruction of evidence, and routine perjury. Moreover, Klan policy prescribes instant and automatic suspension of any member accused of a crime—which enables one and all to deny "truthfully" that the accused is a Klan member. The Klan-cop's first loyalty is to the Exalted Cyclops, not the police chief, and to the oath of Klannishness, not the oath to uphold the law. The highest law of a member is that of the Invisible Empire, not of the United States.

No private armies? The U.S. Constitution is explicit in stating that there shall be no private armies raised in this country. That federal and state authorities look the other way as the Klan, Nazis, Skinheads, and other racist terrorists band together and establish paramilitary training for the avowed purpose of pogroms and takeovers should tell us something. Rest assured that if the NAACP, the Anti-Defamation League, the Hispanic La Raza, or the migratory farm workers union were to establish such camps, they would be shut down overnight.

Who is a traitor? American courts have ruled that to be guilty of treason "by levying war" there must be (1) an assembly of armed force or of a force sufficient to intimidate by its numbers and (2) an intent to overthrow the government or to defeat the enforcement of one of its laws. When our republic was young, it was much more vigorous in prosecuting for treason than it has been of late. In the Shays, Fries, and Whiskey rebellions, for example, citizens were convicted of treason and sentenced to death for such deeds as the tar-and-feathering of federal marshals, intimidation of tax collectors, and effecting jail deliveries—all deeds that the Klan has equaled and surpassed.

Is the Klan above the law? We need not only to deprive the KKK of any legal leg to stand on but to enforce against it "without fear or favor" all the laws of the land. The Klan has always acted as if it were outside and above the law, and it still does, all too often with seeming impunity.

For generations, for example, there has been a law on the books (Section 51, Title 18, Chaper 3, U.S. Code) which provides that "If two or more persons conspire to injure, oppress, threaten, or intimidate any citizen in the free exercise or enjoyment of any right or privilege secured to him by the Constitution or laws of the United States, or because of his having exercised the same, or if two or more persons go in disguise on the highway, or on the premises of another, with intent to prevent or hinder his free exercise or enjoyment of any right or privilege so secured. . . ." That law, providing for up to ten years imprisonment, has been a virtual dead letter, presumably because of a bipartisan gentlemen's agreement not to enforce it.

The Klan has been nothing but a grand criminal conspiracy since the day of its birth, with each klavern hatching new conspiracies every time it meets. The conspiracy shoe fits the KKK to a T, but no one puts it on them.

The nearest thing to a conspiracy charge occurred when Governor Arnall, at my suggestion, had the Georgia Highway Patrol stop and search Klan motorcades on the basis of "probable cause" for concealed and otherwise illegal weapons. The results were astonishing: Not only were some of the Klan's fangs pulled, but projected bloodlettings were prevented and future forays discouraged. News photos of the friskings revealed, furthermore, which of those in "uniform" were on the side of the law and which outside it.

Tax-exempt terrorism. When we can't pin mayhem and murder on the Mafiosi, we bust them for nonpayment of taxes on their ill-gotten gains. Why not the Klux? Hate-mongering and race-racketeering are lucrative enterprises, and ripoff has always been the Klan hierarchy's middle name.

During World War II, President Franklin Roosevelt did put the Klan out of business for the duration by sending the IRS to tack a $607,305 jeopardy tax lien on the door of the Imperial Palace in Atlanta. Wizard James A. Colescott boarded it up and retired to Miami, saying, "What else could I do?" It is a principle at law that a lien follows the property, and the stock-in-trade on which every Klan group since then has cashed in has been the name, regalia, and copyrighted ritual of that same old KKK. If the IRS doesn't want to levy under the old lien, the least it could do is slap on some new ones.

Inciting to riot. It might be said that inciting to riot is the Klan's principal occupation, yet seldom if ever do we hear of a Cyclops or Dragon being so cited, no matter how bloodthirsty they wax over loudspeakers. On the other hand, a worker who mounts a soapbox on a picket line to say something the least bit derogatory about the boss or the scabs goes off to jail. "White supremacy, yes; workers' rights, no!" the premise would seem to be.

This brings us back to the ACLU and its willingness to defend as freedom of expression not only the right of the stripper to disrobe but also the right of the Kluxer to enrobe. The First Amendment, it would have us believe, gives license to the Klan and everyone else to mouth racist epithets, and any attempt to gag them would open the door to gagging the NAACP and other rights groups.

And yet the right of free speech is not an absolute one, and the U.S. Supreme Court has made that abundantly clear in its ruling that we may not wantonly shout "Fire!" in a crowded theater. I submit that the shouting of racist epithets in this crowded world likewise presents a clear and present danger and ought to be proscribed. This has nothing whatever to do with thought control; the *utterance* or *publication* of racist slurs and epithets is an *act* no less than a lynching, one for which we ought to be held accountable. I believe that American jurists and juries are entirely capable of administering such a law.

Such rights as we now enjoy came about through an evolutionary process, and what I am proposing here is not adulteration of free speech but its elevation to a higher plane. Realization of our democratic destiny requires that we abjure such things as racist hate-mongering and embrace such things as Roosevelt's Bill of Economic Rights and the Four Freedoms.

Racism on the air? Even if we opt for the antiquated notion that racism has a right to express itself, does this mean that we owe it "equal time," or any time, on radio and television? Managers of a number of national TV talk shows have seen fit to invite terrorists like J. B. Stoner to sit on their panels and spew forth inflammatory racist slanders coast-to-coast. In some instances, mail addresses are flashed upon the screen for the convenience of any who may wish to join the conspiracy.

This procedure further serves the highly destructive purpose of convincing both the terrorists and the general public that racism/terrorism is a legitimate contender in the marketplace of ideas. To make matters worse, the exponents chosen to defend democracy are often no match for fulltime professional bigots.

We do not put Jehovah's Witnesses on the air to attack all churches and government as instruments of Satan or the godfather to argue that the Mafia is the epitome of The American Way and that he has as much right to rip off as an attorney general or multinational corporation. Why then put on a Grand Dragon to urge us to tear up our Constitution, break the law, hate one another, and persecute minorities?

Who's a terrorist? Uncle Sam talks a good case for counterterrorism, but everything depends upon who is terrorizing whom. If *we* armed and trained them, that is of course because we expect that when they gain power they will do business with us and vote our way in the United Nations. That qualifies them as freedom fighters, as distinguished from terrorists. The other camp defines terrorism in the same way but from the opposite point of view. We would be pleased, of course, if ours were to hold what looked like free elections some day, but this is by no means mandatory.

Despite all the attention given to combatting "international terrorism," little or none of this official concern seems to carry over to Americans engaged in terrorism against Americans in our own country—the Klan, neo-Nazis, Skinheads, and so on. Recent films such as "Mississippi Burning" notwithstanding, the reader of this book will be aware that the FBI has not been at all given to hunting down the KKK and having shootouts with it.

There was a time when the FBI did have agents and informants inside the KKK. Quite by accident, I stumbled upon a news item in the *Florida Times-Union* of November 24, 1980, in which retiring bureau chief David Brumble revealed that FBI investigation of the KKK, Nazis, black activists, and student pacifists had been discontinued some ten years earlier and "has not been taken up by anybody." To me, this seemed a significant bit of news, but when I passed it on to black, Jewish, union, and other civil rights leaders, they showed no interest whatever—enough to discourage any "retired" Klanbuster.

There is considerably more hope when we look to our own resources rather than to governments. A major breakthrough has been scored by the Southern Poverty Law Center and its Klanwatch, based in Montgomery. When the Klan ritually murdered nineteen-year-old Michael Donald in Mobile in 1981 and then strung him up to let the world know it had not forgotten how, the center filed suit for civil damages on behalf of his mother, Beulah Mae Donald. The jury gave her a $7 million judgment against the Klan and certain of its members. When it came time to collect, the court handed her the keys and title to the Klan's "Imperial Palace" as partial satisfaction. It brought only $55,000 on the market, but the proceeding put a damper on racist terrorism unsurpassed since Grant sent an army of occupation back into the South to quell the Klan terror that followed Appomattox.

At mid-century it was unthinkable for a black to sue whites with the expectation of getting anything but killed. Here now is a new weapon, and it is in *our* hands. That old adage "Sue the bastards!" was never more apropos. What's more, the right of claimants to subpoena Klan records and obtain warrants to interrogate Klansmen under oath has turned up evidence that prosecutors could not ignore, and the culprits were put behind bars.

So much for the possibilities of bringing *law* to bear upon racist terrorism. There is also much that *we* can do.

The Klan has always been a symptom, not a cause, although untreated it can do much to aggravate the underlying illness of bigotry. When we lift the hood, who do we find but kinfolk? Just as there would be no drug cartels if there were no drug users, there would be no Klan members if there were no Klan-minded. There being no quick cure for a heritage of bigotry, let us confine ourselves here to ways and means of immunizing ourselves and counteracting the psychological warfare at which the Klan has, through a century of practice, become so adept.

For one thing, we need to create a social and ideological climate offering no sustenance to Ku Kluxery. On top of that, we need to spread the word that bigoted is not the thing to be. A nation of faddists, we must let the Klan know that we are done with it. We must make sure that the public image of the Klan is its true one: un-American, un-Christian, uncouth, cruel, sadistic, lowbrow, cowardly, infantile, ridiculous, anti-labor, bad for business.

The media have ever been sorely tempted to play around with the Klan's sensational stunting, but their responsibility to the public requires that they resist the temptation. The silent treatment is often the best treatment. Certainly no advance billings, no mail addresses, and no blowing up out of proportion are indicated. In fairness to the community, any quote from the Grand Dragon ought to be accompanied (preferably preceded) by quotes from the mayor, city council, police chief, ministerial alliance, central labor council, chamber of commerce, and veterans' and civil rights groups.

Some say that every Klan march should be met by a countermarch, head-on. There may be times when confrontations are called for, but one must expect that, for now, lawmen are apt to side with the Klansmen in any showdown, as in Greensboro, N.C., in 1979, when Klan and Nazi marchers shot and killed five countermarchers. I am convinced that jeering onlookers are a more effective means of discounting the Klan's public and self-image than confrontations, which all too often play into the Klan's hands.

Finally, let me point out that individuals and rights groups can do a number on our homegrown terrorists by tracking down license numbers, publishing members' names, and bringing employer, creditor, and boycott pressure to bear.